# H.L. and Lyda

# H.L. and Lyda

Margaret Hunt Hill
with Burt and Jane Boyar

*August House Publishers, Inc.*
L I T T L E R O C K

Published 1994 by August House, Inc.,
P.O. Box 3223, Little Rock, Arkansas 72203,
501-372-5450.

Printed in the United States of America

10 9 8 7 6 5 4 3 2 1

LIBRARY OF CONGRESS CATALOGING-IN-PUBLICATION DATA

Hill, Margaret Hunt, 1915–
H.L. and Lyda: growing up in the H.L. Hunt and Lyda Bunker Hunt family as remembered by their eldest daughter / Margaret Hunt Hill, with Jane and Burt Boyar.
p. cm.
Includes index.
ISBN 0-87483-337-X : $24.95
1. Hunt Oil Company—History. 2. Petroleum industry and trade—United States—History. 3. Hunt family. 4. Hill, Margaret Hunt, 1915– . I. Boyar, Jane. II. Boyar, Burt. III. Title. IV. Title: H.L. and Lyda.
HD9569.H84H54 1994
338.092'273—dc20 93-49546

First Edition, 1994

Executive editor: Liz Parkhurst
Assistant editors: Nancy King, Debbie Tarvin
Design direction: Ted Parkhurst
Cover design: Byron Taylor



This book is printed on archival-quality paper that meets the guidelines for performance and durability of the Committee on Production Guidelines for Book Longevity of the Council on Library Resources.

AUGUST HOUSE, INC. PUBLISHERS LITTLE ROCK

*To the memory of a great lady*

# *Acknowledgments*

In recalling our family history I have been aided by my sister, Caroline; my brothers, Hassie, Bunker, Herbert, and Lamar; Bunker's wife, Caroline; my cousins Tom, Sherman and Stuart Hunt; and my friends of fifty-five years, Coleen and the late Jesse Johnson. Their comments appear within the text.

# *Foreword*

RECENTLY I ENCOUNTERED my nephew's wife and son at the activities building of the Highland Park Presbyterian Church in Dallas. The child looked at my mother's name, Lyda Bunker Hunt, cut lightly in the stone, done that way deliberately, to be a subtle memorial.

The boy, a Hunt, asked his mother, "Who was Lyda Bunker Hunt?"

"She was your great-grandmother."

"Why is her name on this building?"

"Well ..." she said, "I'm not exactly sure."

I was surprised and disappointed. Perhaps we've been *too* subtle.

In 1948 *Life* magazine published a snapshot of my father captioned, *Is this the richest man in the U.S.?*

Daddy didn't know if he was or not. Just that he had a whole lot more than he had started with. None of us knew that Daddy was that rich. We were aware that we had money and that we lived well, but we never looked around at others to compare ourselves with them. Daddy was an outstanding man, and due to his money and his nature he became highly visible.

Mother was an equally oustanding person, his life's partner all along the road to wealth, over its smooth six-lane highways as well as the bumps and potholes. He often said that ninety percent of his financial success was due to Mother. But during the era in which she lived, the woman's role was in the background. As a result, Mother has around a hundred descendants who know nothing about her.

What *is* known about my family is largely guesswork and most of it distorted. Until 1948, Daddy made a point of avoiding publicity. After the *Life* magazine story, he gave a few interviews, but he never sat down with a reporter and said, "Here's what I'm all about. Here's how I did it." *The Hunt-Bunker and Allied Families* genealogical and biographical documents can be found at the Library of Congress and the public libraries of Dallas, New York, and Boston. But from none of those can one learn what my parents were really like and what it was like for their children growing up in those special circumstances.

If you have an outstanding heritage, if you're fortunate enough to have arrived somewhere that's nice to be, you should know something about how you got there and where you came from. Few of us have made the journey on our own.

My grandnephew's question stayed with me: Who was Lyda Bunker Hunt? If he didn't know, then the remainder of the family could not know either. That is the reason this book has been written—for those hundred descendants of my dear mother. She was exceptional.

# *One: The Bunkers*

MY MOTHER, LYDA BUNKER, was a descendant of William the Conqueror and King Edward I of England, who married Eleanor of Castile in 1254. The first Bunker known in the direct line of the American branch of the family was William Bunker, a French Huguenot who had left Nantes for England to escape religious persecution. The Massachusetts records begin with his son George, who emigrated to Ipswich, Massachusetts. His grandson John Bunker lived in Charleston, Massachusetts, and in 1684, according to Harvard College records, was one of the early donors to Harvard College, founded some fifty years before by John Harvard, an English clergyman who had emigrated to Massachusetts.

My great-grandfather, Charles Waldo Bunker, was a Mississippi riverboat captain. He had a luxuriant black beard, and he used to treat the children by letting them hang onto it and swing back and forth.

Mother's father, Nelson Waldo Bunker—"Pap" as we called him—son of Charles Waldo and Lydia Starbuck Bunker, was born in Cincinnati, Ohio, on May 2, 1846. He was educated in that city's grammar and high schools and at the University of Ohio.

In 1872, Pap, twenty-five and ambitious, having no farm or business to inherit from his father, set off "to make his fortune"—young men in those romantic days did not simply try "to make a living." Pap started as a carpenter on a boat going down the Mississippi River, but he didn't enjoy it, so when it docked across from Greenville, Mississippi, he disembarked and searched the area for work. He landed in Lake Village, Arkansas, and found a job on a cotton plantation.

In 1883 he married Sarah Rebecca Hunnicut Kruse, the young widow of Charles Anthony Kruse, who had died five years earlier. People passed away very young in those days. My grandparents had six children: Willie F., Nelson Waldo, Jr., Lyda (my mother), Lamar F., Floyd O., and Mattie Virginia.

After around fifteen years on the plantation, Pap had saved enough money to buy into Lake Village's general—and only—store. Within a few years he bought out his partner and continued to prosper. When he came home at night he would throw his change on the floor and let his children enjoy scrambling for it. As they owned the only store in town, the kids had no place for children to spend these coins so they would send this money to an aunt in Cincinnati with a shopping list. The parcels would soon arrive by boat.

In 1905, my mother, then sixteen, went to Mattocks boarding school in Little Rock, as there was no high school in Lake Village. Afterward, she attended Potter College for women in Bowling Green, Kentucky, for four years. It was unusual in those days for a female to go away to high school and college, but Mother craved education and Pap indulged her in this.

The riverboat trip to Bowling Green took two days and nights, often longer. Mother studied Greek, Latin, math, and English literature, and graduated with a Bachelor of Arts degree. The young men of Lake Village did not inspire her toward marriage, and having a strong desire to teach, she took a position as schoolteacher in Jonesboro, Arkansas. As Jonesboro was two hundred miles north of Lake Village, Mother could not commute.

The only reason Pap allowed her to leave the security and comfort of his home—returning to Lake Village only during vacations and in the summer—was that in those days the most valued and respected person in a community was the schoolteacher. Custom held that when she came from out of town she was invited to live with one of the leading families. Lyda Bunker was welcomed into the home of the Edwin Pewetts in Jonesboro. Also living with the Pewetts was another schoolteacher, Kate Caldwell Bass, who became Mother's lifelong friend.

# *Two: The Hunts*

One of the earliest Hunts to appear on the American continent was Reverend Robert Hunt, chaplain for Captain John Smith's expedition, which sailed from Blackwall, England on December 19, 1606, and arrived in Virginia on April 26, 1607. He played an important role in the political and civic life of the new Jamestown Colony, where he celebrated communion on June 21, 1607, the first observed by Englishmen in North America. He was responsible for the building of the first Protestant Church in the New World.

Waddy Thorpe Hunt, my great-grandfather, born in 1822, married Melissa Abby Kelly, and prior to the outbreak of the war between the states, they left Georgia for Arkansas. Before crossing the Mississippi, they freed their slaves, an unpopular action in that time and place.

When he was thirty-nine years old, Waddy became Captain Hunt of the Confederate Army. His son, Daddy's father, Haroldson Lafayette Hunt—who had been born in Habersham County, Georgia, October 19, 1843, and who was at that time eighteen years old—served for two years as a private under his father in Company F of the 27th Arkansas Infantry.

It is ironic, given the dangers of a war, that Captain Waddy Thorpe Hunt died not in battle but was murdered. On furlough he was called to the door of his home and shot to death by a gang of marauders called Quantrill's Raiders, among whom were Frank and Jesse James and the Younger Brothers.

At the war's end in 1865, Haroldson—"Hash" as he was known—now twenty-two and the nominal head of the family, took charge. Anticipating the agony of Reconstruction, he loaded his mother, brothers, and sisters into wagons and moved them northwest to Fayette County, Illinois. Hash married Sarah Jane Wear and they had one child, Thomas N., born December 2, 1866, who became a Presbyterian minister in Indianapolis.

Sarah Jane died before 1870, and Hash married Ella Rose Myers Henderson in 1872. The Henderson forebears were also French Huguenots. When exiled they chose not to emigrate to Russia, Tennessee, the Choctaw Nation, or other faraway places as the majority of the exiled Huguenots did, for it developed that they had a close connection to the royal family in Paris and were permitted to cross the border into Germany. But the horrors of religious persecution and exile did not escape them there, and as a result of his mother's heritage, Daddy grew up obsessed with the importance of freedom.

Having no money, land, or animals, possessing only his wits and willingness to work, Grandpa Hunt went into the business of selling other people's animals for them, and before long he was a prospering broker of calves, hogs, wheat, and corn.

Ella Rose, Daddy's mother, had attended Arcadia College in Arcadia, Missouri, in 1859, and during the Civil War served as a nurse on the Union side. Unbeknownst to both of them at the time, she and her future husband were on opposite sides of the war and on occasions within twenty miles of each other.

They had eight children: Robert, Florence, Rose, James G., Sherman, Henrietta, Leonard L., and Haroldson Lafayette, Jr.

The youngest, my father, H.L. Hunt, Jr.—"June" or "Junie" to his family—was born February 17, 1889.

Though she had sent the seven older children to school, Grandmother Hunt chose not to send her youngest child, preferring to teach him herself. She began early, reading to him from the Bible in Greek, Latin, French, and German, translating the passages into English. My father could read when he was three years old.

Grandpa Hash enjoyed showing him off to visitors. He'd hand him the *St. Louis Globe-Democrat* and say, "Junie, I don't have my glasses on, so read me the quotes in the cattle market," and the three-year-old boy would reel them off. This was all the more impressive because in those days there were many adults who were not able to read. By the time he was of school age my father had completed the sixth reader, which was as far as the local school went. His only trips to school came at noontime, when he would take a horse and gallop down to the schoolhouse to play with the other children.

As a child, Daddy worked the farm and the commodities business with his brothers and sisters. By the time he was five he was trusted with the family's weigh station, handling the scales that weighed livestock and calculating their worth. His older brothers did the heavier work. Apparently his father was impressed with him, for while still in his early teens he was sent from southern Illinois to the delta country of Mississippi and southern Arkansas to trade and buy animals for breeding back in Fayette County.

Daddy did have some formal schooling. When he was fifteen, he went to Valparaiso College in Indiana for five or six weeks. In his autobiography, *Hunt Heritage,* which he wrote some fifty years later, he says that he developed such a severe allergy in Indiana that he could hardly breathe or swallow. Afraid he was going to die, he returned home. "When I left I was number two in my class of about fifty." Frankly, I don't remember Daddy ever being allergic to anything; I think he was just impatient with being formally educated.

When he was sixteen years old, Daddy left home and "went west to California, to grow up with the country," and though he was very close to his family, from that time on he seldom returned home. He told us of working as a dishwasher, topping sugar beets, and hauling gravel for concrete. He even tried to play semi-pro baseball. He was well-developed physically and had further built his strength cowboying on ranches, driving ten- and twenty-mule teams, and laboring as a lumberjack.

Daddy told all of us stories of his youth. But those concerned with the harsher side of life he reserved for the boys.

> BUNKER: *I think my father was much smarter than my brothers and me because he'd been out in the school of hard knocks. He was street smart. He understood that there were perils out there. One time he needed to take a train. He had fifty dollars and couldn't spare any of it for a ticket, so he had to grab a freight or ride the rails. There were some rails beneath the cars and you could jump on those and ride there if you didn't see a freight car with an open door. He was lucky and spotted one. But to grab it, he said, he had to wait until it started to move because there were railroad detectives who'd pull you off. Once it was moving, you were OK, because they weren't willing to chase after a moving train. So it became quite a physical feat.*

*The freight car he jumped into carried a load of lumber and there was a little open space near the door. As soon as he landed, there were two hobos who were there ahead of him. He could tell quickly that he was in a bad spot because these two guys looked mean and like they were going to give him trouble. The train was traveling at a substantial speed when they jumped him. He was sixteen but looked twenty. Though he was strong, he was concerned that they might try to kill him.*

*He said, "The only thing I could do was try to defend myself. There was one on each side of me and I got to knocking their heads against the lumber and I figured by doing that I might give them a hard enough time so that we could work out a compromise. I was a little stronger than both of them and after I'd bruised them a bit I said, 'Wait a minute. You guys want some money, and I'm going to give you some money, but lay off. No point in us hurting each other. I'm going to give you ten dollars.'"*

*He said that he was banging them bad enough that ten bucks sounded pretty good to them. He gave them the ten dollars and then real quick he jumped off the train and got away with his skin.*

*That kind of background makes you very wary of life. My father had survived in the jungle and all of his life he had that instinct for potential danger.*

By the time Grandpa Hash died on March 24, 1911, he had become the wealthiest man in Fayette County, a landowner and founder of the People's State Bank in Ramsey, Illinois. Daddy inherited five thousand dollars in cash. His brothers and sisters wanted him to stay home and work with them at the family bank but he had a negative view of banking. Then, and all of his life, he believed, "the borrower has much the better of transactions between himself and his banker."

Nor did he want to work the commodities business. He was only twenty-two and he had the urge to move on again, to get out into the world on his own. He remembered his father telling him that during the Civil War while he had been fighting the Battle of Ditch Bayou in a place called Lake Village in Chicot County, Arkansas, he had seen some of the "richest, best-looking farmland you ever saw." So Daddy took his five-thousand-dollar inheritance and went down to have a look.

# *Three*

ARRIVING IN LAKE VILLAGE, Daddy checked into the Lake Shore Hotel and felt comfortable among the town's twelve hundred citizens, especially the young women. In later years he described himself as being "girl-minded." He had known cowgirls in the dust storm country and allowed as how "the comely ladies of Lake Village with their soft drawls" fascinated him. A handsome, tall, blue-eyed gentleman, he was warmly welcomed into their society of boating on the lake, watermelon parties, and ice cream socials.

Lake Village was a small town on a beautiful, crescent-shaped lake that had been formed by a change in the course of the great Mississippi River.

After studying the area and being impressed by the rich alluvial soil of the Mississippi Delta, Daddy made a down payment on a 960-acre plantation six miles south of Lake Village. This prime cotton-growing land was close to the river, which was essential for transporting the harvest to Europe, the largest market. In those days, an acre of such land yielded a full five-hundred-pound bale, which sold for around $625, a great amount of money. The expression "cotton is king" was no exaggeration: it was substantiated by the great fortunes many cotton planters had earned. Cargo boats would leave America for Europe bearing tons of cotton and return not only with silver and gold but with the other riches of the old world—the silks, porcelains, crystal, and furniture that filled the planters' antebellum mansions.

Staying at the Lake Shore Hotel kept Daddy at the center of town activity. He made land transactions and played poker regularly with the other Mississippi River plantation owners, whom he described as some of the best card players in the world.

Much has been written and said about my father's penchant for risk-taking—poker playing, breaking bookmakers betting on football, matching coins over the telephone with Ray Ryan for a thousand dollars a toss, his passion for horse racing, and his involvement in the notoriously unstable oil business. But he took the greatest risks of all in cotton, a double-or-nothing type of bet that depends on the cooperation of myriad variables: sun and rain in exactly the right amounts, and abnormally good luck against endless varieties of bugs, worms, and insects—at the head of them the boll weevil. Should just one of these forces go against you, you have disaster—the loss of a lot of money and a whole year's labor.

Thanks to a complete levee system, the Mississippi had not caused a major flooding since 1877, and it was now 1912. Daddy's probability for success was enormous. However, after his first cotton crop was barely in the ground, Old Man River rose and flooded out the land—for the first time in three and a half decades.

Daddy prepared to try again the next year. He calculated that if the river had been contained for thirty-five years before breaking loose, then the odds were 70-1 that it would not happen again.

> COUSIN STUART: *He loved to gamble because it was percentages. He had one of the most active minds of anybody I've ever seen. Winning money was the way to keep score. The challenge was what he played for. He understood the percentages. Everything he bet on, cards, dice, horses—his success was in his mathematical ability to calculate the odds. He never bet on hunches; he called himself "a card locater" because he remembered the cards that had been played. He had the guts to bet them if he had them, and he always bet with the odds.*

But the Mississippi beat the odds. It rose for the second consecutive year and wiped him out. Still, Daddy had the resilience, or the simple courage, to pick himself up, brush himself off, and prepare to try again.

The owner of a cotton plantation was not out in the fields all the time. The hired hands were. A cotton planter, like a cattle rancher, takes financial risks but physically doesn't do much except observe and oversee the work he is paying to have done. Daddy's life, therefore, was composed largely of riding around his lands, then into town, sitting in the square with other planters, and playing cards and checkers. While his saturated lands were drying out, he had few options for supporting himself other than playing cards in town. In the evenings the more interesting games were held across the river in Greenville, Mississippi.

And from time to time, when he had accumulated a bankroll, he would travel down the river for the high-stakes games in New Orleans.

During this time, he became acquainted with one of the most prominent citizens of Lake Village, Mr. Nelson Waldo Bunker, who owned the general store and had extensive real estate holdings. A Republican, he had served as the postmaster of Lake Village, as deputy circuit clerk under many administrations, and as commissioner in several improvement districts. He was held in high regard throughout the state of Arkansas.

Daddy was now established as a landowner and planter. Despite his card playing, he had a reputation for being "as straight as a string" and was considered an eligible bachelor. He began escorting Mr. Bunker's seventeen-year-old daughter, Mattie, to the social events that highlighted Lake Village life.

However, in the spring of 1914, Mattie's elder sister by six years, Lyda Bunker, returned home for the summer from her teaching job in Jonesboro. Mattie had introduced Lyda to Haroldson Lafayette Hunt, Jr. the summer before, but this time Lyda took a closer look. And Daddy took a deeper look into this beautiful young woman's brown eyes and at her fabulous, shining, dark hair. He listened to her cultured view of subjects that interested him, and he was entertained by her lively mind. As he caught on to her delicate sense of humor balanced by a touching shyness, the charming band music of Lake Village faded out and he began to hear Mozart and Beethoven—and ultimately *Lohengrin.*

Their wedding took place on November 26 of that year in the Bunkers' home. Mattie played the wedding march on the piano. They went to live on his plantation, in the southern colonial mansion that had not yet been introduced to modern plumbing or electricity.

Daddy put in a third cotton crop, calculating that he now had a 105-1 probability for success. And in fact, his third year as a planter produced a bumper harvest yielding a full five-hundred-pound bale per acre. But there was one factor that he had not anticipated: the total 1914 cotton crop was so bountiful that oversupply drove prices so low that he had little return on his investment. It was then that he came to the conclusion that "probabilities are not always dependable."

Mother had taken a teaching position nearby, which helped financially. I was born a year later on November 19, 1915. She always said that I put my foot in her schoolteaching, because when I came along, she of course she had to retire. Women did not appear in public when expecting. Mother really did not mind; she had only gone back to teaching to help out. But there was another reason that she was happy to retire.

> HERBERT: *Mother really was the stronger of the two. She said Dad didn't turn a lick as far as going out to work. He'd sit around the square and play cards and checkers. So she up and quit teaching before Margaret was born. She told him, "Now it is up to you, June. I have been supporting this family until now. It is your turn. You are going to provide for this family."*

Part of what had attracted Mother to Daddy was his vitality, the sharpness of his mind, his even nature, and the strength to absorb the adversities he had suffered in cotton. She felt that he had the potential to accomplish important things. But she discovered that Daddy needed a push.

> BUNKER: *During the war, in 1942, when women were just starting to work in large numbers, my mother said, "These married girls who are taking jobs are making a mistake. Their husbands will never amount to much. When I got married I was teaching school and I believe if I had not gotten pregnant I would still be teaching school because that is the way men are. Mr. Hunt"—she sometimes referred to Dad as Mr. Hunt—"as long as I had a paycheck, he would do very little. It was obvious to me that he had great potential, but he just did not exhibit much ambition."*

The day I was born Daddy said, "She is beautiful," which was the last compliment he ever paid me. It's not that he was especially hard on me. Daddy simply did not pay compliments to anyone. Except my brother Hassie.

I was not given a name until I was eight or nine months old. They couldn't decide what to name me and were simply calling me Baby. Finally they named me Margaret. No middle name. Just Margaret Hunt. Daddy said, "Never is anybody to call her by a nickname. Never Margo, never Peggy or Maggie ..." And I never have been called anything but Margaret except by my little brothers calling me "Mahdy" when they were unable to pronounce my name.

My mother's best friend, Kate Bass, used to come to visit. They would boil my diapers in a black kettle over an open fire outside. Southern plantations were not all like Tara.

Immediately following Daddy's third financial disaster, the Mississippi flooded so tremendously that everything was inundated, including our house. Daddy and one helper tied some logs together to form a raft, and we literally floated out of the house toward Lake Village a few miles away. As we approached, Pap was standing at the edge of the lake. Suddenly our raft caught on a fence top. It tipped back and forth for about five amazingly long minutes before Daddy dislodged it and we continued on to safety.

That did it for plantation life. We stayed with my grandparents until Mother and Daddy found a small house on the lake front next door to the hotel where Daddy had first lived. I loved being right in Lake Village. My grandparents' house was across the street from the Catholic School that I later attended, and I always stopped off to see Pap on my way home.

Two years after my birth—on November 23, 1917—my brother Haroldson Lafayette III—or Hassie, as we called him—was born. As I had been born on the nineteenth, we always shared a birthday. And one cake. That habit has continued all our lives.

In 1917 the United States was operating on a wartime economy, and business in general was prospering. Land speculation in Arkansas and Missouri was especially active. Good plantation land was commanding $300 an acre, more than double what Daddy had paid. He told Mother that he thought they should take advantage of the moment and sell. She agreed that you are not likely to go broke by taking a large profit. So Daddy sold his plantation for cash. After paying off his notes, he was left with $200,000. That was a huge amount of capital in 1917, comparable to around $2 million today.

If Daddy had not displayed a desire to work hard himself, he certainly expected his cash to labor long and well. He spread his money around making down payments on a number of plantations, later selling them for cash, making several hundred thousand dollars more. Sensing that the market was weakening and that it was time to stop speculating and take a more permanent position in land, he made down payments on plantations aggregating to fifteen thousand acres of the best possible cotton land. He calculated that just one good year—a bumper crop, coinciding with a steady market—would bring him $9,375,000. He figured that even after paying off the notes he owed on the land, he would still be rich.

Again, probabilities were not dependable. In 1920 there was a land bust, and suddenly the rich cotton market began dropping. Daddy's cotton was already in New Orleans, with his brokers, The Cotton Factors, as he waited for the right moment to sell. Closely watching world and economic news, he anticipated disaster coming and ordered them to sell. They came up with a ruinously low price.

Daddy could see no reason why cotton prices should rise in the immediate future, so he took strong positions in cotton futures, selling short. Again cotton fooled him. Inexplicably, the price went up, and he had to use his available cash to post margins with his brokers.

At that hectic moment I developed acute tonsillitis, so I was taken by riverboat to New Orleans to have a tonsillectomy.

After the operation, I lay in my hospital bed, with my mother by my side feeding me ice cream to soothe my throat, when Daddy came into the room. Normally trim and neat, he looked odd. His suit was bulging. He closed the door behind him and, smiling broadly, began emptying his pockets, putting wads and wads of money on the bed. He took money out of his side pockets, his trouser pockets, and the inside pockets of his coat. He even had it folded into his watch pocket. He spread it on the bed in front of my mother. By the time it was all laid out he had counted $25,000.

"I ran into a small game at the Grunewald and then I got into a larger one and got lucky," he said.

"Here I am having Margaret's tonsils out and you were playing poker." But she was smiling.

Mother separated some money from the pile, and that afternoon she came back to the hospital with a new coat and shoes for me and the same for Hassie. That would be her custom for many years.

COUSIN TOM: *Aunt Lyda told me she always wanted to make sure that the children had a new pair of shoes and a new coat. The coat came first. "A coat covers everything but you only stand in shoes." She had the mother's or woman's regard for protecting some money. Uncle June wasn't worried if he lost money. She guided him to make sure that something was left.*

Daddy accompanied us home. When we got back to Lake Village he gave the money to Mother. "Keep this on hand in case you have to cover my futures position." He then packed another suitcase and set out again.

Every day a Western Union boy delivered a telegram from Daddy's broker saying how much he owed and every day, following Daddy's instructions, Mother took the money to the Western Union office and sent it off.

Cotton kept falling. On the fifth day, Mother went through the same routine except that along with the money she sent a telegram saying, THAT IS ALL THE MONEY WE HAVE, SO YOU HAD BETTER CLOSE OUT MR. HUNT'S COTTON FUTURES POSITION.

As we walked home through town, she told me, "If you can believe it, I am relieved that all the money is gone. We are out of that deal and your father's broker will not be sending for more."

Daddy got back in a week with enough cash from his poker games to keep us going for a while longer. He knew from the papers that his cotton futures had required all the cash we had on hand.

Mother was patient but emphatic. "June, I am opposed to gambling on futures—and to speculating in general. I would prefer a less precarious lifestyle with a steady income."

"I understand, Mom. From now on we will try not to put money into anything we cannot control, at least to some extent." He never played the commodities market or invested in the stock exchange again.

Cotton bottomed out at fifty dollars a bale. You could not support an acre of cotton land on fifty dollars a year, so planters everywhere went broke. Those who could not meet the payments on their lands and their taxes had no choice but to give back the properties to the note holders in exchange for canceling the notes. They had lost everything and wanted only to get out from under further liability. Ironically, people like my father who had good credit history were not to be rid of the cotton business so easily. Short on cash to pay his upcoming notes on one four-thousand-acre plantation, Daddy offered to take the loss of his down payment and give back the land, but the note holder refused. He wanted Daddy to keep the land because he was confident he would find the money to pay his notes when they came due. He was right. Daddy found the money and kept the land. So like it or not, and with no foreseeable alternative, he was still in the cotton business. He was not particularly upset, because all his life Daddy enjoyed owning properties. He liked to buy them—but not really to sell them.

Tremendous bargains were available to people with the stomach to risk the gambles cotton land presented. In 1921 Daddy learned that a fine plantation called Montrose, just south of his 2,500-acre Valentine Plantation in East Carroll Parish, Louisiana, was available; the owners wanted to limit their liability, and anyone who would pay $7,000 in back taxes could own the 25,000-acre plantation. In normal times this land was worth between $500,000 and $1,000,000. Daddy reasoned that Montrose would more than double his already vast properties, and if he could hold onto it all until the commodities market stabilized he would be able to make a great fortune in cotton. At the very least, if he could hold onto it until real estate prices normalized, then he could sell for a huge profit.

He called a banker friend, Jim Buck, in Missouri, and Mr. Buck agreed to honor Daddy's draft for what he needed to close the deal on the Montrose Plantation.

His next step was to drive to Tallulah, Louisiana, which is now famous as the place where the idea for Delta Airlines was conceived by a bunch of cotton dusters flying airplanes. He went out to Montrose on horseback, scrutinized hundreds of acres, and found it to be as splendid as its reputation.

He met with the owners, the Noell family of Shreveport, Louisiana, in the office of their lawyer, Judge Snyder. Daddy did not bring a lawyer with him because he was a friend of Judge Snyder, and because he was well versed in land deals, having prepared his own papers in previous dealings.

Naturally the deal was not as simple as paying the $7,000 in taxes and taking over the deed. There was considerable negotiating to be done, and from time to time the Noells needed to confer privately with Judge Snyder. Daddy would excuse himself, step outside the one-room office building and stroll along the boardwalk that surrounded it.

As he walked he pondered the deal he was trying to make, and he tried to foresee the future of the tempestuous cotton market despite the unpredictable weather and the dangerous river.

At one such moment, one of the Noell brothers joined him outside and commented on the oil boom that was occurring in El Dorado*, Arkansas. People from all over the United States were flocking there, he said, overflowing the town, living in tents and in Pullman cars, any place they could find shelter, in the hope of getting in on the current hope for making money.

At first Daddy was only politely interested, his mind being occupied with the business at hand. As the hours passed, however, he began to feel that tingling of excitement that a new possibility offers. He found himself questioning his purchase of Montrose, and the course of his life in general.

*What am I getting into? Am I going to bury myself here for the rest of my life? If this land ever regains its price, I already have fifteen thousand acres and will be rich on that. Why not rent that land out and let it pay for itself until it comes back in price, if it ever does? Instead of buying Montrose and getting in still deeper, with more investment and more notes to pay, why not see about this oil boom?* He was aware that he understood farming and land but knew nothing about oil. Nothing. Yet, he figured in his unwavering optimism, why not learn?

Oil was first discovered in Pennsylvania in 1859 by Colonel Edwin L. Drake and used for kerosene. The first real oil boom came in 1901 with Spindletop in south Texas. In the 1920s, oil was used for gasoline, but there was a larger market for kerosene since there were still a lot more lamps than automobiles. But the market for gasoline was increasing. It was inevitable that interstate highways would be built and more cars sold. So oil exploration offered that most desirable of all things, the opportunity for getting in on the ground floor of a product of the future.

Going quickly to the office while the Noells were in conference, Daddy tapped on the door, stepped in, and holding up his hands before

* pronounced *El Do-ray-do*

they could speak he said, "I have been thinking this over and I believe I should not take your plantation. If it is all right with you, I will withdraw." Daddy went to the Tallulah depot and sent off a telegram to his banker, Jim Buck, saying he would not be requiring a draft after all.

En route to Lake Village, Daddy's usually orderly mind was whirling with images of the Spanish *conquistadores,* imagining how they must have eagerly thought about their El Dorado, the legendary place of gold for which they had relentlessly searched. Now in 1921, parallel to the saga of El Dorado, black gold was streaking out of the ground from lakes of liquid treasure. How appropriate that nearly eighty years earlier the first Arkansas settlers had named their poor little town El Dorado—"the golden"—never imagining the boomtown it would become, or the wealth it would create.

Daddy told Mother about his idea, about getting in on the ground floor of something that might be enormous. Though she had to see that hoping to get rich by drilling a hole in the ground was not exactly what she would consider "a less precarious lifestyle with a steady income," she understood Daddy and did not trample on his enthusiasm, which would surely have broken his forward motion. On the contrary, she gave it her blessing, encouraging him to go there and have a look.

Then Daddy returned to reality, facing the fact that he was broke. Though he had thousands of acres of the richest farmland in the world, his assets—other than the land on which he owed $200,000—were in the form of second, third, and fourth mortgages that he could not collect because nobody had any money. None of the local planters even had cash to lose at poker. Nor could he borrow even fifty dollars for "walking-around money" from either of the two distressed banks in Lake Village. I suppose that borrowing thousands from Jim Buck to purchase a prized plantation at a bargain price was seen as one thing, but borrowing a grubstake to go prospecting was quite another.

Still, Daddy was not about to let a dream be thwarted by these obstacles. He kept on looking as hard for fifty dollars as in years later he might have looked for fifty million. In fact, when you have no saleable assets and no cash at all, fifty dollars is a more distant number than when you can go into a bank and have them listen while you tell them you want to borrow fifty million.

Finally a man Daddy knew said he would lend him fifty dollars if he could get three cosigners to his note. That's how bad the times were in cotton country. Four guarantors for one fifty-dollar loan. He rounded up three friends: Sam Epstein, the leading supplier to the planters throughout Chicot County; R.D. Chotard, a sometime politician, and Pete Mulligan, a timberman. His signature was the fourth.

After telling Mother he would either see her soon or send for us, he cranked up his Ford and headed for El Dorado eighty-five miles away by car, but a million miles from anything he or we had ever known. The man who was to become a legendary Texas oilman was on his way to see Dr. Busey's Armstrong No. 1, the first oil well he had ever seen in his life.

# *Four*

SO MANY PEOPLE WERE ARRIVING in El Dorado every day that there wasn't room for everyone to sleep at the same time in the town's two hotels. Beds were rented by the hour at the Garrett—and later the Randolph—and the boomers slept in shifts. A steak dinner cost 35 cents; it cost a dollar to sleep for six hours. Daddy knew fifty dollars would not go far so he set about playing cards while he figured out how to get himself into the oil business. Risking his grubstake at poker against medium-intelligent fortune seekers was relaxing compared to trying to outthink the Mississippi River and the commodities market.

When oil is discovered in a given place, it causes such quick wealth for some and such dreams of sudden wealth for others that most everyone wants someone to bring the magic wand of a drilling rig onto their land and transform their mundane existences to lives of luxury and leisure.

The normal deal in Arkansas—and later in Texas—was for the oilman to pay the landowner so much per acre per year in cash, starting at 50 cents an acre, reaching up to $5,000 an acre for leases on "proven land"—land that is close to a producing well. The landowner would also retain one-eighth of the oil that was found on his property—called a one-eighth royalty. So landowners made no investment and took no risk. And they could become rich. Often the farmer was so hungry that he'd give the lease to you free if you would promise to drill a well quickly.

Leases ran an average of five or ten years, giving the prospective driller that much time before he had to drill or lose the lease. After the initial lease period, the lease remained in force as long as he was drilling or producing oil.

> LAMAR: *Dad understood land and he quickly learned how to trade leases, which was a fundamental part of it. He'd go out near where the oil play was going on and buy a lease from a farmer for twenty-*

*five dollars. Then he'd come back into town and sell it for fifty dollars. Then he'd buy another lease for fifty dollars and sell it for sixty dollars keeping a one-eighth interest in it.*

And so it went. Daddy saw the opportunities others missed, partly because he was smarter than some and partly because he had the will to drive himself on, working eighteen and twenty hours a day. He would go out into the farmland and buy a lease, then return to the hotel lobbies and the courthouse square, where all the buyers and sellers gathered and did business, sort of a lease exchange. There he sold the lease and then went out and bought others. When other lease hounds were confined to town because their cars would get bogged down in the mud, Daddy would ride on horseback from house to house. Hearing of a farmer who wanted to sell, he would gallop out to make an offer. After six months of lease trading and observation, Daddy felt he knew enough to buy his first lease for himself—a half-acre in the El Dorado South Field.

His next step was to find some drilling equipment. He heard of a rig sitting on a railroad siding because of unpaid freight charges. He paid the demurrage, which was storage fees and charges, then found a man with a team of mules who moved the old-fashioned wooden structure three miles from the freight yards to his lease. He hired some local rig men to build the necessary wooden platform and a 114-foot derrick. The way Daddy set up his operation was known in the oil fields as poor-boying—patching up and borrowing materials whenever possible so you don't have to buy them.

Following oil-field tradition he called his well the Hunt-Pickering No. 1, for the producer, the landowner, and the number of the well in drilling sequence. Though his site was surrounded by splendid producers, the Hunt-Pickering No. 1 came in flowing in small heads, bringing up two large spurts of oil and then going dead for two to five minutes, then spurting again.

Daddy came back to Lake Village regularly and during meals gave us detailed reports of life in the oil fields. "Hunt-Pickering No. 1 should have been a big producer, and it would have been except that reservoir pressure has been so badly depleted due to the area being highly overdrilled. There are no controlled oil-field practices, no plans for the future. It is every man for himself, so when they hit a producer they flow them at capacity ..."

Mother was concerned. "June, it sounds to me like we are getting involved in another uncontrollable business. The oil business seems to be fraught with risks."

Daddy said, "Calculated risks. You invest ten thousand dollars to drill a well, knowing that you will either lose your ten thousand or strike oil and make hundreds of thousands, maybe a million."

She was not convinced. "Ten thousand dollars is a fortune to risk."

"Ten thousand dollars can buy a lot of food and medical care but it is not a fortune. If you have ten thousand dollars and you have done your homework, and you risk it all to make a hundred thousand, then that is a fair risk. A bad risk would be if you have a hundred thousand and you expose it all to make ten thousand. For business purposes, there is no difference between a hundred thousand and a hundred and ten thousand."

Pap died in February. I was seven. When I heard that he had died I hid in the laundry basket while I cried. Mother was a restrained person. I had never seen her cry. So I did not want anyone knowing that I cried, and no one did.

Daddy did not make money on Hunt-Pickering No. 1, but neither did he lose his interest in the oil business. On the contrary, he committed to a forty-acre lease on land belonging to Mr. Tom Rowland, who took Daddy's note for $20,000. The Rowland lease was considered proven land because it lay between two oil-producing leases. Still, many a dry hole has been drilled on proven land. The site was about two miles southeast of the Pickering well. He liked the fact that lease prices there were not nearly as high as they were in the center of the field, and he was gambling on a hunch that the oil extended to where he had bought. Fortunately, this time his hunch turned out to be right.

Obviously Daddy had no schooling as a geologist. None of the wildcatters had. By definition a wildcatter is one who goes out and gets himself some acreage on which there is little or no geological information and drills a well. It usually proves to be a dry hole and is marked on the map with an X.

Daddy and the other wildcatters were what he called creekologists. Though it sounds humorous, he was entirely serious. He termed this inexact method of discovering oil creekology because, as he would say, "You are walking along, thinking only about where to find oil and you wonder, 'Why did that creek make a bend for no apparent reason? And why is that ground a little high over there?'" These creekologists assumed that these aberrations were caused by some underground forces and were willing to take a chance that it was oil. And sometimes they were right.

When Hunt-Rowland No. 1 began spurting oil it went straight into Daddy's blood. H.L. Hunt Incorporated was formed. He was in the oil business to stay. He sent Mother a telegram: START PACKING. AM LOOKING FOR ACCOMMODATIONS.

Locating a home for his family of four in a small town to which suddenly thousands of people were flocking was nearly impossible, but Daddy was always able to search out what he wanted. Soon another telegram arrived: HAVE LEASED FURNISHED TEMPORARY APARTMENT.

Meanwhile he was drilling on other leases as quickly as he could finance his efforts. When you struck oil, the normal procedure was to sell your production to a big oil company. They would run a trunk line over to your well and move your oil away in their pipeline. Daddy recognized that this meant he would be selling his production to them at their prices and that they would resell his oil to the refineries at substantially higher prices. Though Daddy did not start out like a house afire, once he got going he did not ever wait and let things progress in the conventional manner if he could think of a better one. He took the attitude that if he was going to spend his time and energy working, being away from his family, risking his money, then he wanted the maximum compensation for his investment and effort.

So he ran his own pipeline from well to well and then to the railroad line, marketing his oil directly to the refineries at higher prices. By creating his own gathering system, Daddy received his proceeds from runs and could pay out his royalties faster than the other operators, who were not willing to make the investment in a pipeline. Daddy was always willing to spend money to earn money.

At first he was so lucky that the word was "Follow Hunt and strike it rich." Then, after drilling six dry holes in a row, the saying changed to "Follow Hunt and go broke." But luckily, in the oil business a string of producers more than compensates for a string of dry holes. There was no stopping him.

Mother, ever conservative, would wonder aloud, "Are you drilling too many wells, June?"

> BUNKER: *Dad believed in drilling. He always said, "The more wells you drill the more chances you have of finding oil."*

> COUSIN STUART: *Everything he did was based on percentages. He told me, "Have lots of acreage because you are going to hit a lot less than you are going to miss, so if you hit it then hit it big. Do not go out there to drill one hole. Give yourself a chance to find oil."*

Daddy did, however, see a great difference between drilling with a lot of space between the wells—and hopefully reaching independent deposits of oil—and overdrilling one small area and probably tapping the same reservoir more than once. That was economically useless, as well as a waste of the underground pressure that pushes the oil to the surface.

From the moment he got into the oil business, he had a sense of responsibility toward the industry. Abuse or waste of this amazing natural resource bothered him and he became involved with its regulation and conservation. He sought and promoted the most effective use of oil reserves, maximizing profits and minimizing loss.

Daddy had influence with the other independents and managed to persuade some to ease up when they were overdrilling, to leave much more space between wells—saving them the millions they would have spent in equipping and operating unnecesary wells.

When we got the telegram to START PACKING, Mother did not delay. She had no qualms about uprooting from Lake Village—to move away from her home, her widowed mother, her brothers and sister, her childhood friends, and give up her status as a member of the Bunker family. She had lived away from home at boarding school and college and as a teacher, and she knew she was bigger than Lake Village. Nevertheless, Mother was a cultured lady, and it must have seemed onerous to her to transplant to a place that Daddy bluntly charactered as an uncouth boomtown. But if that was where he felt his destiny to lead him, she wanted to be there, too. Further, it appealed to her very rational sensibility: it was unfair to cause her husband to be commuting eighty-five miles a few times a month, which in 1922 took five hours each way.

Daddy came to get us in his Ford. We all piled in, with me sitting on a suitcase to make room, and off we went to El Dorado. Though it had rained there for the better part of the past three years, I remember it as a sunny day.

Daddy was exuberant. He had his ever-present cigar. As he drove, he told us what changes we could expect in El Dorado. "Life is going to be different. A boomtown attracts many undesirables, and so for your security, ladies and children are not allowed on the streets after dark." That was to affect Hassie and me more than Mother. At that time she was expecting Caroline, and custom did not allow her to appear in public anyway.

Our apartment was the upstairs of a two-family house. As Daddy showed us around he told us, "In order to get this apartment—which hundreds of others would love to have—I had to agree not just to pay the inflated rent but to buy the belongings of the man who previously lived here, a rather famous oilman called Deep Rock Foster."

Mother stared at the bathroom towels. They all had *F*s embroidered on them, but the monograms were all different sizes and colors. "This F is not for Foster," she said. "These towels have been stolen from hotels..."

"That is entirely possible."

She rolled her eyes.

We unpacked our clothes and, with a sense of excitement, sat down for our first dinner in El Dorado. Though there was no moon that night, it did not seem to get totally dark outside. Through the window we could see a bright glare coming from miles away. Mother was astonished by it too.

Daddy said, "That light is from the flares that burn all night and all day." He explained, "As oil comes up out of a well, with it comes natural gas, which is not very saleable. However, it is too dangerous to leave floating in the atmosphere, so it is flared. The flares you see are from different wells that are over twenty miles away."

The next evening I looked for the flares, and sure enough, the sky around El Dorado was lit up all night.

Daddy took me to enroll in school. Though Hassie was two years younger than I, he was big for his age and we brought him along. Having completed the first grade at the Catholic school in Lake Village, I was being enrolled in second grade. The administrator turned to Hassie and asked him, "What about you? Would you like to go to school?" Daddy had prompted him, should he be asked, to say, "Oh, yes." In those days there were no kindergartens, so Hassie started the first grade at age four. It was hard on him, but formal education, as with my father, was not to prove as important in his life as his natural genius as an oilman.

Daddy bought a touring car, open on both sides with a canvas top. Every morning, when he started the engine, Hassie and I tore out of the house and jumped in the back seat. Pregnant with Caroline, Mother had little strength for us. There were no picture shows yet, nor were there such things as playgrounds. School lasted only half a day, in the afternoons, so Daddy took us wherever he went and we spent all of our free time in the oil fields.

We drove on one-lane gravel roads between the towns, but to get out into the fields we had only narrow dirt roads. Whenever two cars met, one had to pull off and let the other pass. Where it had rained and the ground was marshy, cut pine poles were laid side by side across the road for as far as a mile. But then the cars couldn't pull off into the marsh when they met, so the one who was closest to the end had to back up. They called them corduroy roads, and whether forward or backward, when riding on those roads it was all you could do to stay in your seat.

Closer to the fields, we drove across board roads that had been put down because rains caused so much mud that it was difficult to to move the equipment in otherwise. Board roads were a bit less uncomfortable than corduroy roads.

Fortunately, it was an open car, because I often got carsick. When I did, Daddy didn't stop, he would just call out over his shoulder, "Hang your head out the back." No matter how sick I got, the next day I would still tear out of the house and jump into the back seat.

Whenever he saw a patch of green grass, Daddy would pull the car over and we'd all get out and look for four-leaf clovers. He had a strong superstitious belief that they brought good luck and he was extra-talented at finding them. I know it is odd that a man who lived by percentages and probabilities was also impressed by the power of four-leaf clovers. But that's how Daddy was.

Herbert's experiences in later years were very similar.

> HERBERT: *Dad's idea of babysitting was to throw you in the back of the car and have you spend all day in the oil field with him. He felt that the best way to teach someone something was to expose them to it and let them absorb it to the best of their ability.*
>
> *There wasn't a lot of conversation, except for when he was involved in something, then that was all he'd talk about. There usually would be someone with him in the front and two of us kids in the back.*
>
> *He'd flip his cigar ashes out the window. They'd blow right back inside the rear window and I'd be rubbing them out of my eyes.*

Daddy was distinctive, even to us kids. For instance, he would always wear a white shirt. He wore khaki pants like everyone else— except his were always pressed—but always a fine white shirt and a necktie. Beautiful, long staple Egyptian cotton. Everybody else wore khaki shirts open at the neck. Daddy never owned one. I don't know why. Somebody might say that he did it to set himself apart, but I doubt that. He did not need a costume to stand out from other people.

When we went to the oil field with Daddy we did not eat in a "greasy spoon," one of the makeshift lunch stands or barbecue places along the road. Daddy was very particular about what we ate. We'd stop at a general country store and buy crackers out of a big barrel and rat cheese. There was always a big wheel of yellow cheese from which you cut off a slice. There was only one kind of cheese and it was also used to catch rats, so it was called rat cheese. He would also buy cans of peaches and apricots. And watermelon, he was big on watermelon, "Because, you see," he'd say, "you need the water. The most valuable commodity in the world is water. Oil can drive you places and keep you warm. But water is life and death. You can live without oil, you can live without almost any single thing. But you cannot survive without water." We'd stop at the side of the road and he'd find a boulder, slit the watermelon end to end with his pocket knife, then tap it against the rock. It would split open and the heart of the watermelon would be standing up on one side, and he would slice it so that you could take it out with your fingers.

Daddy never let us eat potato salad because of the mayonnaise. Refrigeration was inadequate, and if the mayonnaise was old the uncooked egg in it might have spoiled. We could eat canned Vienna sausages and crackers or canned sardines, but he would not let us eat a pork chop because the pork might not have been thoroughly cooked and there was a chance we could get trichinosis.

As Mother was indisposed, I did the shopping. Besides getting groceries, I went down to Sample's Dry Goods Store when they had the white sale. Though I could hardly reach the counter, I felt the sheets and towels, in search of linens without an *F*.

When Caroline was born, on January 8, 1923, we borrowed a laundry basket from the people downstairs, the T.P. Marks family, who had the Ford automobile agency, and that was Caroline's crib. In El Dorado there were no real shops and not much of a selection of anything.

The phone rang in the middle of the night. Discoveries of new oil fields seem to always happen, like appendicitis, in the middle of the night.

We were all awakened by it and came out into the hall. Daddy was listening to the caller. He jotted a few notes on the back of an envelope and hung up. He told Mother, "It looks like something is happening in Mount Pleasant." He got dressed, stuffed a suitcase with cash, and headed out. It was a freezing cold night. Cars at this time were not equipped with defrosters, so he took some candles with him and put them on the dashboard to keep the windshield from freezing. I could see that Mother was distressed by his going out in the cold of night.

> STUART: *But there was a boom in Mount Pleasant, and when you had a boom, boy, you went. When there was a lease play Uncle June would take all this cash with him and pay the farmers straight out. Everyone else was offering bank drafts, so fifty or a hundred farmers would sell their leases to Uncle June. He got the jump on everybody that way.*
>
> *He carried ten or twenty thousand dollars. He needed all he could carry because he was paying a dollar, five dollars, maybe ten dollars an acre. The farmers really liked his cash. There was a ten-day waiting period for bank drafts to clear. Uncle June would make deals on the shake of a hand, make payment in cash and hope the titles*

*were clear. I never knew of any that were false. He was willing to take that risk. Playing the percentages. Always playing the percentages.*

Daddy returned thirty-six hours later, and we all sat in the kitchen while Mother prepared a hot meal and he explained, "When there is an oil strike, the idea is to be there ahead of everybody else and buy all the leases you can in the surrounding area."

"I would think," Mother said, "that the people who made the strike would keep it quiet and buy all the available leases themselves."

"That would be logical. But wildcatters are usually pressed just trying to finance the well they are drilling."

I asked, "Then how about the landowners, the farmers? Why would they sell leases and keep only one-eighth? Once they know there's oil, why don't they just drill it themselves?"

"Generally they are unable to drill it themselves or cause it to be drilled for them because they have neither money nor know-how. Drilling is complicated. To be in the oil business, to be the person who is investing and drilling and doing it, this is not peanuts, these are not dumb people. They are people with a lot of imagination and intellect, and a lot of courage to take that risk. Seventy-five hundred or ten thousand dollars to drill a well is a fortune, especially as the banks just sit on their cash and will not invest in oil."

Suddenly there was a frightening blaze of light, as if it had become morning again—as if a huge golden sun had just lit up outside our window. We left the table and ran to the porch.

The light was coming from far away, a radiance so vast that where we were standing we could have read a newspaper by it. Peering through the night and the distance, Daddy said, "It has to be that a well has cratered. It can only be the Smackover discovery well, seven miles away."

"But that large, June?" Mother asked. "Can a well be that large?"

"I know of blowouts that covered a radius of fifteen hundred feet. It is not just a well with oil coming out of a pipe, Mom. When a well craters, it explodes, and the earth caves away, and the derrick and the platform, the people on it, and everything topples and sinks into the blowout, and this mass of oil burns like a lake on fire."

The light went out. And then suddenly it flared up and boomed thunderously. It had blown out, cratered and caught fire, blowing cantaloupe-sized rocks hundreds of feet high.

In the morning our porch was covered with red sand, which had traveled all that distance through the air. Until then, I would have imagined that oil was below the ground in a liquid pool. As a matter of fact at that point in my life I had not thought very much about oil at all. I had no idea how much I had ahead of me to learn. In fact, oil is contained in sand or carbonate or limestone—in some porous rock formation that has the permeability for the oil to move through or it can't be produced. In this case the oil was in a sandy clay soil that burned as the oil burned off of it and then floated in the air, blanketing everything for miles around.

The four of us—and Caroline in her laundry basket—always had breakfast, lunch, and dinner together. When there was something he felt worth passing on, Daddy would lower his newspaper and turn to Hassie and me. One morning he said, "You might want to remember this. In a speech made yesterday in Washington D.C., President Coolidge said, 'The business of America is business.' Bear in mind that like our country, this family's business is business. A constructive citizen does not sit on his hands. He produces something, or performs a service that is useful to the community."

I remember wondering what I could possibly do to be useful to the community.

Lunch talk always consisted of reports from the oil field. Dinner conversation did too, but often it was less intense.

As we were having dessert, Daddy might say, "Margaret, tell me the capitals of Wisconsin, Maryland, and Colorado."

"Madison, Baltimore ..."

He would look at me questioningly.

"I mean Annapolis. And Denver."

He'd give me a dime. That was a lot of money then.

Then he would turn to Hassie. "Let me hear the Pledge of Allegiance."

We were questioned on subjects including the presidents of the United States, the cabinet members, the Bill of Rights, and the Preamble to the Constitution. Daddy paid us a dime for everything we got right—the incentive system. He did not pay us for good grades in school. He paid us for knowledge we had gained. And we did not miss much. For relaxation he would say, "Let us think up six-letter company names beginning with P." I don't know where he got the idea that six-letter names beginning with P were lucky, but he believed it was true and our companies were later given such names as Panola, Parade, Placid, and Penrod.

Hassie and I were frequently corrected on grammar, especially contractions. Mother and Daddy never used contractions and if I said something like, "What'll I do if ..." I was interrupted, "What *will,* Margaret, not what'll."

We were spanked or paddled, mainly for bad manners, like talking with our mouths full. Arguing at the dinner table was a major transgression. But mostly we got punished for fighting, for not being willing to share.

CAROLINE: *They were permissive parents. But they did not allow unpleasantness. You could not argue at the table. I was only spanked once by my father. For that. It was just a love tap. But it hurt my feelings.*

BUNKER: *Mother would take a switch to you. "OK," she'd say, "I'm going to have to switch you. Go out and get your switch. And make sure it is not too small." She was a pretty good Bible student. The old saying, "Spare the rod and spoil the child" comes from the Bible—not in that exact form, but it's in there.*

*Today if you see an undisciplined kid it's almost a sure thing that his parents were afraid or intimidated about disciplining him. My mother was not like that and neither was my father. Dad was pretty strict with my brother Hassie. He would not take any lip from the children. What he said was what you did.*

Mother had grown up as a Methodist in Lake Village, Arkansas, where the Bunkers were the pillar of the church. Mother had a nice voice, and her sister, Mattie, played the piano and the organ at church. But when we moved to El Dorado the people who lived downstairs, the Marks family, were Presbyterians. While Mother had been pregnant with Caroline, Mr. and Mrs. Marks and their daughter, Theodosia, and son, Russell, took Hassie and me to the Presbyterian Sunday school and Church. Hassie and I were pretty active at church. That was the fanciest thing you did in a small town.

After Mother had the baby, she came with us, and soon she was an active member of the Presbyterian Church. Mother sang the hymns in such a strong voice that with my childish values it embarrassed me. Daddy did not go to church. His attitude was, "Save the seats for the sinners. I see the people who sin the most sitting in the front row."

We lived upstairs over the Marks family for a year, and then we moved to 303 Peach Street, a little brown frame one-story cottage close to downtown. It wasn't much of a house, but it was all ours and there was room for Mother to have servants to help her.

After we moved to Peach Street, men would come and knock on the door at night and say to Mother, "Lady, I'll pay two dollars if you'll give me a pillow and a blanket and let me roll up on your front porch." There was just no place in town for them to sleep. It was difficult to get a bed even for one shift at the Garrett or Randolph. Though initially we had no extra pillows or blankets, Mother sent me to Sample's to buy some. She always accommodated the homeless. And of course she would not take their money.

My baby sister, Lyda, was born February 20, 1925. One night when she was about two weeks old I was awakened by a commotion.

Lyda's nurse was in the hall, distraught. "Mr. Hunt, the baby's face is blue ..."

Daddy went into the nursery and lit a match. From the sound it made, he knew that gas had leaked from the stove that was kept on for heat. The rubber hoses sometimes leaked, and the baby had been breathing the gas. These were the days before odorant was put in gas so that its presence could be identified.

Daddy ordered, "Take the child out into the fresh air, massage her chest, try to get air into her lungs ..."

Wearing an overcoat over his pajamas, he rushed to his car to wake up the dentist and get his oxygen tank, but it did not help. She lived two weeks.

Lyda died on March 20, when she was exactly a month old. I remember it was a Friday. I came home from school and there was a wreath on the front door. I went around to the back.

Daddy was waiting for me. "We lost the baby, Margaret."

The funeral was Saturday. It was a major tragedy in our family, yet when I went back to school on Monday, no one knew about my baby sister's death. Mother and Daddy kept their pain to themselves. A neighbor who couldn't help but know paid a condolence call, and when Mother courteously entered into conversation, he marveled, "If it had happened to me I'd've collapsed." Mother thanked him for what she understood to be a compliment, but when he had gone she said to me and Hassie, "Ignore what you just heard. We do not collapse."

Daddy took Mother to New York in an effort to distract her from her grief. When they got back to El Dorado, he and Mother decided to build a house. Though nobody then even knew the expression "good therapy," I think that my father looked upon the work and responsibility of building a new home as a healthy diversion for Mother.

By this time most of the residents of El Dorado had money, and I guess we had as much or a bit more than most. The boomtown days were behind us, and the town had become an orderly, affluent, comfortable community. Women and children could once again go out at night. Downtown, they built a five-story skyscraper, the Exchange National Bank Building. I used to go to our office there all the time.

Mother and Daddy bought a whole city block in a new subdivision that did not yet have streets or sidewalks, just outside of El Dorado. The house was built in its center. It was a three-story, red brick, English-revival house with a living room, large dining room, and a sunporch. It had a basement with an oil-burning furnace. The second floor had six bedrooms and four baths, and the third floor had two bedrooms and a bath. There was a downstairs guest room and bath. We always had family guests. Daddy's sister and brother, Aunt Nettie and Uncle Jim, spent a great deal of time with us. Aunt Nettie was an old maid who had paid her own way to France during World War I and drove an ambulance on the front lines.

We had excellent help, two women and a man who stayed with us for many, many years: Gertrude Sanders, our cook, Pandora Batchler, who cleaned and helped in the kitchen, and Earnest Lewis—known to us as Lewis—who served the table and drove.

Mother did her share. She ran a meticulous house. She used to say, "Never go up the stairs or down the stairs empty-handed. There is always something downstairs that needs to go upstairs and vice versa." And it's true. All my life I have found something to carry when I go upstairs or downstairs.

Our new home was called The Pines because of the large number of tall, beautiful pine trees surrounding it. Though we had lived in small towns, Mother's horizons were worldly. Before tulips were commonplace in the United States she had read of them, she ordered hundreds of bulbs from Holland, and we had beds of tulips banked around each pine tree.

Mother was big on Easter egg hunts because the church ladies in El Dorado dyed eggs as a money-raising project. She ordered many big wooden crates of dyed eggs from the church, and Lewis, Pandora, and Gertrude hid them in the tulips while we were at Sunday school. In the afternoon we had egg hunts and homemade ice cream served in cones.

Ours was the largest house in El Dorado, a mansion! There was a concrete driveway that went up under the porte-cochère and then circled around and out the front entrance. Roller skates had just become popular, and our driveway was the best skating rink in town. Everybody we knew, and some we did not, came over to skate.

I took a spill and skinned a knee. When Daddy got home and saw it, he got out a bottle of Absorbine Jr. He was an absolute believer in Absorbine Jr. and always had a bottle of it at home and on his desk at the office. If you cut your finger he would say, "Come here," and he would pay us a dime to let him pour Absorbine Jr. into the open wound. He blew on it, mightily.

Then he would say, "Now you blow on it."

And we'd blow on it.

"Harder."

In retrospect I realize that he made it into a game to distract us from the pain. It burned like crazy. But it is a fact that none of us ever did end up with an infection. Daddy had learned the virtues of Absorbine Jr. working on a horse farm as a teenager in California. In later years he tried to buy the company just for the fun of owning it, but the owners had so much cash on hand that there was no reason for them to sell.

When the city sent crews of men out to where we had moved to pour cement and build streets and sidewalks, Hassie opened a lemonade stand at the end of our driveway. I was shocked. He had flatly refused to work with me when I had a lemonade stand over on Peach Street. I asked him about it.

"You didn't have any customers," he said matter-of-factly. "But with all those guys working and sweating on the street there's a market."

Again the phone rang at night. This time it was news of a shallow discovery in the Tullos-Urania Field in La Salle Parish, Louisiana. Daddy and his man Friday, Mr. Bailey, left within a few hours.

"The oil is so thick it is ready to blacktop a road," Daddy told Mother when he returned from Tullos-Urania. "You have to heat it to separate it from the water that comes up with it, it is that thick."

In those early days, without chemicals and the advanced methods of separating oil from the water that came up with it, oil was produced into open pits and it was the action of the sun, heating the oil, that separated it from the water.

"I would like to see that field, June." Mother was not a retiring housewife, she was always keenly interested in what was going on. So a few days later we were all out there in rubber boots wading through the mud in the Tullos-Urania Field.

A few weeks later Daddy reported, "Standard Oil moved quickly and bought six hundred thousand barrels of the first oil produced in Tullos-Urania but now they have stopped buying. This oil is a disappointment to them as fuel oil. It is too heavy." It was as thick as Vaseline, only black.

Daddy, however, was not one to follow the leader, even a major company like Standard Oil. He bought a lease in the Tullos-Urania Field and started drilling. He brought in a well that produced crude with a high lube content but with an unpopular asphalt base for which there was no market. It looked bad for him as he was producing four hundred barrels a day and had no buyers. This heavy black oil was accumulating in earthen pits alongside the drilling rig.

Interested in this unusual crude, wanting to understand it in every aspect, Daddy worked in the fields himself, getting the heavy oil on his hands.

At dinner one night he said, "Cleaning that sticky stuff off is the hardest to do of anything I have ever experienced." Holding his hands out he stopped, stared at them, and observed, "But, look! There has been a marked improvement of the skin of both hands and especially of my right hand, which has been subjected to the most oil."

Mother examined his hands.

He always brought home Coca-Cola bottles of oil from new wells, stoppered with pieces of cloth, and we would taste the oil to check for a hint of salt water, which will destroy a well. I remember seeing Daddy out in the fields put his tongue to the core samples that the drillers brought up.

Mother took those bottles of oil to her bedroom and experimented with this thick crude, applying it to her hands, then to her neck. After a week of such treatments she was of the opinion that this oil had a decidedly beneficial effect. And she suggested that it just might have more value to a cosmetics company than to fuel-oil refineries.

Daddy took the train to New York. Once there he made the acquaintance of a buyer for Sinclair Oil. He told him about the cosmetic properties of the Tullos-Urania oil. Always on the lookout for new ways to sell petroleum or its by-products, Harry Sinclair's company had its research department look into this new idea. There was less corporate insecurity in those days, and in two weeks the research chief decided that this oil could be in demand in the cosmetics business and placed an order for 4,500 barrels a day, the entire field's production. The other producers, desperate for a market for their heavy crude, were delighted to unload it to H.L. Hunt Incorporated. Daddy got a bank to finance him, added a half-dollar a barrel to his cost, and shipped it off to Sinclair, turning a failure into a $2,250-a-day profit.

Tullos crude ultimately produced one of the finest lubricating oils in the world, able to withstand the greatest pressure and friction, enduring 500-degree temperatures that caused other oils to break down and fail to serve as lubricants. It became a premium crude oil during World

War II. Yet at the beginning, only the cosmetics industry saw a value in it.

Lewis would come to school to pick up Hassie and me every afternoon. As we came out of the building, Lewis would slide over, and Hassie and I took turns driving home in the big, new Packard limousine Daddy had bought. It had a glass window that rolled up between the chauffeur and the back seat. There was a bud vase for a single rose on each side in the back. It also had a big trunk that stuck out on the rear end of the car. Within the trunk were suitcases that had come with it, shaped to fit perfectly.

I had developed the habit of ruthlessly chewing up my fingernails. Every afternoon when Lewis picked me up at school, we stopped at the barber shop—there were no beauty parlors in those days—and every day the manicurist filed my nails smooth so I would have nothing to bite. Daddy objected to my biting my nails and he was curing it.

He was also concerned about our teeth. Each night after dinner he would say "Come here, Margaret," and I'd go into the living room and stand between his knees. He would take his thumb and press it firmly against my front teeth. As I held my neck stiff, he pushed my teeth with his thumb. Today I have perfectly straight teeth. Maybe I would not have had them otherwise. They must have needed something or he wouldn't have done this every single night.

Then he would go to his desk and work on papers.

HERBERT: *He never did anything but work. He did not fish. He did not hunt. He took up golf for a little while but that didn't last long.*

His sole interest was business. Consequently, we have always been a business-oriented working family.

BUNKER: *Dinner conversation was mostly business. My father and Hassie would talk about business together. They both had mathematical minds. Dad understood figures. Not geology, which is more artistic.*

CAROLINE: *When my father was there he was the center of the conversation. I learned to "cut out" because I was not interested in business at that time. We talked a lot about politics. During the war, dinner was very quiet because we had to listen on the radio to the different commentators, Paul Harvey, Gabriel Heatter, and William L. Shirer.*

It was always business and current events—and sometimes sports. Daddy discussed everything with Mother in front of us. And he gave us his views.

"The United States is the most generous country in the world, the only place where an individual can own both the minerals and the surface of land. Everywhere else an individual can own the surface but the government or the state owns the minerals."

He repeatedly said, "Do not ever serve on a bank board. Do not own bank stock. And do not use a bank trust department. You cannot rely on them. They will sell good growth stocks and buy whatever bonds the federal government tells them to."

None of us ever served on a bank board. Time and again we were asked, and it was flattering, but fortunately we had been told this early in life. Many people we know, beguiled by the prestige of serving on bank boards have, following the S&L disaster, become implicated in devastating lawsuits due to the misdeeds of others. Daddy's advice and foresight saved us a lot of grief.

Because Mother and Daddy both read the newspaper daily and thoroughly, we had duplicate papers delivered. Mother would be at one end of the dining table, Daddy at the other, so two papers were a convenience.

Reading the newspaper one morning, Daddy said, "The Republicans want to nominate President Coolidge for a third term. Sure they do! He has reduced the national debt by two billion dollars in three years. But he says, 'I do not choose to run for president in 1928.' You have to take your hat off to a man who loves his country more than the power of the presidency."

I was puzzled. "If he's been a good president why shouldn't he stay on?"

"Because historically republics have died or drifted into dictatorship rather quickly, usually because of a popular figure remaining in power too long. George Washington knew that when he refused to run for a third term. Everyone knows that we do not want a king. The Founding Fathers left the king in England. Another reason not to risk the chance of one man staying in office permanently is so that fathers can truthfully say to their sons, 'If you want to, you can be president.' No-third-term is a tradition that has been handed down over thirty presidencies. I admire Coolidge for not being tempted or flattered into breaking it."

Hassie and I were best friends but we had a major problem. We jointly owned a four-door blue DeSoto with a yellow two-inch band stripe around it. There were no driver's licenses in those days. All you needed was a car and you could drive. Hassie had it at night and I had it in the daytime. When I went to use it in the morning it would reek of perfume and was always littered with cigarette ashes and butts and even beer and whiskey bottles.

I would complain bitterly. "Ugh! What kind of tacky friends have you got that you drive around in our car? It takes me an hour to air it out and clean it up every morning. I would almost rather not use it at all if I have to keep sharing with you."

Then I discovered that Hassie was using our DeSoto as a taxi. In those days the black people had large dance halls, so he would go out to these dance halls and load up as many people as he could get in and charge them ten cents each to take them home or wherever they had to go. He was about eleven or twelve.

I was infuriated but I was also impressed by my brother's industriousness. I did not tell on him. We never told on each other. Neither did my parents. If one of them caught us doing something wrong, they never told it to the other.

Every night after dinner Mother played the piano. We had a baby grand. That was the evening's entertainment. Daddy loved to sing. He would put his arm around Mother in exaggerated theatrical gestures, singing "I can't give you anything but love, baby ..."

But nobody in our whole family kissed anybody. One time Hassie kissed Mother and Daddy shooed him away. "Stop that. Don't be kissing people." Daddy was not demonstrative about love. One of the few out-of-character things he did was give Caroline a little bracelet made of letters that read I LUV U.

Years later, in the 1980s, I was at a Petroleum Club luncheon in Fort Worth and was touched to hear the speaker, Van Cliburn, remember, "I grew up in El Dorado, Arkansas. My father worked for Magnolia Petroleum Company. My mother was a concert pianist and music teacher, and she used to play concerts on Mrs. H.L. Hunt's fine Steinway baby grand piano in their living room."

Home entertainments like video, cable TV, situation comedies, and football have eliminated the family life that we knew. The hours we spent at home were always filled talking, visiting, telling stories, and consequently developing our values and our close family relationships.

Daddy was a very present figure in the house, always talking or singing. He was usually "up" and we'd hear him while he was getting dressed in the morning, "Sometimes I'm happy, sometimes I'm blue, my disposition depends on you ..."

He was not a joke teller, though. He was pleasant, but he was a strong personality. If he came into a room there was no question as to whose would be the dominant voice.

> HERBERT: *Dad didn't do idle chitchat. If you were talking about something and it was nothing, you'd be interrupted. Dad took over.*

On Sundays we always had fried chicken and ice cream. Gertrude made ice cream the old-fashioned cranked way—caramel ice cream, peach ice cream, strawberry ice cream—and we served it in bowls.

We were not treated as kids except when we acted like kids. On my twelfth birthday, in 1927, Daddy took me downtown to the Exchange National Bank and helped me open a checking account so I could learn to take care of my monthly allowance.

Daddy's brother, Uncle Sherman, lived in Miles City, Montana, and was married to a lady with a sensational personality. As a young girl, Aunt Tot went east to boarding school in Boston. That was a long train ride so she only got to come home once a year, until she got kicked out for dying several classmates' hair with ink. Tot played golf and was the first woman to drive a car in the state of Montana. Her family, the MacLeans, had gone to Montana in a covered wagon.

Uncle Sherman and Aunt Tot had two boys, Sherman and Stuart.

STUART: *My grandfather [Tot's father] came from Scotland. Most of the West—it's amazing how much of it was settled with Scottish money. He and Teddy Roosevelt were friends. They had a big problem with rustlers up in that part of the country. Real tough killers. So Teddy Roosevelt put together a group of people and they killed about seventy of them. I don't believe it's ever been written about. Grandfather told Dad about it.*

If cousin Sherman was studying his schoolwork and Aunt Tot felt like going to the picture show, she would not hesitate to say, "Come on, Sherman, you don't need to be studying, let's go to the picture show"—and away they'd go. Although Aunt Tot was high-spirited and my mother was a lady of the old school, they became close friends.

In early February 1926, Uncle Sherman and Aunt Tot came to visit from Montana and stayed in the room downstairs. Mother was pregnant with Bunker at the time and two weeks overdue, but she wanted privacy and was determined not to give birth until Uncle Sherman and Aunt Tot had departed. As under normal circumstances they were always more than welcome, and being unaware of mother's sensibility at this particular time they stayed with us two more weeks until February 21. Bunker was born the next day. He weighed twelve pounds. Daddy sent a telegram to Aunt Tot and Uncle Sherman at the railroad station in St. Louis to tell them that Bunker had arrived.

In later years we always said, "Poor Bunker, he really can't help being overweight because he came into this world a month old and weighing twelve pounds."

Daddy wanted us to see and understand our country, not just El Dorado, Arkansas, so we began to travel. It was 1928. The trains featured marvelous sleepers and drawing rooms and delicious, well-served food in the dining cars. It took two days to get to New York, two nights and a full day. As the train raced along the countryside, Daddy suggested, "Look out the window and remember the size and the shapes and colors of the greatest, freest, noblest nation on earth."

As soon as we got to New York, Hassie and I were taken to Bradford Bachrach for a photo portrait. The days were meant to be pleasant but also instructive. Serious museum-going was part of every day's activities.

Daddy was fascinated with the New York theater, so we stayed at the Piccadilly Hotel in the theater district. The first Broadway performance Hassie and I saw was *Whoopee,* starring Eddie Cantor, at the New Amsterdam Theatre. Daddy had already seen it but he took us for the fun of watching our amazement upon seeing a live, white horse on the stage. We saw shows every night we were in New York.

Daddy loved the unusual, the mysterious. Magicians fascinated him and he would load us on the train from El Dorado to St. Louis to see Houdini, Thurston, Blackstone. We saw them all. In 1928 he took Caroline, Hassie, and me to Mardi Gras in New Orleans. Mother and Daddy were not intimidated by distance. They thought nothing of taking a train for an overnight trip to see something they thought we should see that was not available in El Dorado.

Mother had more cultivated musical taste than Daddy and was interested in symphony and opera. She would take us to Shreveport to hear Ignace Paderewski. Today you see one-year-old babies on planes, but in those days it was very unusual for children to be traveling for pleasure.

Herbert was born on March 6, 1929, and was so named because Herbert Hoover had recently been inaugurated. That spring we left El Dorado on a summerlong excursion west in the huge Packard limousine my father drove.

Herbert started that trip on a pillow, as he was three months old, but by the time we returned to El Dorado he was sitting up and looking out the window with avid interest. Herbert was my little toy. He had curly hair. Bobby pins had just come out and I'd shampoo his hair and roll it. He was like a little doll.

When we reached the edge of the Mojave Desert Daddy put Mother, Caroline, Bunker, and Herbert on the train, for he knew the drive was supposed to be very uncomfortable. Hassie, Daddy, and I made the ride across the desert.

We picked up Mother and the kids in San Diego and drove on to Los Angeles. All the way from San Diego, Hassie and I had been fussing and picking at each other over who was going to drive next. As we unloaded the car, Daddy said, "All right now, we have been subjected to excessive strife. I want you two to get out there on the grass, have a good fight, and get it over with." We wrestled and fought for awhile but we both understood that we had been imposing on the others and, embarrassed, we ended it fast.

Daddy took us to a Chinese restaurant for dinner. After studying the menu he suggested, "You will probably want to try the bird's nest soup."

The sound and thought of it made me ill. I grimaced.

He was disappointed in me. "That shows a profound lack of adventure." But he did not insist that I try it. Daddy exposed us to things that were new to us but he never forced us to do anything. He and Mother taught by example.

> CAROLINE: *Important guidelines were established, but few rules. I always felt free to express myself with my father and my mother. They were very accepting. You didn't have to be in any mold.*

> BUNKER: *My father expressed his opinions to us. He did not insist that anyone agree with him.*

As we drove around southern California Daddy sought out specific orchards, taking pleasure in showing us bushes and trees he had planted as a teenager.

We went to Yosemite and stayed at a famous Indian lodge. One morning Daddy told Hassie and me to go ahead downstairs for breakfast. "This hotel is 'American plan,' which means that you can order anything that you want and we still pay the same price."

Seated in the dining room, Hassie said, "Let's start at the top of the menu and eat one of everything."

When Daddy came down to join us the maitre d' greeted him urgently, "Hurry! They are killing themselves. They're eating everything on the menu."

We continued on to Salt Lake City. Mother believed in travel for education, so when we went sightseeing we saw everything.

Daddy received a phone call from a scout who was closely watching a well being drilled in east Texas. So he hastily departed by train for Texas to check out the report he had received of a possible discovery.

That October, Daddy called Mother from New York. "I have information that the stock market is becoming violent. Go to the bank, *at this time"*—when something was urgent he would say to do it *"at this time"*—"and withdraw all the cash you need to have on hand for expenses until this settles down."

Mother and I came back with so much cash that it made her nervous. Even though El Dorado had settled down it was a larger, less protected environment than Lake Village had been when she had had $25,000 in cash and never gave it a thought. We took the money into the room where Daddy worked, a sort of library, and she made piles of a hundred dollars each, which we placed between the pages of twenty or thirty books.

The next day the newspaper reported the stock market crash of 1929. People lined the banks trying to get their money, but there wasn't enough cash on hand and the banks had to close. For that week we were among the few people in El Dorado who could pay their bills with cash.

Daddy smoked La Corona Belvederes, a box a day. He did not drink alcohol. He was a teetotaler, though not a prohibitionist—he did not mind others drinking.

> COUSIN TOM HUNT: *Once we were taken to the Chambord in New York and served chilled Polish vodka and caviar. I'm not much of a drinker, but I will have a drink. Uncle June didn't want the vodka so he slid his over to me. I had them both. Then the host asked if anyone would enjoy another round. Uncle June said yes. And they served the caviar and the vodka and again he slid the vodka over to me. I said, "Look, Uncle June, don't have any more caviar. It's killing me."*

Daddy had the reputation for being against alcohol, but it was not a moral judgment. He had seen things that turned him away from it. "When I was a boy working the wheat fields, in 1909, I was in the town of Evanston, Wyoming, which was among other things the home of an insane asylum. There were a number of tie-cutters working there because Evanston was near the main line of the Union Pacific Railroad, and I saw frequent examples of man's inhumanity to man. Here were these big, powerful men who cut the ties, and they wore these caulked boots—which is to say, boots with steel runners on the soles to give them traction when they had to walk on top of logs. They drank themselves stupid after work, which invariably led to fights. Whoever was knocked down would be marked in the manner of the Heidelberg scars, but not with the subtlety of a rapier's flick leaving just the trace of a wound. These men used hatchets to make horrible gashes across the other men's faces.

"Worse, when they became especially inebriated they would get hold of the inmates of the asylum who were on parole and peacefully walking the streets, tear off their clothes, force them to lay down naked on the ground and then walk on them with these caulked boots that tore their flesh open. During the day they were normal human beings, working, singing, helping each other. But the alcohol turned some of them into savages."

Things had been good for us in El Dorado. But oil fields decline and wells wear out. El Dorado was becoming depleted, and Daddy's income was dwindling.

Around the first of September, 1930—again, in the middle of the night—Daddy received a phone call that not only changed our lives but affected the lives of all Americans.

# *Five*

LAMAR: *Everybody is born to do some one thing, as opposed to something else. Dad was definitely born to be an oilman. He must have been one of the great wildcatters of all time.*

The phone call to Daddy was from his friend Judge M.M. Miller, who, with his brother Charlie, had perfected a drill-stem testing tool that was the best in existence. "There's a wildcatter working down in east Texas and he may have something going," Judge Miller said. "We're running a drill-stem test on his well tomorrow and I thought you would be interested."

Drill-stem testing was a means of obtaining information about a well's oil potential before the well was finished being drilled. In laymen's terms, a drill-stem testing tool was a device that was lowered into the hole on the bottom of the drill pipe as far as it had been drilled. The tool was then opened for some time to collect a sample of what was below.

The wildcatter Judge Miller was talking about was Columbus Marion Joiner, who was about to discover the greatest oil field in the United States prior to the Alaskan field discovery nearly forty years later.

Daddy drove the two hundred miles to Rusk County, Texas, and was at the well site on Friday, September 5, 1930, when the drill-stem test was run on the Joiner well. When the tool was run in the hole and then opened, oil blew through the top of the derrick. Impressed by the volume and velocity of the oil, Daddy instinctively knew that the well would be a producer, though others observing the test were not as sold on drill-stem testing as he was and preferred to reserve judgment until there was a production test of the well. This was considerably more time-consuming because before you could produce oil, casing had to be run and cemented, a process that prevented the sides of the hole from caving in and closing the well. Once that was done, you could open the valve, let her flow wide open, and gauge how many barrels a day it could produce.

Skepticism about finding oil in east Texas was not unfounded. Prior to the Joiner discovery in 1930, seventeen dry holes had been drilled in Rusk County—and not one producer. Further, some highly regarded geological and oil books stated that absolutely, positively, the last place to look for oil was in the east Texas area.

On October 5, the well was swabbed in and a colossal column of oil shot over the top of the crown block on the derrick of Mr. Joiner's Daisy Bradford No. 3.

Money was nearly nonexistent following the 1929 Wall Street crash, but Daddy invested all he could get his hands on in leases east of the Joiner well. He also acquired a twenty-acre lease as a south offset to the Joiner discovery well and commenced drilling the H.L. Hunt-Miller No. 1.

Fortunately for us, the major oil companies were still influenced by those negative geological studies, so they did not rush in and buy up all the leases. In fact, being hampered by Depression cutbacks and big company red tape, the majors got pretty well shut out of the discovery area by the independents.

Then, on Saturday, December 27, 1930, a well blew in on the Lou Della Crim farm, flowing 22,000 barrels a day. That well was nine miles from the Daisy Bradford No. 3. No one reckoned for what was then a geological phenomenon. No one could know it at the time, but the field was sixty miles long and ten miles wide—one big deposit of oil that was so huge that it came to be referred to as the Black Giant.

Historically, no oil field had ever encompassed so much land. Extending through the towns of Arp, Wright City, Overton, Kilgore, Longview, and Gladewater, it could not be named for one locality as most fields were; instead, it was named for the entire region and became known as the East Texas Oil Field.

Daddy came home to El Dorado every week or two, totally consumed in his new involvement, full of praise and enthusiasm for east Texas. "The biggest, greatest oil boom of all time is on. This is the California gold rush, the Klondike, the Florida and Oklahoma land rushes, Spindletop, El Dorado, all of the past booms rolled into one. From a business point of view, east Texas is an oilman's dream: near pure gasoline as it comes out of the ground. Over in west Texas, in contrast to our shallow, two-thousand-foot wells, they are drilling up to five and six thousand feet, which takes months and is costly, and it is sour crude, the oil has a lot of sulphur in it. The sulphur is poisonous. Two or three breaths of the sulphur gas and you are dead. In contrast, our sweet oil hardly needs to be treated.

"East Texas is the simplest possible drilling. You can drill with almost any mud. The bottom hole pressure is not so great that you have blowouts, yet it is strong enough that few wells have to install costly pumps to extract the oil. It gushes up and licks your face."

Once Daddy got the drilling going in east Texas, he would call the Tullos warehouse every evening to see how much oil they had produced. That would let him know whether he had $200 or $500 to spend the next day on his new drilling operation in the east Texas fields. Though the Sinclair Oil contract had terminated and he was selling only what his Tullos wells produced, a few hundred barrels a day, the money was crucial at that time because it enabled him to commit himself accordingly in east Texas, making Tullos a thread in the history of Daddy's growth in the oil business.

The perfume of oil was wafting across the entire United States and calling to people who saw no work where they were, no chance of making a living, only soup kitchens and apple sellers on every corner, and so they made their way to east Texas, on foot or by rail. Somehow thousands of them got there, to the one place where there was hope.

> JESSE JOHNSON: *People would do anything they could to survive. One would put up a little stand to sell something; another would find a place that had water, hang a pipe pointing down and have curtains around it and men would pay fifty cents to have a shower.*
>
> *Things were really, really bad. In west Texas those of us who had rifles would go out and kill jackrabbits and bring them in to be cooked in the Salvation Army stew pots to feed people.*
>
> *I was in the drilling business. When I got to east Texas there were so many people looking for jobs that at noontime when the leftovers from the plates were taken out to be dumped in the garbage there were people standing in line to get them to eat.*

Along every paved road—from Gladewater to Longview, to Kilgore, to Henderson, to Overton, Arp, and Wright City—people who owned the land sold or rented little lots where people parked tents or old buses and lived in them. They formed an unbroken line on both sides of the road. Whereas only a month earlier, Kilgore had been a town of four hundred people, overnight there were tens of thousands. I can never think of an oil boom without thinking of rain, and there was almost incessant rain that year. There was no underground sanitation system, so raw sewage ran down the streets of Kilgore and Gladewater. If any kind of a disease had erupted, it would have been epidemic. You dared not drink the water anywhere around Rusk County unless you knew it was state certified. There was a lot of sickness, a lot of flu and colds, and a lot of people died. There were few doctors and no hospital. Only Tyler, twenty miles away, had a small clinic with only a few beds.

Employees of major oil companies who were sent to east Texas were required to take typhoid shots, just as if today they were going into a third-world country. The majors had finally come in; they made their headquarters either in Kilgore or Longview and built boarding houses and operated kitchens for their people in compounds guarded by fences and armed guards night and day.

Even twenty miles away, in relatively untouched Tyler, hundreds of men were sleeping on the ground wrapped in newspapers, for lack of constructed housing. The courthouse in the middle of town was left open all night so people could use the bathrooms.

East Texas was a nightmare in all of these ways, but it was an oilman's dream, and it would be grossly incomplete to describe it without also describing the oilman who dreamed it, hustled it, conned it, and prayed it into a reality.

Columbus Marion Joiner, later called "Dad" Joiner because he was considered the father of Rusk County, was born in Alabama in a log cabin with a lean-to kitchen on March 12, 1860. Like my father, he was the son of a Confederate veteran and largely self-educated.

Despite having only seven weeks of formal education, he practiced law in Tennessee. He then served in the Tennessee Legislature from 1889 to 1891.

Lawmaking was not enough to satisfy him, so he went west in 1897, moving to Ardmore in the Indian Territory to try his luck in the oil fields. He drilled a hole in Seminole County but ran out of money and had to abandon it at 3,150 feet. Later, the Empire Gas & Fuel Company, working nearby, drilled 200 feet deeper and discovered the great Seminole Field. Another exploratory hole he drilled near Cement, Oklahoma, was abandoned just seventeen feet above what later became a big producer for Fortuna Oil Company. After that, Mr. Joiner wryly urged wildcatters, "Never stop drilling until you have gone another seventeen feet."

He barely made a living until he was seventy. He could have ended up as "Dry Hole Joiner," but with the courage and conviction unique to the old-time wildcatters, he managed to convince people of his ability to discover oil and he eked his way through thirty-three years of drilling and missing—leaving a string of seventeen dry holes behind him.

Mr. Joiner arrived in Texas in 1926 and became convinced that there was oil beneath the red clay soil of Rusk County in east Texas. The land at that time was dedicated mostly to cotton acreage and pasture—and to breaking the hearts and the backs of those who toiled to scratch a living out of it.

Major oil companies ignored him. C.M. Joiner's only support was testimony from a Fort Worth geologist, Dr. A.D. Lloyd, who was neither a doctor nor a geologist. He had no schooling in geology, yet be it talent, luck, instinct, whatever—in this particular case he performed as well as any trained geologist. He concurred that C.M. Joiner would find oil in Rusk County and he told him almost exactly where and at what depth in an impressive, scholarly-looking document that Mr. Joiner used to induce investors.

Joiner believed so devoutly in Rusk County's oil potential that he leased between five and six thousand acres before he had drilled a well or smelled oil. For his test site he chose the farm of a widow, Mrs. Daisy Bradford, which lay between Henderson and Arp a few miles southeast of Overton.

The poor-boy rig he assembled was nearly worn out, but he was able to begin drilling the Daisy Bradford No. 1 in August 1927. The makeshift old pine rig and the rest of his equipment were no match for the tough east Texas earth, and the drilling became a series of fishing operations to recover a drill bit that stuck or twisted off and had to be fished out. All of those physical woes ran up the cost of the operation, and Joiner had to sell off some of his leases to raise working cash.

There were plenty of con men who sold and resold the same percentage in a well to as many people as they could fool, dreading only the day when they might actually find oil and be revealed as con men. Some never even drilled a hole. Mr. Joiner had, out of his desperation to keep drilling, sold one lease to eleven different people, but generally he was simply an oilman struggling to keep going, trying to strike oil as he believed he would. In the course of surviving from day to day he elevated poor-boying to a creative art, paying for meals and a night's board with a certificate for a dollar's worth of interest in an oil well. The farmers and small business owners of dust-dry Rusk County, Texas, were so badly off that a boarding house owner would happily forsake a dollar in cash in favor of a "certificate of hope" that might one day bring in a thousand dollars. Joiner issued so many certificates that they were passed from person to person as money.

Six months after starting Daisy Bradford No. 1, the bit got stuck at 1,098 feet and could not be brought up. Inextricably wedged in, the only option was to sacrifice the bit and stem, leave them in the ground and start another well. The crew skidded the rig a hundred feet away and Daisy Bradford No. 2 was begun. Mr. Joiner had sold participation certificates for twenty-five dollars each to finance this well, but bad luck hit him again—another wedged-in drill bit, this time at 2,000 feet.

He was practically broke and unable to interest more investors. He hoped that a more professional crew would give credence to his quest, so he went to Houston in May 1929 and talked to Ed C. Laster, an experienced and successful driller who coincidentally was between jobs. To obtain Laster's services, Joiner made a deal for some cash, around $10 a day, plus an interest in the east Texas well. With Laster's track record as window dressing, he knew he could attract some fresh money.

When Laster arrived in Rusk County and saw Joiner's equipment, he almost went back to Houston. Further he stated that the No. 2 site would have to be abandoned. It would be too time-consuming to fish out the drill bit, and he did not like the location. The consensus was to go uphill. But that was not to be.

The creaky rig was skidded downhill, because it was cheaper. Fate was now calling the shots. If he had gone uphill, he would have been beyond the eastern edge of the pool and drilled a dry hole. But poor-boying it, they skidded it down a hill toward the No. 3 location, which was staked about five hundred feet southwest. Abruptly, after dragging the rig three hundred and fifty feet, a sill snapped and the rig could move no further, which is why the historic Daisy Bradford No. 3 was drilled at that spot.

Joiner was too pressed for cash to pay a crew, but he got help from farmers who gathered around when they were not working in the fields and pitched in to lend a hand on the rig. Even an Overton banker who believed in the possibility of east Texas oil came out to work in the late afternoons. It was not a professional crew, but the drilling bit continued to bore into the ground.

To raise cash, Joiner was now reduced to reading obituaries and calling on recent widows, whom he was often able to charm into investing their inheritances. He worked hard at his "fund raising" and rewarded those investors with poetically written love letters.

On October 3, 1930, Mr. Joiner's worn-out drill touched the prayed-for Woodbine formation. Laster cut a core and found oil-saturated Woodbine. There was no doubt in his mind that they were about to strike oil.

> JESSE JOHNSON: *When you hit the Woodbine and you pull your bit up and you smell the sand and there's oil what you do is discreetly return your bit to the hole. You pretend to be still drilling, but you're just faking it, giving your people time to go out and buy as many leases on the surrounding land as possible. You did your best to keep a discovery quiet, but there was usually some smart cookie either up close near your rig or on the next field with binoculars. And if he saw the roughnecks hurrying around the deck or something going into the pit, he'd know why and spread the word: "He's circulating." If you were real lucky, no one would notice and you could close down at dark.*

The moment Laster could leave the drill rig without raising suspicion among his crewmen, he rushed off to a telephone to reach Mr. Joiner and cryptically pass on the news.

Returning to the rig, he remembered that in his excitement he had left the evidence of the find—a bucket full of oil-saturated cuttings—on the rig floor. Now driving back at dangerous speed in his old Nash, he screeched to a halt and ran across the drill-site clearing. Out of breath, he clambered up onto the floor of the rig. The bucket was gone.

Who had taken it? It could only be one of the scouts working for the majors. Fearful that with this proof of the existence of oil the majors would rush in and buy up all the available leases in east Texas, Laster sat by himself for hours agonizing over the damage he had done to his employer. If he had been more careful, Joiner could have bought back leases he had sold for survival money, leases which were now worth a thousand times what they had been worth that morning before he hit the Woodbine.

He heard a car approaching and looking up he saw Henry Conway, a scout from Amerada, approaching, waving a telegram. When Laster read it he saw that it was a negative report from the Pure Oil paleontologist at Van Field, saying that if Joiner found the Woodbine, it would be at over five thousand feet and would carry salt water, making it worthless.

Obviously it was not Conway who had taken the bucket of cuttings.

A while later, the despondent Laster heard his name being called and he saw the young Sinclair scout, Donald Reese, climbing up onto the floor of the rig.

Reese snickered, "Well, I found your bait."

"What bait?"

"That bucket full of cuttings. You've gotta be kidding with that sucker trick." He shook his head ironically. "Did you really imagine you could fool me with that phony bait?" Reese was laughing. "Salting the well so you could inveigle us to come in. Kid stuff. You ought to be ashamed."

"I guess I am." Laster laughed at himself with Reese and played glum until Reese had left.

# *Six*

C.M. JOINER'S COMPLETION OF Daisy Bradford No. 3, his discovery of the immense East Texas Oil Field, set off the greatest boom in the history of oil and also a chain of circumstances that would harass him mercilessly.

After a lifetime of failure, he had discovered oil in such a massive quantity as to make him rich beyond imagination. But those billions of barrels of oil that he had found were not legally his because his leases were not firm.

Joiner's lease block consisted mainly of small farms. Many boundaries had changed through the years by handshake and agreements between the farmers, and many of the tracts had been in one family for several generations, with the heirs scattered all around the country. Joiner lacked abstracts—concrete proof of ownership—to any of his block with the exception of one paltry two-and-a-half-acre gin lot to which he could prove title. The more than five thousand remaining oil-saturated acres were not legally his.

The problem was not entirely due to carelessness and informally drawn leases. Sometimes you bought a two-hundred-acre lease and when you surveyed it you might have six hundred acres, because the original deed called for a line from this oak tree north to such and such a creek and then it might say, "following the meanders of that creek back to this corner." But instead of the creek going straight as it had when the deed was written, it had changed direction in the next hundred years.

> JESSE JOHNSON: *The leases were further complicated by the fact that all the land of east Texas was Spanish-grant kind of land and it had been surveyed not in yards but in varas, an ancient Spanish measurement form, which could vary from thirty-two to forty-three inches.*

A lot of little tracts in the Joiner leases belonged to descendants of slaves who had been freed and given five or ten acres of plantation land to farm and scratch out a living, and nobody had spent much time or money making surveys and registering deeds for them. For years nobody bothered them or cared about a few acres of dust here and there—until the dust was known to have oil under it.

Creditors stormed down upon Mr. Joiner. The courthouse clerks in Henderson were overwhelmed trying to handle dozens of lawyers litigating debt and titles. Local sentiment was strongly for Joiner. Judge R.T. Brown of the Rusk County District Court, sitting in Henderson, threw out the first receivership suit against him, announcing, "I believe that when it takes a man three and a half years to find a baby he ought to be able to rock it for awhile."

His judgment offered only a brief reprieve because the creditors moved to Dallas and brought suit for receivership. As Joiner's troubles mounted, Daddy had completed his first east Texas well, a minor producer that might better be called a trickler—not worth the cost of drilling except that it showed him where *not* to drill. It was located south of Joiner's discovery well. Obviously the oil was not flowing south of Daisy Bradford. Therefore he was closely watching a test well being drilled by Foster & Jeffries on the Claude Ashby farm, which was north and west of the Joiner discovery.

He was extremely interested in the strange behavior of the Joiner discovery well, the likes of which he had never seen before. When it had first come in, it had produced 6,800 barrels a day, but that fell quickly and dramatically. Daisy Bradford No. 3 would produce a head, a huge spurt, of some 200 barrels of oil, and after flowing the head would cease producing for that day, then repeat the whole cycle the next day. He calculated that the casing of the well, the shaft, would hold 127.6 barrels of oil standing full, thus the heads were of a slightly larger volume than the pipe within the well.

The knowledge of reservoir engineering and production practices in 1930 was not what it is sixty years later. Much of today's technology is based upon what early operators like my father discovered and proved by trial and error and common sense.

Geologists were not impressed with the Daisy Bradford No. 3. They called it a freak.

As Daddy studied it, he deduced that oil was feeding slowly into a thin section of the Woodbine sand at the bottom of the well from a thicker parent sand body that could only lay west and north of the discovery well—and not east where he had purchased his leases. Foster & Jeffries' big producing wells brought in northwest of the discovery confirmed his feelings.

It was common knowledge that by this time Mr. Joiner was backed to the wall by his creditors, and that his situation was becoming more precarious every day. There was little interest from anyone in trying to make a deal with him because his titles appeared so weak.

Daddy estimated that even if Joiner's titles could be sustained, about half of his lease block would be dry because it was situated to the east of the discovery well. The part of Joiner's block that lay to the west, however, would be highly profitable—but only if the legal difficulties could be resolved.

To subsist, Joiner was selling the unrefined oil his well produced as boiler fuel for other rigs. It was such a high-gravity oil that in its natural state it was nearly gasoline. Oil is graded by gravity. If the gravity runs from fifteen to forty, by the time you get up around forty-two or forty-three it is close to gasoline. The east Texas crude was thirty-six. The refineries would take out the gasoline and be left with just a little residue from which they made fuel or lubricating oil. Therefore the commodity was highly marketable, which is why it was getting so much attention.

Yet no one was trying to buy Joiner's leases.

Daddy made the decision to make an offer to buy Joiner out lock, stock, and barrel—problems included.

Candidly, Joiner responded, "Boy, you would be buying a pig in a poke!"

Ever "straight as a string," never one to denigrate a property he wanted to buy in order to get it for less, my father replied, "I don't think so, Mr. Joiner. I foresee a lot of aggravation and struggle but with a great pot of oil at the end."

Joiner sighed wearily, shaking his head and holding out his hand. "That's the beauty of youth, son. You can look at trouble without getting worn out by the sight of it."

At that moment poor Mr. Joiner would have had a hard time believing that in a few years the area around the Daisy Bradford No. 3 would be named Joinerville in his honor.

Daddy pursued the deal and went to see Joiner in Dallas in late November, 1930 to work out an agreement. At that time the best place to stay in Dallas, for comfort and prestige, was the Baker Hotel, but getting rooms there was difficult, and Daddy not only wanted a suite, he wanted one next door to Mr. Joiner.

Daddy always had a sidekick, a troubleshooter, who did a lot of things for him that he had neither the time nor desire to do himself. First there was Mr. Bailey and then came Mr. H.L. Williford, a gray-haired, elegantly spoken Southern gentleman from Memphis, Tennessee, who always dressed in a navy blue suit, white shirt and necktie. Mr. Williford went to the manager of the Baker Hotel and, taking him aside, confidentially suggested, "I think I can do you a great big favor. I think that I'll be able to get H.L. Hunt to stay here instead of at the Adolphus."

The manager asked, "Who's H.L. Hunt?"

Mr. Williford, a consummate actor, appeared stunned. "Oh, my Lord, man, you don't know who H.L. Hunt is? How could you ever have come to be in the position you are?"

By the time he got through telling him who Daddy was, the man quaked, "We'll be honored to have Mr. H.L. Hunt and provide everything he wants or needs."

Within an hour Daddy was installed in the suite adjoining C.M. Joiner's, and from that day forward we always had all the rooms and service we needed at the Baker.

Wherever Daddy went, the telephone was a critical tool of his work. In those days there were no dials on telephones—you relied on the switchboard operator to place your calls for you. If you did not have a connection with her, you were in trouble. When Daddy and Mr. Williford arrived anywhere, one of the first things Mr. Williford did was to pay a visit to the switchboard operator. He would bring her a box of candy and flowers and say, "I want to introduce myself because we'll be having to make a lot of very important calls ..." I'm sure there was always a fifty-dollar bill or two mixed in with the flowers.

The Joiner deal consisted of separate transactions for each of three land areas: the 80-acre lease on which the Daisy Bradford No. 3 was located; a separate 500-acre Bradford lease situated west and southwest of the discovery well; and then the balance of the Joiner block of leases, being forty-two leases covering 3,329 acres, more or less (which was the source of his problem), and scattered over an area of several miles.

These three separate agreements were signed on November 26, 1930, between C.M. Joiner, individually and as trustee, and H.L. Hunt as trustee; in total, they called for the payment of $30,000 in cash, four short-term notes totaling $45,000, and ultimately $1,260,000 payable out of stipulated percentages of production that might be obtained and marketed from the leases.

The Joiner deal was an innovative, workable form of transaction and was the prototype for later agreements among the oil fraternity. Unique to the oil business at that time, it established a new method of transferring leases by means of a a large-scale payment out of production.

Despite the fact that Daddy was counted among the more successful independent oil and gas operators and had around one hundred wells to his credit in Arkansas and Louisiana, and though it is a fact that H.L. Hunt "got rich," it was "finally," not "quick," for at that moment in time his money was all invested back in the ground. To be precise, Daddy had only $109 cash with which to pay the $30,000 needed to close the deal.

Daddy had initially asked several friends in major oil companies if they would be interested in going in with him, but Joiner's shaky titles scared them all. Banks were not yet sophisticated about oil. You could borrow on your car or get a few dollars if you had a horse. But you could not get a dime against millions of dollars worth of oil in the ground.

Daddy came home to El Dorado but he had no interest in stopping by to see Charlie Murphy, a prominent banker of his acquaintance. It would have been pointless. Even during the boom in El Dorado, Mr. Murphy had sat on $2 million in cash, not lending any of it for leases.

With neither the major oil companies nor the banks interested, Daddy needed a private investor. While looking over some new shirts at the Star Clothing Company, a haberdashery in El Dorado, Daddy mentioned to P.G. "Pete" Lake, the owner, that he thought he had a wonderful oil deal lined up. He mentioned that he was looking for an investor with $50,000 to close the deal and provide some operating capital.

Pete Lake said, "I've got thirty thousand saved. What about me?"

Daddy had been thinking of someone much more affluent. He understood that Lake had saved his money over a long period of time, in nickels and dimes. "Now, Pete, the oil business at its best is highly speculative." He wanted to be painfully clear to this hardworking haberdasher. "You could easily lose your life's savings overnight."

Lake was not to be put off. "But how much could I make if we're lucky?"

Daddy told him what he believed. "Millions."

"How much of your deal will thirty thousand buy?"

"Twenty percent."

They shook on it and went together to the bank. Pete Lake's savings were withdrawn and turned over to Daddy.

The deal was closed with Mr. Joiner, who walked away with the $30,000 in cash, more money than he had ever owned. He could also look forward to short term payments totaling $45,000 more in cash and immense potential income from production. Further, freed from his legal spider web, he could finally breathe freely.

And H.L. Hunt took a major position in the East Texas Oil Field and assumed full risk of proving his titles.

Fred Mayer of Continental Oil Well Supply Company extended my father credit and furnished all of the equipment needed to drill wells and build the Panola Pipeline to deliver the oil to the tank cars. Mr. Mayer understood the business and had faith in Daddy. He had been sent to Texas from Pennsylvania by his company. He and Daddy became close, lifelong friends. Without his understanding and extension of credit Daddy could not have made it, and Daddy never forgot it.

But cash was still needed to pay the derrick crew and to buy water to make the steam that powered the drill. Water for boilers was a precious commodity. To meet immediate operating expenses he sold off some of his leases, the less certain ones to the east, but he was not a seller so he was not going to let go of much. He knew that he needed bank funds and therefore connections with a sophisticated bank.

Daddy went to Shreveport, contacted the head of one of the city's large banks, and presented a detailed financial statement along with a request to borrow $50,000.

The banker snorted, "You are broke and your statement shows you are broke."

Daddy was startled. "I am here to borrow money because I have no cash. I prepared a factual statement for your information, confident that you would appreciate that oil in place, recoverable oil, is a bankable asset ..."

"Bah! I've seen you oil fellows"—he named some Arkansas and north Louisiana operators—"You oil fellows drill a well, and it begins to flow. Then you take a trip to Europe, you buy a couple of expensive automobiles, and when the well quits flowing you are broke and you disappear! I will not lend you fifty thousand dollars, and I do not wish for you to open an account in this bank."

That was unjust. Sure, there were overnighters and con men, but you couldn't last in the oil business as Daddy had unless you had a good name. These were handshake times. One shady or questionable deal, and no one would have anything to do with you.

> BUNKER: *Any deal that was ever mentioned that wasn't clean, that had a kickback, he'd say, "I won't have anything to do with that."*
>
> TOM: *In 1937, W.O. Woodard, Uncle June's chief land man, made a twenty-five-thousand-dollar deal on what looked like a tremendous lease near a wildcat well that was drilled—but the next day the well was dry. Mr. Woodard said, "Mr. Hunt, I could probably say that we hadn't checked title yet and done everything ..." The money really meant something to Uncle June then, but he said "Did you commit the company?" "Well, yes, but ..." "No, you pay off, and we'll go on to the next deal. Let's just forget about that one."*
>
> SHERMAN: *Nobody every questioned our fathers' integrity. Deals were made on a handshake or over the phone, and the deal was the deal. They might not get around to doing the paperwork for a week or ten days, and somebody meanwhile would offer a higher price—and I* know *people offered a higher price because I was there—but Dad or Uncle June would say, "I'm sorry, I just made a deal with Charley Jones. It's too late." There wasn't anything signed, but that was that.*

When Daddy returned home to El Dorado, Mother said, "Discouragement is not you, June. There are lots of banks." She showed Daddy a newspaper article about the newly formed First National Bank in Dallas, a merger of two sizable banks, which had just started doing business under that name on January 1, 1930. The president, Mr. Nathan Adams, was quite a famous banker. Mother reasoned, "If these banks have put their assets together then they must have a lot of cash. And they are losing money every day that it is not out on loan. I would hazard the guess that a more metropolitan bank like this one is looking for reliable borrowers as eagerly as you are looking for a loan."

Daddy called for an appointment with Mr. Adams and then traveled to Dallas to meet with him. He described his accomplishments in the oil business to date, and the extraordinary leases he owned in east Texas.

Mr. Adams said, "We will lend you the fifty thousand dollars."

Daddy did not try to conceal his delight. "I am gratified and appreciative. What collateral will you require?"

"Your signature, sir. Nothing more. We'll draw the papers at once."

Daddy called Mother to tell her the good news and then had lunch at the Baker Hotel's Peacock Terrace. When he returned to the First National Bank and signed the papers, Mr. Adams handed him a checkbook. "There's fifty thousand dollars to your credit, Mr. Hunt, at our going interest rate of one and a half percent. I'll be grateful if you will consider us your principal bank and therefore do your principal banking business with us."

Shaking his hand, Daddy said, "I take pleasure in that thought. This has been a satisfying experience."

He offered Mr. Adams a cigar, and they sat together for almost an hour while Daddy educated Nathan Adams about the oil business. Mr. Adams was one of the first bankers to foresee the value of oil in the ground.

As they were about to part, Mr. Adams said, "I'm sure you understand, Mr. Hunt, that when I received your statement and request for an appointment I asked around about you before we met." He showed Daddy a letter from one of the El Dorado bankers whom Daddy had given as a reference.

> H.L. Hunt opened an account with us ten years ago. He has not given us any trouble.

That was a high compliment, considering the boom-and-bust nature of the oil business. Below the banker's signature was a handwritten postscript.

If you want to lend him money, he will borrow all you have.

Before leaving town, Daddy called on Judge J.B. McEntire, his Dallas lawyer, and persuaded him to move to east Texas to take on the massive job of handling three hundred separate lawsuits connected with the Joiner deal and proving all the leases. Although it would take him ten years, he managed to see every lease sustained.

H.L. Hunt Incorporated made the first runs of east Texas crude through its Panola Pipeline to the I-GN Railroad's main line track at Friars Switch on December 1, 1930, and delivered the oil to Sinclair's tank cars waiting on the railroad siding.

There were a hundred tank cars to a train in those days. Like commuter trains, as soon as they reached the refineries they would turn around and come back to reload. One tank car carried from 100,000 to 167,000 pounds. Thirty gravity oil was heavy, weighing about seven and a half pounds to the gallon. You had 10,000-gallon and 8,000-gallon tank cars, which cost the same to rent, so our people always tried to get the tens.

The first tank cars brought Daddy 62 cents per barrel. That was down from $1.19 earlier in the year, but his east Texas operation was off and running.

Satisfied that he was in the oil business to stay, Daddy decided that Hassie, who was now thirteen, would join him in Henderson, where he had been staying. He moved out of the Just Right Hotel and rented two rooms in a private house. Daddy always said that Hassie was the smartest of us all. He was always complimentary about Hassie though he never, ever complimented any of the rest of us. It didn't bother us. We were never a competitive group. Each of us just did what was expected of us. Daddy spoke of Hassie as being "an oil finder," the highest praise he could utter—and he was right. Though Hassie was young, he had grown up in the oil fields and Daddy believed that he knew as much about the oil business as anyone.

When Daddy came back to El Dorado to take Hassie to Henderson, he told Mother during dinner, "You should begin thinking of a move to east Texas. That is where our future operations are likely to be."

The moment I heard it I thought of how Mother had already uprooted from Lake Village, built this beautiful house in El Dorado, and developed a satisfying, active life bringing us up and participating in local school and church activities. Uprooting from what she had built as a young adult had to be distressing to her. But I knew that even if she was feeling that she would not let it be known.

She said matter-of-factly, "We are ready whenever you say. There is no need for you to be traveling two hundred miles back and forth to see your family."

Daddy enrolled Hassie in the Henderson school. But, without my father's knowledge, Hassie went to work in the oil fields instead of attending classes. He loved it out there. When Daddy learned about it, he really didn't mind; he'd take Hassie out with him, letting Hassie drive. As Hassie sped over the board roads at sixty miles an hour, he explained, "If we go off the road we have enough speed to get back on."

When Daddy laughed about it to Mother she was concerned, but Daddy said, "Don't expect him to be like everybody else. He's a genius."

Bringing a teenage boy to Henderson was perfectly acceptable, but moving the rest of us there was out of the question. The towns composing the heart of the oil field overflowed with roughnecks and drillers, thieves and gunmen, and a generally hard crowd of boomers, rougher than El Dorado had ever been.

> JESSE: *Gambling operations ran wide open; all of Texas was dry, but bootleggers peddled fruit jars of corn whiskey; tent cities sprung up and thousands of people lived in them without sanitation. In Kilgore, prostitutes literally paid the salaries of the police department. The city had been incorporated so quickly that by error they had made no provisions in the budget for the policemen, who were urgently needed. The practical solution was to "fine" the prostitutes twenty dollars per week, which paid the police. Everybody was happy—especially the prostitutes, who ended up with the protection of the law.*
>
> *If you could get ahold of a couple of bottles of good booze you could get some attention. It wasn't easy, but we managed. When we*

*sent a train of tank cars filled with oil to the East, after it started back we'd get a telegram—CHECK CAR NUMBER TWELVE—and when the train was on the siding we went there at night, climbed on top of the specified car, and opened the hatch. There, hanging from a wire attached to the valve under the opening on top were a couple of cases of the best Canadian or Scotch booze.*

*Our hangout was the fifth floor of the Blackstone Hotel in Tyler. There wasn't any air conditioning in those days. The oil people got together and made a deal with the management that no one except oil people be allowed on the fifth floor. Therefore we could open up all the windows and let the air blow clear through the floor. Women weren't allowed. When we'd come in everyone would strip down to their shorts, and we had a rule that everyone was supposed to have two kinds of cigarettes. I'm darned if I can remember why, but we had to have either Chesterfields and Luckies or Pall Mall and Old Gold. That's about all the brands there were then. And a little booze.*

*Pete Lake had a room on the fifth floor. And that was where the card playing took place. There wasn't a heck of a lot of gambling because no one had much money. Titanic Thomas, one of the famous gamblers of the day, was down there but he didn't stay very long because there wasn't enough money for him. But while he was there he pulled a few interesting stunts. He bet us he could throw a lemon over the top of the five story hotel. Well, we all took him up on that because we knew a lemon wasn't heavy enough to travel that far no matter how hard even someone as strong as Titanic Thomas threw it. So we pooled our money and he went downstairs to the lemon stand on the street, bought a lemon, wound up and threw it clean over the top of the Blackstone Hotel. After he'd gone we found out that he'd visited the fruit stand earlier and injected one of the lemons with about six ounces of mercury so that it flew like a baseball.*

*But he wasn't only tricks. Titanic would beat you left-handed and right-handed playing golf. He was a great golfer. Played for a lot of money. One day out at the Willow Brook Country Club he won a lot of money. When he got home the caddy master who'd worked for him was hiding in the bushes. Titanic shot and killed him. Believed he was there to hold him up.*

*Mr. Hunt didn't go to the Blackstone. He wasn't one to hang out. But he was known to bet on sport at the Just Right Hotel.*

Kilgore had Mattie's Ballroom, which featured nationally known bands, among them Ted Lewis, Louis "Satchmo" Armstrong, and Jack Teagarden. Mattie's also attracted hustlers and rustlers, new oil-rich millionaires, and muddy-booted roustabouts. Four miles east of Kilgore was Newton Flats, where every form of gambling known to man was available to please everyone from the ten-cent shooter to the thousand-dollar high roller. Four miles west was Pistol Hill, a den of thieves, stickup men, murderers—all the hard cases who had come from miles around.

East Texas had all the potential for being the dirtiest, wildest, most dangerous place in America. People got hijacked as they stepped out of the bank. At the beginning there were so many homicides and armed robberies and other crimes of violence that oilmen questioned the wisdom of trying to get rich in a place where you might not live to spend your money.

So they did something about it. J. Malcolm Crim, who had just been elected mayor of Kilgore, sent for the Texas Rangers. They answered his call. But they did not come galloping into town shooting outlaws like in the movies. They had their own way of operating.

One day, an unshaven stranger walked into Kilgore—just another impoverished, dirty face and disheveled soul among many. He hung out on Pistol Hill and around Newton Flats, his beard growing longer and his clothes dirtier by the day. Who bothered to pay attention to him? Just another boomer. He stayed for two weeks. Then he was gone.

When he next appeared on the main street of Kilgore, he rode a magnificent black stallion. He wore clean boots and shining spurs. The white Stetson on his head was immaculate. An automatic rifle was in the saddle holster, and he wore a double holster rig bearing a pair of pearl-handled, silver-mounted Colt automatics. He was a handsome man, bronzed by the Texas sun, clean-cut, clean-shaven, with broad shoulders and a slim waist.

"It's Lone Wolf Gonzaullas," murmured every mouth on the street. People came out of barber shops and stores to stare at the most famous Texas Ranger of them all: every child in Texas knew of his Herculean strength and the greased lightning style in which he drew, fired, and killed. This was Sergeant Manuel T. Gonzaullas, known as "Lone Wolf" because he could handle almost any civil disorder by himself.

Lone Wolf had not come to town just to break up fights among roughnecks or to impede the trades of the prostitutes and bootleggers. He was interested in the robbers, con men, and murderers he had spent those two weeks researching incognito. Yet for another two weeks he took no action, allowing the mere fact of his presence to cleanse the area of hundreds of hard cases who had seen him mop up other Texas boomtowns. Others, not so wise, stayed.

Then he struck. With the help of four other Rangers, he staged raids at Pistol Hill, Newton Flats, and other trouble spots around Kilgore and beyond. The morning after the raids, they marched three hundred men down the main street of Kilgore. As there was no jail, the prisoners were brought to the vandalized and abandoned Baptist Church where Lone Wolf had earlier prepared a heavy chain running from one end of the nave to the other. At intervals along the heavy chain were lighter trace chains, which he looped and padlocked around the necks of his captives. This became known as "Lone Wolf's trotline."

The identification process was then begun by the local police captain, Leonard Pace, and two fingerprint experts from Dallas. Within hours it was established that a majority of these men were wanted for serious crimes by police departments in Dallas, Houston, and other municipalities both in and out of Texas. Thus identified, they were removed from the trotline and sent under guard to where they were wanted.

Being escorted away in chains to be brought to justice almost compared favorably to being kept on the trotline. Prisoners were fed once a day, and a tin can was passed up and down the line for their physical necessities. The chain was padlocked tightly behind their necks to prevent them from picking the locks, and it was rough on the skin. Furthermore, there were so many men on the trotline that they had to remain standing day and night.

Those who were not found to be wanted by other authorities were offered freedom from the trotline—provided they were gone from town in four hours. Lone Wolf added one condition: "If you come back, you're dead." With no exceptions, the released prisoners took the four-hour offer and gave back three hours and fifty minutes.

Lone Wolf had been called in to establish order and preserve the peace. He and his men had not had the time, the jails, or the courts to wait for the judicial process. Though the way they operated would not be possible today, it was appropriate then. If the criminals they sought resisted arrest, the Rangers' attitude was: "A first-class killing is sometimes the best sermon you can preach to some people."

The Rangers brought in an average of a hundred criminals per day for around three weeks, until there were none left to arrest. The crime wave Lone Wolf had been brought in to stop came to an abrupt halt. The East Texas Oil Field was cleansed of all major crime. The lesser, non-life-threatening varieties were allowed to flourish as harmless amusement for those who were interested.

# *Seven*

THE MOST APPROPRIATE PLACE for Daddy to bring his family was Tyler, the seat of Smith County and the oldest city in east Texas, located about twenty-five miles west of the discovery area. God had landscaped the area with an astonishing variety of evergreens and magnolias and pecan and peach trees. But the most unusual beauty of Tyler was in the air. This was the rose center of the United States, and the scent of millions of roses being grown for miles around pervaded the air.

Tyler had a population of around 25,000 and a fine residential section in which the more substantial independent operators were beginning to take permanent residence. Most importantly it was far enough away from the oil fields to offer security from the less desirable elements who would not travel there.

In June 1931, as soon as school was out, my family and our three servants moved out of our home in El Dorado, Arkansas, to Tyler, Texas.

Tyler sported tree-lined brick streets around the square and along a street called Broadway. A brick factory in the little town of Pittsburgh in Camp County had overproduced so many bricks that they couldn't sell them. They offered the Tyler officials such a bargain price that the city hauled them there and laid them on the streets.

Since Tyler was an agricultural town, the leading families were well-to-do farmers, and many of them owned extensive pieces of land throughout the east Texas field. So although Tyler was unaccustomed to oil people, we were not unwelcome.

Daddy had rented a small red brick house on Woldert Street with just three bedrooms and two bathrooms for the seven of us. He had to pay $275 a month, a colossal price at that time. But to find a house in Tyler with two bathrooms was a major feat. There was a front bedroom and a bath and then another bedroom. Then one more bedroom and a bath. Daddy always had his own room. He shared his bathroom with

Mother, who had the next bedroom with Caroline. I had the third bedroom with Bunker and Herbert.

Hassie went to Culver Military Academy. He hated being removed from the oil business, but my parents felt that as he was only thirteen he should take more interest in education. Reading was a problem for him because he tried to read from the right side of the page. Today we know this as dyslexia. Mother and Daddy chose a military school because Mother felt that Hassie, who was a bit of a nonconformist, could benefit from the discipline.

Even office space was hard to come by in Tyler and H.L. Hunt Incorporated was lucky to find a second floor room over the Brookshire Grocery Store, next door to the Presbyterian Church on Broadway.

The Woldert Street house was unfurnished. What was there was what we brought, which had to be little because of the limited space. The living room had only a few chairs and a huge piece of furniture, which was a radio. They were very large in those days with as many as twenty tubes inside, the size of small light bulbs. The most important furniture Mother moved from El Dorado was the dining table and its fourteen chairs. We had fourteen of everything, and the table was always set for capacity. Though we were only eight or less, depending on who was away at school, the table needed to be ready for fourteen because Daddy often arrived with guests for lunch and dinner, unannounced.

At the beginning, Mother said, "June, call and let me know you are bringing people."

"No. That does not work." It was not an oversight or lack of consideration that caused Daddy to just arrive with guests without warning. He said, "When I call and indicate there are extras the food is just not as good. Gertrude must try too hard."

Gertrude did not allow us in her kitchen because there were so many people to feed. All my friends could make candy and cookies at home—that was a big deal—but we were never allowed to because Gertrude was feeding a lot of people three big meals a day. She needed room and never stopped working.

In 1931 you did not go to the supermarket and come home with a ready-made frozen dinner—or even a pre-cleaned chicken, for that matter. You plucked every feather out of every bird and then you had to singe the skin over fire, and it smelled terrible. You shelled every pea and made every batter, starting with the flour. There were no mixes, no shortcuts. Everything was done from scratch. The only "time saver" Gertrude had was Pandora, when she wasn't busy cleaning the rest of the house. The meals were planned, and we had a fixed menu for every day of the week. In those days restaurants were nonexistent.

CAROLINE: *We always dined at a set hour and that was partly because of the help, so they could leave on time. Meals were at eight* A.M., *twelve noon and six in the evening. On the dot.*

Because east Texas was one of the few places in the country with money at that time, it attracted major entertainers. Will Rogers came to Tyler to perform at the high school auditorium. Daddy appreciated his humor and took all of us to see him. Rogers was a homespun cowboy type, the Bob Hope of his day. He stood on the stage, twirled his lariat, and said witty things, often about politics: "The politicians put such a high inheritance tax on us that it makes patriots out of everybody. If you die from this time on, you die for your country."

Mother was not going to have us jammed into a house like sardines for any longer than absolutely necessary, so she searched Tyler for an alternative and found the Mayfield home on Charnwood Street. It was more than a hundred years old and had been used as a school and a hospital until it was abandoned for lack of indoor plumbing and electrical wiring. She bought it immediately and hired an architect to make the extensive renovations necessary to turn it into our new home.

We went to school in shifts and for only half days. Built to accommodate five hundred children, the Tyler school had never reached capacity. But that fall there were fifteen hundred students. They seated us alphabetically. I went in the afternoons and shared a desk with a boy named Hubbel. Out textbooks were state owned and there were so few of them and so many students that we only had books one night a week.

Caroline and Bunker went to Hogg Junior High, named for the late Governor James Stephen Hogg. Governor Hogg had a daughter named Ima, who was a lovely lady. I suppose there was humor intended in her name, but it always escaped me.

CAROLINE: *Mother sent Lewis with my lunch from home every day on a china plate to be sure I ate a properly balanced diet.*

I attended the high school, and it was there that I met my lifelong best friend Coleen Baughn. Coleen was raised in the Duncan, Oklahoma, oil play. Her father, who worked for Mudge Oil Company, moved his family to Tyler the same year we did.

At the end of my first semester I received a passing but not glittering report card. When Daddy got home from the oil field, I surrendered it to him.

He ignored it. "Your mother will sign that."

Mother asked me, "How do you feel you have done?"

"Nothing to get excited about."

"Try harder next semester."

I knew that my father had received wonderful teaching from his mother but that he was not formally educated, so his disinterest in my grades was no surprise. But I was curious why my mother, with her background, did not expect and insist on more from any of us. I can only surmise that she understood the limitations of the Tyler school system and, pragmatically, accepted the fact that we had to be there.

Mother and Daddy wanted me to go to Hockaday, a fine boarding school in Dallas, but as I pointed out, I was needed at home. I did all the grocery shopping and outside errands. Mother was not only running the household and remodeling the historic building which was to become our future home; she was expecting again.

Uncle Sherman and Aunt Tot had begun having hard times ranching in Montana when the depression hit. So when we moved to Tyler, they did too, with their sons Sherman and Stuart, and rented a small house on Donnybrook. Sherman went to high school and Stuart to Hogg Junior High.

One day, Daddy and Uncle Sherman were driving from Tyler to the east Texas field when a car in front of them, a convertible, hit a slick spot, skidded, and turned over. The driver was pinned under it. The traffic stopped, and everyone jumped out of their cars to lift the car off the trapped man. Suddenly Daddy staggered back and started screaming. In lifting he had torn a ligament and a disc in his back.

Uncle Sherman called us from the hospital. When we arrived, the doctor was in the room with Daddy saying that he needed to go to Dallas for surgery.

"No."

The doctor stared at him. I guess he had never heard a patient tell him no.

Daddy didn't believe in operations because his brother Leonard, to whom he had been especially close, had died of peritonitis after an operation for a ruptured appendix—this was before sulfa or penicillin. Daddy understood that his death was not the fault of the surgery, yet that was the beginning of his obsession against operations.

"Mr. Hunt, you need to be treated in a large hospital."

"I will be treated here."

"But we aren't equipped to treat you properly."

"I will cause you to become equipped."

Daddy ran everything. There was no question about it. He was not always right, but whatever he said went. It did no good to question either him or Mother. What they said was law.

Daddy was on his back at home for weeks, but he kept a male secretary busy taking dictation. Since the middle of 1931, east Texas had produced 300,000 to 400,000 barrels of oil a day. Everybody was recklessly trying to produce as much as they could sell, which not only brought the price down to 10 cents a barrel but squandered the bottom hole pressure that pushed the oil to the surface.

Fervently believing in the need to conserve this great natural resource, Daddy spent most of his time writing articles on proration, urging the government to control production. His articles ran on the front page of the *Dallas Morning News.* He wrote:

> East Texas can literally flood the oil markets of the world at this time. We need to control production. The independents want only to hit a producing well, produce it wide open, get the volume and go on to find another one. Why not be in this for the long pull? If we limit the daily volume we will conserve the bottom hole pressure, give the field longevity and we will get the price of a barrel up from ten cents. We would be a lot better off keeping nine barrels in the ground and selling one for a dollar than producing ten barrels and selling them for a dime each. I am the last one to want the government in my business, but as

long as the independents will not shut their valves proration is essential.

His secretary did not work on weekends or at night so almost every evening and Saturdays and Sundays I would sit at his bedside with a steno pad and he'd dictate to me.

"Daddy, not so fast."

"Try to write faster."

"I'm not a trained secretary. I can't even spell."

"Just get it down. Let them fix it at the paper."

His articles tried to explain to the other independents that even if the government prorated them to twenty barrels a day per well, the wealth was still there in the ground; it continued to belong to them, and this practice ensured them of a background of reserves. The other independents did not have Daddy's vision. A lot of them were poor farmers or make-it-for-the-day-and-be-gone wildcatters. They accused Daddy of being a tool of the majors. But history has proven him to be the father of proration in the oil industry.

In 1931, there was a half-block in downtown Kilgore called "The World's Richest Acre." Twenty-four wells were drilled so close to each other that the derricks overlapped. The front yard of the church was being drilled by two rigs. A bank had been dynamited and the rubble removed to make way for two other rigs. Merchants tore down their buildings to provide space for drilling sites. Others, wanting to have their cake and eat it too, cut off the rear ten yards of their stores and continued to do business up front while drilling for oil in the back.

Daddy campaigned for the regulation of the number of wells per acre, a practice called spacing, which today is standard procedure. Today a permit from the state to drill a well might allow only one on eighty acres, instead of the old practice of placing rigs side by side like two straws in the same Coke bottle.

BUNKER: *Dad understood spacing. Many people drill too many wells. They drill twenty when five are enough. They waste their assets. My father understood that. You lose the cost of the wells. In those days you were talking about maybe a ten-thousand dollar well, whereas today it's a million-dollar well. But if you drill twenty million-dollar wells when you could get by with five, you'd be spending fifteen million more to ultimately recover the same amount of oil.*

As always, unless one of us had something worthwhile to say, such as a political question or a serious family matter, business talk dominated mealtime conversations. Daddy told us, "Hunt Oil has rented a warehouse over at Wright City. It is really a barn on a peach orchard owned by the Fair family. But we need to build our own accommodations on our own land somewhere. Everytime some oil drops on one of the peach trees, it kills it, and Hunt Oil Company has to pay Mr. Fair for his peach tree. He gets a lot more for the tree this way than his peaches would be worth. And I really do not enjoy buying a dead tree."

Daddy also kept us up to date on the sharp operators who were always attracted to boomtowns. One time he said, "There are two geologists who have dreamed up a slick scheme. They go around to the farmers who have leased their land and own one-eighth royalty, and they buy that royalty for a few hundred dollars cash per acre."

Mother was incensed. "That is chicanery. Those farmers obviously do not realize that their royalty is worth millions, June."

"*If* it is drilled and *if* there is oil. You have seen how it is possible to bring in one well and think you have a field and then drill dry wells all around it."

"Not in east Texas," Mother said.

"Are you sure, Mom? Nobody knows where a field ends. But it always does. Somewhere. And to poor landowners, cash in the hand looks awfully good. If a man has forty acres of royalty and sells it for three hundred dollars an acre, that is twelve thousand dollars. More money than he has ever heard of."

"Because they have no understanding of the potential. Those poor souls are having their only hope in this life all but stolen from them."

Daddy said, "There is no excess of purity on either side. The farmers look upon it that if some goof comes along and offers them cash money for one-eighth interest in something that has not even been proven—and with oil at only ten cents a barrel—then they might just as well take advantage of his stupidity."

After all the proration articles and speeches, the State of Texas finally decided to enforce proration. Officials sent in the Rangers to shut down the entire field from August 17 to September 3, 1931, until they could establish controlled, limited production. Then, from October 13 until the following February, they cracked down hard on the "hot-oilers," those who continued to produce illegally.

Most refineries were in the Gulf of Mexico or in New Jersey and Pennsylvania, but there was one small refinery in east Texas that was still receiving "hot" oil secretly through the pipeline, passing it through the stills to be turned into gasoline and then trucked to market. Men with machine guns stood guard on top of the refinery in case anyone tried to stop them.

Daddy was unable to speak about anything else. "I, and the others who are obeying the law and not producing, waiting for allowables to be set, can not get the Rangers or the National Guard to shut down this refinery."

Mother was startled. "You do not mean that somebody is paying off the Texas Rangers!"

"No. They say, correctly, that there is no law against the operation of a refinery. We tell them the refinery could not operate without crude and nobody is supposed to be producing crude, yet obviously it is coming in through the pipeline because there is gasoline going out every day in tank trucks. They agree, but they can not find anyone who is producing oil.

"The hot-oilers are ingenious. They have valves made in reverse so that when they are inspected you think they are closed, when in fact they are wide open. Instead of having the lines come up from the surface they have them going down with well heads tied in on the bottom side of the pipeline. These hot-oilers are doing sleight-of-hand right under our noses and ruining the field for all of us."

Daddy was even more worried about the physical danger created by all the unflared gas they were producing. Since the hot-oilers were violating the law they could hardly advertise it by flaring the gas, so they were venting it into the air. On a damp night the humidity will hold gas close to the ground and anyone who comes along and lights a match or has a cigarette will cause it to ignite. The legal producers, pumping only their allowable barrels per day, were flaring, and it produced a small flame. But a hot-oiler, producing a thousand barrels instead of twenty, would produce a flame fifty times larger that could be seen for miles and immediately give him away. So the hot-oilers were taking an unconscionable risk by not flaring all that floating gas, merely keeping their fingers crossed that there would be no explosion. The odds were short, because they had fires in the boilers that made the steam power for the drill, and they had plain old light bulbs on the derrick, not the safety bulbs we have today—some even used kerosene lamps.

Mother said, "June, when there is a burglar and the police fail to come, you need to consider handling that thief yourself."

"Now, Mom, we cannot take the law into our own hands."

"Absolutely. But I *was* thinking that until the field is reopened those hot-oilers do not have any way of selling their hot-oil except via the refinery ..."

"Correct."

"That refinery has created a mortal danger to everyone for miles around, as long as it is functioning."

So the Hunt and Humble oil companies made a deal with Halliburton, a company they each employed to cement the wells, which kept the sides of the hole from caving in. A few nights later Daddy reported, "Well, while the refinery guards were on watch with their submachine guns last night, about a mile away a substantial mixture of cement and water got pumped into the refinery pipeline, and when that cement hit those hot stills and the hot pipes, why, it wreaked havoc with the whole refinery operation. It hardened and clogged up everything so bad that the refinery has had to shut down."

Daddy's dinner conversation with Mother in front of all of us was not just for the sake of chat, I am sure. Many times Mother contributed ideas that helped him, and I am certain that he expected that what we heard would not go in one ear and out the other but would be absorbed and put into useful practice in our adult lives.

The headlines were big and black: LINDBERGH BABY KIDNAPPED! After the shock and initial sympathy for the ordeal of the Lindberghs, Daddy sighed heavily, "Ohhhh, my goodness, this is going to start something. This is going to suggest a lot of things to a lot of people."

A week later, a waterproof canvas-like package was dropped in some shrubs at one end of our yard.

COUSIN SHERMAN: *It was a threat to kidnap Margaret and Hassie. It said to meet the kidnappers at the Blue Moon Night Club. Uncle June turned it over to the Rangers. A few days later there was a call from the sheriff, and I was told to drive Uncle Jim over to Ranger Hill at Kilgore to meet Lone Wolf Gonzaullas. Luckily he was nearby, due to the hot oil crackdown.*

*We went into the Ranger headquarters and were told that Lone Wolf Gonzaullas was still in bed, asleep, so we went back to his room and knocked on his door. He was getting dressed. He carried two pearl-handled automatics around his waist. He had a little pistol in his coat pocket, a knife in the back of his coat, and a derringer in his boot. He said, "I'll follow you." He was driving a Chrysler. It had a split windshield that you could loosen and raise from the bottom to let the air in, and he had a Thompson submachine gun mounted on the right-hand side so he could fire this machine gun while he drove.*

*Captain Gonzaullas followed us in the Chrysler, and we went out to the Blue Moon Night Club between Gladewater and Longview. A great big Ranger came out leading four handcuffed cats, real tough-looking but scared to death, with him. They were driven to the train station, put aboard the express to Chicago, and told, "Don't ever come back to the state of Texas. If you do you're dead." And nobody ever heard of them coming back. Lone Wolf said they were from the Mafia out of Chicago trying to extort money from the oilmen.*

A week later somebody called and told Daddy there was a crew of people who were going to try to kidnap him personally. Lone Wolf came over and gave Daddy a revolver to keep handy. Daddy held it with distaste.

BUNKER: *He would never keep a gun. Normally he didn't want a gun around the house. Wouldn't have a shotgun. He'd done some hunting as a kid and he'd seen people get hurt and it didn't appeal to him.*

Lone Wolf told him, "Mr. Hunt, the house across the street will rent me the front room, so I'll be staying there and watching out for any movement."

This event coincided with my first date. I had taken hours to get dressed and was waiting for my date to arrive to take me to the movies.

He drove up in his Model-A, left his motor running, and started up the walk. He was carrying an extra-large bouquet of flowers. Two Texas Rangers materialized out of the bushes and held guns on him while they frisked him. I saw it all from inside. He looked scared to death. I rushed out to identify him, but all I saw was the taillight of his car disappearing up the street.

I went back inside and fumed at Daddy, "It is a real disadvantage to have money, having everybody know you have money."

He said, "If you get sick or anyone in the family gets sick and you need attention and care, it is desirable to be able to pay for it."

Lone Wolf came into the house and said, "I'm sorry, Miss Hunt. But I'm real pleased there wasn't anything in those pretty flowers." He turned to Daddy. "Mr. H.L., maybe we need to bait the hook. If you could be a bit visible coming and going during the day ..."

Uncle Sherman, who was at the house for dinner, said, "You're too busy for that, June. But give me your hat. I look enough like you, and I'll play the role of H.L. Hunt until some fool shows up to make trouble."

Though he wasn't as tall, Uncle Sherman wore Daddy's straw hat slouched to the angle Daddy wore it, and drove his car playing decoy, with the Rangers nearby ready to grab the threateners if anyone showed up. No one did.

> CAROLINE: *I was not allowed to walk to school because of the kidnapping threats, but I was not given the reason and considered myself deprived that I could not walk to school with the other girls.*

Lamar was due in mid-July 1932. When school was out, we all drove back to El Dorado so mother could be cared for by her own physician, Dr. Murphy. Hassie and my father came from east Texas when the baby was expected and waited two weeks.

Finally, Mother said, "June, you and Hassie need to get back to the field."

Daddy said, "No, Mom, everything can wait."

"No, it cannot. Our business needs attention so do go on back." She was adamant. "I have done this six times. You two get on with the drilling, and Margaret will take care of me and the baby."

Mother and I sat together and talked about the new baby she was so happy about, but she worried about having time to give it all the attention it would need. "Your father was set on having a lot of children to pass his genes on to. Thank heavens you and Hassie are grown. Four children is the right number for someone to have. It is really too difficult to spread oneself efficiently over the activities of more."

That evening, before I went to sleep, Mother said, "I feel fine, Margaret, and I am sorry to put this burden on you, but people of forty-three do not customarily have children. So just in case anything should happen to me, the clothes I want to wear are in a suitbox in the closet."

I had never before imagined life without Mother. I would never have let her see what I was feeling, so I went to bed as I had been instructed. Putting out the light I lay there thinking of Caroline and Bunker and Herbert—and Daddy—without Mother. Daddy would be the worst. Strong as he was, he would not be able to handle that.

I realized that I'd fallen asleep when I suddenly heard Mother calling my name. She was shaking me urgently. "Please drive me to the hospital." She shuddered, withstanding a pain. I was terrified. I'd never been with her or with anyone when they were having labor pains and about to give birth.

Lamar was born August 2. In later years when he was in business and began to display a tendency toward being extra careful with money Mother said, "We should have known that about Lamar long ago. When he was born, the hospitals were not air-conditioned, so they had 'August Specials' to encourage people to have operations in off-season. Lamar waited till August to be born so he could take advantage of the cut rate."

Mother continued to work on the Charnwood Street house. Aunt Tot went to Dallas with us and the architect, Shirley Simons, to select bathroom fixtures. The latest fashion was black washbasins and toilets and tubs and black tile walls, and when it came time to select the tiles for my bathroom I said, "I have to have the black."

Mother said, "It will be a mess. Every drop of water will make a spot on the black tile. That is so impractical."

Aunt Tot was a pal. "Let the child have whatever she wants. It's not that important. And if she thinks it's so great, let her be happy with it."

And that is what I wound up with. A black bathroom that was always full of spots.

Mother had been working for nearly a year getting the Mayfield house remodeled. Finally, we were able to make the move. Her renovations had transformed the outdated three-story structure into a comfortable and elegant home, with separate bedrooms for each of us and a third-floor ballroom that later was made into two more bedrooms. There was a guest room and bath on the first floor which were in use most of the time.

The stables were converted into the servants' quarters. A tremendous magnolia tree stood in front of the house. The side street was an "oil street," a dirt road with oil poured on it to keep the dust down, as was the street behind the house.

Mother decided Oriental rugs would be practical, so Daddy had Mr. Haddad, the biggest Oriental rug dealer in Shreveport, come to Tyler. He arrived in a mammoth truck, which was parked behind our house for a week while the rugs were tried out. After at least six were brought into the living room and put down and then replaced, Mother asked me, "Which one do you like best?"

"None. I hate those mixed-up patterns and colors."

Though all our lives we had been geographically removed from mainstream culture centers, we susbscribed to every magazine there was, from which Mother learned much of what there was to know about such things. Growing up, I hated those rugs but the fact is they didn't spot, they lasted forever, and were beautiful. I treasure one now.

Mother was especially knowledgeable about furniture. She appreciated English antiques and her home was very eclectic, including an elaborately carved Victorian bedroom set she brought from Lake Village.

In any boomtown, some people were always doing great, but many more people were not as smart or as hardworking or as lucky—and they were starving to death. The country was in the throes of the Great Depression. Out on the screened back porch Mother had a long table, and every day she fed ten or fifteen people who had come to town to get work, had not found any, and didn't have anything to eat.

HERBERT: *Times were tough, and a lot of people would knock on the back door and Mother would have Gertrude feed them. I'm not talking about bums, I'm talking about people who were fairly well dressed and seeking work. I don't know if someone put a mark on Mother's front door or something, but they knew where to go.*

BUNKER: *Mother was much the same to everybody, be he the King of England or a hobo at the back door. She treated everyone politely and never looked down on anyone except to give them a hand up.*

We never locked the front door or had occasion to think that we should. People were desperate, but they did not steal. It was a different moment in time, a different world, a different set of morals. There was little street crime, little robbery. I don't remember ever having a key to the house, and we left the keys in the car. Those men on our porch had not come to Tyler to rob, they had come to work.

Mother had unlimited human sympathy but she was not a push-over.

BUNKER'S WIFE CAROLINE: *What did try Mrs. Hunt's patience were people who loafed on the job. She did not loaf, and she did not expect anyone else to. She got so mad at the yard man. She would catch him back of the garage sleeping and she told him, "You either work or you leave."*

*She did not believe in loaning anyone money. That was one of the first rules of hiring help. "You never loan money. You just give it to them." One maid needed a loan and Mrs. Hunt said to me, "Oh, no, she'll leave you and you'll never see her again. If she needs it, give it to her."*

*But she didn't believe in giving money to relatives. "That messes up the whole family fabric. Help them to borrow it from a bank. Keep it on a business basis."*

*Mrs. Hunt said, "When you have money people who are in need will find you." And she was generous when she thought it was needed and always very private about what she gave.*

Uncle Sherman became vice-president of H.L. Hunt Incorporated. He was Hunt Oil's top land man. His presence in Tyler relieved Daddy of the job of traveling around east Texas to buy leases, which was a big help because Daddy believed in owning a lot of leases.

TOM: *Uncle June didn't just sit like so many people in the early days of the oil business, who made a strike and that was the end of it, they let it play out. He thought in terms of expanding.*

Sherman, Jr. went right to work in the oil field for the summer and would have gladly stayed there if he'd been allowed to, instead of going to school.

SHERMAN: *Our fathers placed little emphasis on formal education. They could have all the graduate engineers you can say grace over for seventy-five dollars a month, whereas I could go to work in the oil fields and even on a roughneck's rate make a hundred and fifty. Just a very few of us went off to college. If you were big enough and knew somebody, you could work. There wasn't any child labor law, and we were big stocky kids. Every summer we worked in the oil fields.*

*We got five dollars and ten cents a day, and there wasn't any withholding. We got every cent. Tool pushers came out and wrote the checks.*

*One summer Stuart and I worked as roustabouts. Roustabouts did the hardest work, mixing cement and drilling water wells. We would put chain-tongs on a piece of drill pipe and walk around it, four of us, actually drilling the hole for the well. Around in a circle all day in the Texas heat. We were the oxen.*

*Nobody had hard hats or safety shoes. They used to say "Son, if you ever set your foot down at the hole just walk on away 'cause you don't need to tell the driller to take it up, you've cut it off. You have no toes left." You could always tell the old-timers by their missing fingers. They'd lose them handling the pipe.*

*We wore leather-faced gloves with a cuff, which had elastic on the back, but everyone would cut the elastic off. That way if something happened and your glove got hung up on a pipe splinter it would slip off. If the elastic was still on, your hand would go with it. There were cotton gloves that cost fifteen cents a pair, but two towers was about all you could get out of a pair of cotton gloves, whereas you could make a whole well out of a pair of leather-faced ones.*

*There was not a lot of money in those days. Gasoline was down to ten cents a gallon. Roughnecks and drillers were paid so much in cash and so much in gasoline books. They used the coupons to buy gas and to go to the picture show. It was almost legal tender. The coupons were narrow, two to a page.*

*Hunt Oil did not use gas coupons. They paid one hundred percent cash. Hunt was the most prosperous company around.*

*There wasn't work for everybody who came to east Texas. If you weren't standing on your designated street corner when the driller went by in the crew car, there were a minimum of six men standing there ready to go to work in your place and you were out of a job. So you didn't oversleep. You were there when that car came by.*

Our years in Tyler were some of the best we had as a family. When Hassie came home from school he and Daddy were in the oil fields all the time. Hassie looked just like Daddy. He wasn't even that much smaller now that he had reached fourteen. He and Daddy went to a father-and-son banquet and won first prize in the lookalikes contest.

One day Hassie and Daddy came back in time for lunch. Hassie had left in clean white buck shoes. As he walked in the house I saw they were spotted with oil. I whispered, "You'd better get those downtown and have them dyed before Mother sees them." The next day he wore them for dinner. He'd had them dyed a bright apple green.

The rest of us could not go to the fields. I was a teenage girl and it was no longer possible for me to wander around in that rough man's world. The kids—after Hassie and me, the other children were always referred to en masse as "the kids"—were too young to go near the oil fields because it was so dangerous. The type of oil being produced in east Texas was as flammable as gasoline. Back then, when you brought in a well you would flow it into an earthen pit; every well had a little film of oil over these pits, fumes that rose from the oil and were called light ends. In cool weather, those light ends would stay in the oil, but when it got warm they'd come out. I saw a welder working two hundred feet from a pile of oil when the wind changed and carried those light ends to his torch and the whole thing went up like an inferno.

Tyler, a town of twenty thousand people, had a football stadium that seated twenty thousand. The Tyler High School football team were the Texas state champions, which gave us a lot of events and rallies to attend. There were special trains to Tyler from Corsicana, Kilgore, Longview—everybody went to football. Mother was a major fan and never missed a game. The only other social activity for teenagers was to go out in a car and circle the square. There was a picture show, but until a few years later when Tyler developed into a more prosperous town, there wasn't much else going on.

> HERBERT: *Margaret, being a teenager, would offer to take me with her when she went places, so I spent a lot of time with her. I was virtually her kid on afternoons. We were going somewhere once and there was a crowd blocking our way and someone said, "OK, guys, make way for the young mother and her little boy." Margaret didn't*

*care for that at all. Yet I guess I saw her as a second mother, an adult who I minded and had a good time with.*

Our traveling was curtailed for the first six or seven months in Tyler because cash was scarce. Daddy was producing and selling plenty of oil, but he was drilling wells and putting all of the money into the ground. Nobody yet had any idea exactly how big the East Texas Oil Field was. But they were beginning to realize that it was impossible to drill a dry hole anywhere.

When the Humble Oil Company drilled a dry hole, the geologist was incredulous. "This can't be!" he exclaimed. So they dropped a bit of dynamite to shock the well and widen it a bit, and sure enough, it came in producing.

After dinner one evening, when we'd retired to the living room, Mother said, "This morning I gave a meal to a young fellow who knocked on the door asking for work. I had nothing we needed him to do, but he looked like he had missed more than one meal. Gertrude made two big chicken sandwiches, gave him some peach pie and a quart of milk. Two hours later, when I came around to the back of the house, there he was, chopping firewood and making piles of kindling, to pay me back. It is a bad thing when a man with working hands like that cannot find a job and have his self-respect."

Daddy said, "Well, Mom, if we went to four six-hour shifts, instead of two twelves, we could hire one hundred percent more people." Oil rigs worked around the clock, and the crews worked twelve-hour shifts. "Considering we are drilling twenty new wells, with six-man crews we could create jobs for two hundred and forty more families."

"Do it. We enjoy the privileges of wealth. We also have responsibility."

This was right up Daddy's alley. He looked at the kids and me."The greatest good we can do is to provide the opportunity for a man's personal progress through his own work. The government is talking about handing out money to the unemployed." He shook his head impatiently. "There is a saying: 'Those who cannot remember the past are condemned to repeat it.' And history proves that 'relief,' as they are talking about now, has been tried time and time again throughout the history of mankind and it has never worked. On the contrary, it humiliates the beneficiary. It corrupts all but the absolutely helpless and smothers a vital spark in those who are forced—or who allow themselves—to exist for too long on the fruits of another man's labors. On top of the pain of their material poverty we inflict spiritual poverty of the worst sort."

I was figuring out loud, "By putting on two more shifts, the men who have the jobs now are going to get less money. Our crews are not going to be happy about a cut in pay."

"Are you sure, Margaret?" That was one of Daddy's favorite questions. You did not want to say things to him that were not fact.

> BUNKER'S CAROLINE: *On Bunker's tombstone it's going to say* ARE YOU SURE*? Because he and his daddy insisted that you be sure of something you're saying, not that you're just quoting a statistic or something that wasn't a certain fact.*

Mother interjected, "If your father asks our present crews to hire the other shifts, they will surely hire the relatives and friends they are supporting anyway. That should be a welcome financial relief to them."

"Exactly," Daddy said. "Further, if we could afford to pay them forty cents an hour instead of a quarter, to help make up for the six hours they lose, they would only be taking a twenty percent cut in net pay."

That's when Daddy introduced the flexible work week. He and Mother were correct about the men. They were pleased to work six hours for $2.40 a day as opposed to twelve hours for $3.00. It cost Daddy some money, but that's what he worked for.

> TOM: *He didn't think of money so much for himself as, "This will enable me to drill here, to employ more people, provide for my family ..." The money was a tool to be used. He created more than two hundred new jobs in his own company, and the roughnecks and drillers were elated. It heightened the camaraderie with his men. Believing that he was looking out for them, they solidly supported him and would take pride in saying, "I'm a Hunt man."*

> TOM: *People followed him, worked for him, as if it were a cause.*

Despite Daddy's shortage of cash, we did travel some. He took me to Chicago with him to a meeting of API, the American Petroleum Institute. "If you listen to everything, you will learn a lot that you may want to know," he told me.

> HERBERT: *Dad was one of these guys who when he got into a cab would talk to the cab driver all the way to town, ask him about politics: Who's going to win the race for Mayor? How's the Mayor doing? Whatever the topic of the day was. Same with the elevator operator. That was his way.*

API had meetings all day long. Women were not invited. One day, Mrs. Charlie Rosier from Fort Worth took me to lunch and she ordered a beer and smoked a cigarette. I had never seen a lady drink a beer. I was fascinated.

I went to the dinners with Daddy. Though I was very interested in the oil business and wanted to please my father, my interest had its limits. We were staying at the Drake Hotel. One morning after a heavy dinner conversation about the flexible work week, spacing, allowables, and depletion allowances, I went down to the hotel cashier and signed for enough money to buy a train ticket back to Tyler. I left a note on Daddy's night table: *I've caught the train. Going home.*

When he returned a few days later, Daddy did not react at all. If he had had something to say about it he would have said it. He was a tireless talker about what he thought was constructive. But he never wasted words on criticism. None of us can remember being criticized. We were corrected, even punished, but never criticized. He wouldn't use his time or breath on the obvious.

Daddy was home only as long as it took him to repack his suitcase and board a train to Washington. Several other oil companies had followed his lead and successfully changed over to four six-hour shifts. Then why not the whole country? Troubled by the nation's unemployment, Daddy spent a week talking to senators he knew, urging them to make the flexible work week a national policy.

The reasoning would seem inarguable: doubling the amount of available jobs would instantly eliminate unemployment and spare people the indignity of soup kitchens and standing on street corners begging others to buy apples and pencils. Businesses would gain more customers, as those formerly unemployed would have money and become consumers. Daddy was certain that most reasonable citizens would accept a slight lowering of their own incomes to see the country as a whole made well.

Senator Hugo Black, a Democrat from Alabama, introduced the Black Bill establishing the flexible work week, which passed the Senate. In fact, to meet some technicality it was voted upon and passed a second time. The Ways and Means Committee of the House of Representatives reported the bill favorably, which by precedent practically ensured passage by the House.

Before Congress had time to complete passage, President Franklin Delano Roosevelt sidetracked the Black Bill in favor of the National Industrial Recovery Act. The NIRA became law June 16, 1933, supplanting and killing the flexible work week. Daddy left Washington and returned home feeling painfully disillusioned by what an individual citizen could hope to accomplish for his country. He went back to his own business.

"Pete Lake does not belong in the oil business," Daddy said. He was sitting in the living room, waiting for dinner, fatigued from yet another impossible meeting with his partner. "In two years, Pete has received a four hundred percent return on his investment, with a fortune to come. But whenever I speak to him about the need to reinvest some of our income he looks at me as if I'm crazy. Today I wasted two hours trying to explain to him that if we invest two million dollars into expanding Panola Pipeline this year, it will be able to handle all the oil we'll be flowing into it five years from now. He says, 'Five years from now! Who cares about five years from now? I'd rather have my six hundred thousand dollars today.' The man has no vision. He never wants to do anything that costs money, like the flexible work week or expanding Panola, which keeps us independent of the majors and increases profits."

Hassie told him, "This is ridiculous. Whatever it takes to get rid of Pete Lake—do it. He doesn't belong in the oil business. Buy him out."

Daddy was reluctant. "Pete's OK … he helped with his savings when I really needed it."

Mother didn't buy loyalty to Pete Lake. "Friendship and kinship do not sail a good business ship.'"

I hated seeing my father frustrated and handicapped. I said, "Daddy, you can't live with a partner like that. You can't operate in your own way, you're hampered and confined ..."

> BUNKER: *My father had a loyalty streak about him. If he believed in somebody it was almost impossible for him to consider that they would do anything wrong.*
>
> *If he had somebody working for him who he liked very much, he never wanted that person to retire because he had read and observed that people who retired would die, they wouldn't live very long, so he wouldn't let them retire.*

He sat there rubbing one thumb against the cuticle of the other, something he did when he was disconcerted.

Mother read him clearly. "Your problem is pure sentimentality, June."

Daddy made a settlement with Pete Lake that amounted to a return of many millions of dollars for his initial $30,000 investment, but Daddy was happy to pay it and be a free, independent operator again.

# *Eight*

I GRADUATED FROM HIGH SCHOOL in 1933. During the Depression you could go to any college you chose as long as you could pay the tuition. Mother decided on Mary Baldwin in Staunton, Virginia. Though her great-grandmother had gone there, that was just a coincidence. I don't know why she chose Mary Baldwin, but I am elated that she did. In retrospect I realize that though my father would appear to be the stronger of my parents, I often challenged or disagreed with him; I never, however, questioned anything Mother said or decided. None of us did.

Mother said, "We need to go to Neiman's for your school wardrobe."

My allowance did not include clothing because Mother knew I would not buy good enough clothes if I were paying for them out of an allowance. She was very particular about personal appearance. Mother and I frequently drove to Dallas to shop at Neiman Marcus, which had opened in Dallas around ten years earlier, bringing quality and international style to a hitherto rather plain-dressing region. Neiman Marcus taught all of Texas how to dress well. The founders were Mr. Herbert Marcus and his sister, Mrs. Carrie Neiman. Miss Carrie always waited on us. Tyler to Dallas was a hundred-mile drive. Though bridges were being built, sometimes along the road you'd reach a dip where the river had risen three or four feet high over the road. A man with a team of mules would be ready to pull your car through for a dollar.

We meticulously timed our trips so that at lunchtime we would arrive at Wills Point, the halfway point, where there was a fabulous boarding house. You paid a flat amount and sat down at a table on which there were huge bowls of mashed potatoes, corn, meats, fried chicken, and pies and cakes. It was a sit-down buffet where everything was passed around. Invariably, we would eat too much.

BUNKER: *Mother weighed one hundred and fifty pounds and was five feet tall. Quite short. She tried to watch her diet but she did love Southern cooking.*

That was about twenty years before we read Adelle Davis's *Let's Eat Right to Keep Fit.* Once we learned that we were eating our way into the grave it wasn't nearly as much fun.

I had no compunction about leaving home and going off to school. We had traveled a great deal, and I knew Hassie was happy at Culver.

HERBERT: *We had to drive to Mineola to put Margaret on the train to go to school. That was exciting because when we put pennies on the track, the heavy steam engines would flatten them into long ovals. We were guilty of destroying currency, which was against the law, but we didn't know it at the time.*

Mother gave me a subscription to the *Tyler Courier-Times,* which I received every day. I was not even deprived of the substance of lunch and dinner conversations. Daddy wrote five- and six-page letters on airmail paper—in pencil on both sides of the page—on the current subjects: prorationing, new wells he was drilling, how poorly he regarded President Roosevelt, and all the family news:

October 2, 1933

Dear Margaret,

While in New York I hired a Swiss governess, Eugenia de Tuggenier, for Lamar as I would like Mom to be less tied down to family obligations. Raising the first five of you has not left her adequate time for the traveling she enjoys and needs to do with you all to expose you to more of the world. I hired her on the basis of impressive references, however, Miss Tuggenier's previous experiences had not prepared her for living in Texas. Upon arrival she expected to be threatened by Indians. Also, she has never before experienced devoted colored servants. Bunker calls her "Toogie" to her face which he manages to get away with although she is quite strict otherwise. "Toogie" is teaching Bunker and Herbert to speak French which I do not suppose will damage them. Toogie has some *Flying Elephant* books which the boys read out loud with her in French.

> Hassie wants to play football at school but Mom and I are not giving our permission. I never knew of a football player who didn't end up with some permanent injury.
>
> Caroline is not greatly enjoying being away at Hockaday. She comes home as often as she can and from time to time brings a lot of girls with her, foreign students, boarding students who are her friends.
>
> *Daddy*

Mother and I wrote to each other daily. Writing every day is easier. You do not have to get caught up, you just describe the day's activities.

At Mary Baldwin we were allowed two free weekends per semester. We organized groups to go to New York. Everyone paid $5 a night at the Weston Hotel because students received special rates, and besides, we tripled up. We rode to Washington in a Greyhound bus, then sat up all night in the coach car in the back of the train from Washington to New York. When I traveled with Daddy we had drawing rooms, parlor car seats, and great meals in the dining cars. But on school trips few of the girls could afford that. I would certainly not have let my friends know I could pay for a berth. Once we were in New York we spent most of our time in museums, as admission was free or inexpensive. In pairs of two, girls could stroll the streets around Broadway. There was no danger in those days.

Mary Baldwin had classes on Saturday but we were allowed to leave at noon. We could board a Greyhound bus at Staunton and be in Lexington in an hour, go to Washington and Lee for a football game and dinner, and return to school in time for the eleven P.M. curfew.

Scholastically, I was mediocre. I had no background. Probably my best year of schooling was the first grade at the Catholic school in Lake Village. In El Dorado—and later Tyler—the schools were entirely inadequate because of the crowded boomtown conditions. Lacking a proper foundation, I had severe academic problems. A foreign language had not been offered in high school but was required at Mary Baldwin. I chose French, but it was difficult for me.

Mary Baldwin also required two years of Bible. Despite Mother's devoutness I was never much of a Bible student, so when I was assigned papers to write, it posed a problem.

Mother's friend, Mrs. Melvin Wilcox, was a graduate of Bryn Mawr. She was an ardent Presbyterian and a Bible teacher. Her husband had been injured while riding horseback and they had chosen Tyler as a tranquil community in which to live simply and raise their family. They had five sons and a lovely home out on Bullard Road. The last thing they expected was for Tyler to become a boomtown.

I can hardly believe it now, but I had the nerve to write Mrs. Wilcox and give her my Bible assignment—and bless her heart, she would send me an outline. Having that as a start I could get out the Bible and prepare my papers. Of course, Bible was my best subject.

What I did accomplish very easily at school was to gain weight—twenty-five or thirty pounds in two months. Mary Baldwin had excellent meals—with hot bread, fried apples, and honey. The Shenandoah Valley is apple country, and a basket of apples was always available in the hall outside the dining room.

Mother came to visit me on my first Thanksgiving away from home. She left Lamar, who was a year and a half, and Bunker and Herbert, who were seven and four, with Toogie. I did not appreciate at the time how hard it must have been for her to make the trip, as she was totally unaccustomed to turning her children over to someone else.

Stepping off the train she gasped at the sight of me. "What will your father say when he sees you? You are substantially overweight."

When I returned home for Christmas, Mother and I went straight to Neiman's and bought all new, larger-sized clothes. While I was there, I bought my mother alligator luggage for her Christmas gift, which I now have. It is beautiful but weighs a ton. My gift for Daddy was a brass four-leaf clover for his desk. There was always very little pleasure in buying him presents because anything he wanted he bought and when you gave him a present he would fail to get around to even opening it. He had no curiosity about what was in a package. He always wore a dark suit and white shirt so he was not excited by a new sweater or the current hand-painted necktie.

TOM: *When we went to meetings Uncle June carried his papers in a red cardboard expansion file. His assistants carried the expensive briefcases.*

*When you have the status, you don't need the symbol.*

The first day home from college, Mother told me, "You are always writing you need money for books and such. Please get better organized. Figure out exactly how much you need for the year and you will be given that amount at the beginning." I added up tuition, books, train tickets, two weekends a semester to New York, and miscellaneous expenses. From that day forward, I was given a flat amount in September to cover my expenses for the entire year. I always stayed on my budget.

My roommate was a girl whose father was a minister in a small town called Stanley, Virginia. When I visited her one weekend I slept in a feather bed. It was a new experience, like going back in time. There were other things I'd never seen before, such as an outdoor water pump. They did have one inside bathroom, but life in Virginia was a different world. The state of Virginia was very poor in the 1930s. I felt continually saddened by the disparity between my financial situation and that of my friends and I confided it to Mother.

Dear Mother,

I never lived anywhere where we were not prosperous. We are fortunate and I know we are fortunate. But sometimes it can be uncomfortable. When I'm out with the girls I'm careful. I would feel sad if I made the other girls feel badly because I can do more than they.

It concerns me because the friends I have in school hear about Texas and read about Texas, they are fascinated with Texas and I would love to bring them home to visit in the summer. But, what will happen when they see our house, the cars and Lewis and Gertrude and Pandora? I wonder if they'll think it strange that I've never said anything, though what would I have said? Or will they be impressed in a way that I'll never know what they really like me for?

*Margaret*

Dear Margaret,

It is good to be sensitive to other people's feelings, but do not go to the other extreme and become a victim of what you have. "Do not let your possessions possess you." You must not isolate yourself by trying to avoid what has not, might not, and should not happen. Bring your friends home without worrying that they may be critical of you or extra nice to you because of the comforts you enjoy and can provide for them. If what we have negatively influences their feelings

> toward you then you have to regard it as unfortunate. Envy is probably the most destructive of all human feelings.
>
> *Mother*

I wanted to bring them to Tyler without causing them to pay for railroad fares, so Lewis drove the car to Mary Baldwin and picked me up with three other girls and we drove home. They stayed two or three weeks and loved Texas. I did not lose any friends.

Mother had had her own experiences with being affluent while having friends who were not as fortunate. Kate Bass's husband had suddenly just taken off, deserting her and their two young children at the height of the Depression. Kate was a fine, genteel lady, a person who should have money. But fate does not deal in shoulds and shouldn'ts. Kate was a very strong Roman Catholic. She never said a word about her husband to Mother, though his absence and her sudden need to work made the situation obvious. There was no way she would accept even the most discreet offer of financial help. So her friends could do little more than hurt for her.

Mother was creative at finding ways to at least divert her friend's mind from her hardship. In the spring of 1934 she told Kate, "We made plans to meet Margaret in New York at the beginning of summer vacation, and now suddenly June has to stay in Texas on business and I just cannot imagine being in that big city by ourselves for three days before he can join us. Would you mind keeping us company?"

Kate was pleased to help and admitted that she would greatly enjoy the diversion of the trip.

Daddy never took any of the sumptuous Presidential or "Rich Texan" type suites that were available in the Waldorf Towers. He felt comfortable enough in the main hotel with a normal bedroom and living room. Kate and Mother and I had a wonderful time window-shopping.

Daddy arrived, as arranged, three days later. He took us to dinner at the hotel's Starlight Roof. The ceiling was open and we could look up and see the stars. Daddy was a wonderful dancer so we took turns foxtrotting and waltzing with him. The orchestra leader was Xavier Cugat, who would come to your table and draw caricatures of you if you wanted him to. Kate and Mother didn't want caricatures, so he did one of me and one of Daddy.

On Saturday we went to the races at Belmont Park. Daddy and Mother were both good handicappers, and they often won. Daddy always sat in the grandstand because the bookmakers were never in the clubhouse area.

Daddy announced, "Ladies, I'll tell you what we are going to do to make this an interesting afternoon. I am going to bet five hundred dollars for each of you on Four Leaf Clover in this race. My conditions are that if Four Leaf Clover wins we are going to bet our winnings on Daily Bread, in the next race."

Kate became so nervous her smile of pleasure froze on her face. Fortunately, there wasn't much of a delay before the horses were off and running.

Four Leaf Clover won the first race.

After we'd all congratulated ourselves, Kate ventured, "How much did we win?"

Daddy said, "He was six to one. We each won three thousand dollars."

It was more money than Kate had ever had in her life. "June," she said, tentatively, "I'm real happy with three thousand dollars. Do you think we should take a chance ..."

"Now, Kate. We made a bargain."

She nodded and clasped her hands together. She tried to smile. "Is Daily Bread a ... favorite?"

"Oh, no. He is only four to one."

Then the horses were off and running. Kate could not bring herself to look at the track, only at us and our reactions to what was happening.

I was thinking, *Give us this day our Daily Bread*—but I wouldn't have dared say it.

In a few minutes pandemonium erupted and we were all congratulating ourselves, especially Kate. Daily Bread won and paid us each $12,000. Daddy distributed the winnings and turned Kate's share over to her in 120 hundred-dollar bills.

When we got back to the hotel she was exhausted from the excitement and from clutching her handbag containing all that money. She could have put it in a safe-deposit drawer at the hotel for the night but she still had to get it home. This was Saturday, and the banks would be closed Sunday, when we were leaving.

Mother understood. "June, take Kate's cash and give her a check in her name."

When the three of us were upstairs changing for dinner, Mother turned to Daddy. "I am simply delighted that Kate made all that money. It will carry her for a year—and longer if you invest it for her in a surefire producer. This cash fund could solve her problems permanently. But June, how could you not have let her keep the three thousand from the first race? What would you have done if after all the excitement of having some money she had lost it? You could not have given her money. You know she would never accept it."

"It was an all-time low in bad judgment, Mom. I didn't think to control my gambler's instinct. And then I couldn't think of a way out without embarrassing her."

In 1934 I was chosen to be Queen of the Third Tyler Rose Festival, an honor as well as a civic responsibility to promote Tyler's largest industry. The president of the Rose Festival Association selects the Queen from one of the most "prominent" local families—it is a great honor as well as a great responsibility.

Mother and I met in New York and ordered my out-of-the-movies gown from a Broadway theater costume maker. The theme of the festival that year dictated that the gown be gold because I represented the "rising sun."

It took special permission for me to be absent from school for the Third Rose Festival. Air travel was in its infancy, and being curious about it, I took a train to Atlanta and then booked myself on a Delta airplane from Atlanta to Dallas. Mother and Daddy naturally assumed that I was coming home on the train as usual. As I was leaving the Atlanta airport, I sent a telegram asking Lewis to meet me at Pounds Field, the airport in Tyler.

It was quite an experience, me and the pilot and the mail. The plane landed at practically every city between Atlanta and Tyler. It was thrillingly modern and fast compared to the train, lacking only the great dining car meals. Little did I realize that sixty years later I would see that plane in a Delta museum.

Coming into the airport in Tyler, I saw Daddy standing at the gate. Not a word was said on the way home.

At home Mother got me alone. "That was a thoughtless thing to do. From the moment the telegram arrived your father never sat down."

The Rose Festival was the major occurrence in Tyler—and still is. Business stopped from Thursday until after the weekend to allow for all the festivities. There were Duchesses and Princesses from other cities throughout Texas. There was a Queen's Tea, the Coronation of the Queen for each of two nights, and, finally, a lavish parade of thirty floats on Saturday morning with a Duchess on each one.

Mother was especially excited about a new rose that one of the growers had developed and named the Queen Margaret Hunt Rose. It was a dark red velvet, extremely beautiful. It would take three or four years to see if it had the strength to be grown in quantities and become popular or if it would disappear. About one out of a thousand new roses survives and the "Margaret Hunt" ultimately turned out to be too fragile. Being too young I did not share Mother's excitement, but I realize today how flattering it would have been to have a Margaret Hunt rose being grown all around the world.

My parents gave the Queen's Tea in our rose garden. Mother had arranged for Boedecker's in Dallas to make a rose-shaped mold and freeze ice cream in it. There were no freezer trucks in those days, so these beautiful vanilla ice cream roses arrived packed in dry ice. Due to our lack of experience with commercial ice cream no one thought about the thawing of the frozen roses. On the contrary we worried that they'd melt before being served. Therefore, the ice cream roses ended up being served hard as a rock. The guests were equally inexperienced so when they stuck their forks into the roses naturally the ice cream roses careened off the glass plates and ended up in the flower beds. The next morning it looked like a snowstorm because the hundreds of white roses had melted all over the yard.

One of my main concerns was my weight and how I would look on the float in the parade riding through the center of Tyler. Until then the parties had all been with friends and acquaintances. But now the public was going to be lining the street, and somebody could very well say something unkind about the fat Rose Queen. After nearly two years at school even my lavish "royal gown" could not disguise the results of all the hot bread, fried apples, and honey.

With five-year-old Herbert beside me in white tie and tails, I passed through the crowds on the Queen's float. Among the spectators was an old man with an ear trumpet. I saw his wife gesture and say what appeared to be "Oh, look, here comes the Queen."

Being nearly deaf, he spoke louder than necessary and could be heard clearly. "Look at *her!*" he bellowed. "Well, thank goodness. The Queen last year was so skinny she looked like she wouldn't make it. But this one's really nice and plump."

Forty-seven years later, driving down to Tyler for the fiftieth anniversary of the festival, my husband, Al Hill, joked, "I hope they don't introduce you as 'the oldest living Rose Queen.'" It was funny because I was and obviously still am.

Before I went back to school, Mother and I drove to Dallas to go to Neiman Marcus, stopping at the Wills Point boarding house, naturally. In Dallas, we parked the car at Nob Walters' garage behind the Baker Hotel, got out, and started around the corner to Neiman's. Women were selling newspapers on the street in those days, and an old lady was screaming, "Extra! Extra! Read all about it! Joiner sues Hunt for ten million! Joiner sues Hunt for ten million!"

We bought the paper and lost our appetite for shopping.

Mother didn't say much in the car home, but obviously she was furious. You could do a lot of wrongs but you could not abuse her family.

> BUNKER'S CAROLINE: *With Mrs. Hunt it was God first, family second, and everybody else afterwards.*

Mother asked Daddy, "How much has Joiner received thus far?"

"A million four hundred thousand."

"That is two hundred thousand more than he was due."

"Well, Mom, I saw no reason not to go ahead and keep paying him royalty, we have done so well while his luck soured ..."

"Then his complaint is made out of whole cloth. You could easily win the lawsuit."

"I would say so, but you do not win any lawsuit 'easily.' There are lawyers' fees, time, aggravation, notoriety, public opinion. Joiner is an old man ..."

"A *greedy* old man. It would have been one thing if he had come to you and said he wanted to talk. But to bring suit makes it look like you did him wrong."

"People make mistakes sometimes, Mom. I'll have a talk with him ... We'll work it out."

Aware of Daddy's loyalty streak, Mother asked, "If pushed to the wall, do you believe you could win the lawsuit?"

"Yes. But all things considered, winning a lawsuit is almost as expensive as losing one. Life will be happier for all if I win the negotiation."

Daddy had a talk with Mr. Joiner, and the lawsuit was withdrawn and never brought up again. I don't know what it cost, but Daddy believed in never going to court.

November 18, 1934

Dear Margaret,

This is nothing to be alarmed about but Herbert has had pneumonia. He is fine and recovering now. Of course we kept him here at home and the doctor had him in an oxygen tent. Mrs. Wilcox has volunteered to tutor him and help him catch up at school. Herbert, for his part, could help Mrs. Wilcox in business matters. We have to bribe him to take his medicines. It has gotten to where he is charging five dollars to take castor oil.

*Daddy*

Just before we were supposed to leave Mary Baldwin for Christmas vacation of 1934, the school's business manager called me to his office. "Margaret, I've had a visit from the FBI because there has been a threat against your safety. The train going home will have additional security..."

It seems that a man who had been in the lobby of the Blackstone Hotel in Tyler had remarked that he would do "almost anything to make a little money for Christmas." He was approached by someone who told him that they were going to kidnap me off the train when it laid over for an hour in Texarkana coming from St. Louis to Dallas and they could use another hand.

The first man's remark apparently was motivated by despair and bravado. Frightened, he went to Daddy's lawyer, Judge McEntire, to warn him. The judge and my father questioned him for two days trying to figure out whether he'd made the story up or not, perhaps hoping for a reward. Finally, convinced he was telling the truth, they had called the FBI.

I was distressed to learn that the FBI had moved me to a drawing room. We Texas girls had an entire car. Washington and Lee students were also on the way home, and the train was full of boys. The real disaster was that when we were underway there was an FBI agent at each end of our car and no one was allowed to leave or enter. We were locked in, and the boys were locked out.

The federal agents were changed at stops along the way. As we were pulling into St. Louis, the conductor and a woman and man came into the car asking, "Margaret Hunt? Margaret Hunt?" I put my hand up and they came toward me. My friend, Annie Terrell from San Antonio, whose father was a famous judge, stood, shielding me from them and said, "Show me your credentials."

The other girls in that car would be switched through to Dallas stopping in Texarkana, but the FBI decided to take me off and transfer me to the Katy—as we called the M-K-T line, which traveled through Oklahoma—so I would not be on that car if an attempt were made to kidnap me.

Walking through the enormous Union Station in St. Louis, with FBI agents on either side of me, I heard a whoop and up rushed Hassie. He was wearing a great big floor-length raccoon coat, and was on his way home from Clark School in Hanover, New Hampshire, having graduated from Culver by then. He rushed over and threw his arms around me, and the agents stuck guns in his ribs. I screamed, "It's my brother! It's my brother!"

We were escorted to a drawing room on the Katy. Even with an FBI man outside in the passageway, Hassie barricaded the door with our luggage until we arrived in Dallas the next morning. As with the other threats, happily, nothing happened.

Though we never spoke about kidnapping or threats, it had its effect on us. One night that week we couldn't find Caroline, who was only eleven. She wasn't in her bed. We searched the house. I'm sure that Hassie and my mother and father were fearing, as I was, that she had been kidnapped. We looked in every room, in every closet. Mother was losing her normal calm; I saw tears in her eyes. "June," she said, "call the Rangers."

It occurred to me that we had not thought of looking on the third floor, which we never used except for storage. I ran upstairs, and there was Caroline asleep on a chaise longue. She had been walking in her sleep.

But in general, life in Tyler continued tranquilly, even serenely, with the exception of occasional minor emergencies.

> HERBERT: *Our governess, Toogie, was very, very strict. She insisted that we learn how to speak French. Lamar and I spoke French before we spoke English. We had a dog called Willie. Dad came home one day and called Willie, and Willie wouldn't come to him. So I called Willie in French and the dog came running over to me, and Dad said, "That does it. That is the end of Toogie. I can't even talk to my own kids. Or their dog."*

While we were still home on vacation, Daddy said to Hassie and me, "We need to think of a name for a company you are going to form. Panola Pipeline and Parade Oil have been rewarding. What other six-letter words beginning with P would you suggest?"

Hassie grinned, "Paltry? Putrid?"

"This is a business conversation," Mother said. "No levity."

Hassie shaped up. "Placid?"

Daddy rolled it around on his tongue, "Placid … Placid Oil … good. More?"

I had just been reading Booth Tarkington. "What about Penrod?"

"Perfect. You might want to name your new company Penrod Drilling. Sounds excellent."

"Our new company?"

"Hunt Oil has been paying outsiders to drill more than twelve hundred wells, and we have a great many more to go. You and Hassie can have Hunt Oil's drilling business provided you work well and do not overcharge."

He said to me. "You are nearly twenty-one and legally of age. Hassie is still underage, but Mom and I have signed the appropriate papers and removed his legal disability, so he qualifies as an adult."

Knowing that my father always had everything thought out and planned before he spoke, I asked, "What do you want us to do?"

"You and Hassie have an appointment in Dallas at two P.M. tomorrow with Mr. Nathan Adams. If you impress him with your knowledge of the oil business, with the fact that you are serious young people, and if you mention that as prospects you have contracts with the Hunt Oil Company, then he might wish to loan you the funds to start a drilling company.

"What contracts do we have?"

"You have *unwritten,* verbal contracts. Be sure to state that clearly. Do not imply anything that is not a fact. Good bankers invest in people. When you begin a banking relationship you are an unknown, but as my daughter and son the indication is positive because I have had a good relationship with the bank. However, the slightest deceit, any negative surprise about you or your integrity can permanently injure your business relationship."

The next day, Hassie and I got into his car, with him at the wheel and me seated beside him. He started off as usual like he wanted to win a race. As we got to a stop sign, he hardly slowed and ran right through it. He did the same thing at the next one.

"Hassie!" I said. "That's two stop signs you ran. Didn't you see them?"

"Sure I did, but it's less expensive to pay the traffic ticket, *if* and when I get one, than to replace the brakes and tires. Plus you use less gasoline."

I muttered, "Daddy may have made you legally an adult but you're acting like a kid."

As he went through a third stop sign I looked around us in all directions. Fortunately, there was little or no traffic, so it was not very dangerous. I still didn't like it.

At the First National Bank on Main Street in Dallas we presented ourselves to Mr. Adams's receptionist. As we waited to be called, Hassie said, "Let me do the talking."

"I'm older. And obviously more mature."

"But I know more about the oil business."

"I'll be the spokesman." We were nervous. We were both too inexperienced to understand that Daddy had guaranteed the loan merely by calling Nathan Adams and making the appointment.

When Mr. Adams had seated us in front of his desk, a beautifully polished dark wood surface that didn't have a paper on it, he asked, "Tell me, what gives me the pleasure of your visit?"

"My brother Hassie and I plan to go into the drilling business"—Mr. Adams nodded, reassuringly interested—"and to buy materials and equipment we need operating capital."

"Of course. Have you had any experience in the oil business?"

"Well, Hassie's had eight years' experience in the fields. He has helped my father select drilling sites."

"Excellent. And you, Miss Hunt, have you had similar oil experience?"

"No, Mr. Adams, I have not. I used to spend time in the oil fields with Daddy when I was a child. But oil has been the major subject of conversation in our home since I was a child."

"Since you were a child? Really?"

"Yes, sir. Also, I'll be watching the books with the help of Daddy's accounting department."

"How much capital do you think will be required for this venture?"

Hassie said, "Twenty-five thousand will be a start."

"And what collateral do you wish to put up?"

"None," I said. "But we have verbal drilling contracts with the Hunt Oil Company. We'll start drilling for Hunt Oil, but we hope soon to be drilling for others."

Hassie and I signed the papers and Penrod Drilling was launched.

February 12, 1935

Dear Margaret,

As you know, your father has put me in charge of his mathematical handicapping system. For a year I have been his sole handicapper, working hours on end to dope out the horses he would bet on. His system has been quite successful, but I have become exhausted by the endless lists of numbers. I told him that I could not go on doing this anymore and that he would have to hire somebody. I resigned. So when you return for vacation, do not be surprised to find the downstairs guest bedroom converted into an office for Messrs. C.G. Johnson and John Lee, who work full time on Daddy's horse-racing venture which we should probably name Hunt Horses, which does not begin with P and therefore will probably not be very lucky. However, he enjoys it and is fairly successful.

*Mother*

During dinner in early June 1935, Daddy announced that he and Mr. J.K. Wadley had bought the Jumbo Gold Mine in Winnemucca, Nevada, and that we'd be going out to have a look at it. "I like gold mining because precious metal is inflation- and deflation-proof. But one of the difficulties of gold mining is keeping the miners from walking away at the end of a shift with nuggets concealed in their mouths and elsewhere. We have hired some local experts, but their hazy reports give credence to the saying, 'An expert is somebody a long way from home talking about something you know nothing about.'"

In those days there were no airport-style metal detectors to walk the miners through. Other than a complete body search, which was tantamount to calling all your employees thieves, there was no way to police that sort of thing.

Aunt Tot, Uncle Sherman, and cousins Stuart and Sherman, Jr. were having dinner with us. Daddy turned to cousin Sherman. "How about you going on out to Winnemucca and applying for a job at the mine as a mucker with a shovel and pick. Without letting anyone know who you are, snoop around and see what you can find out. I believe we need a family source of information. We will be out there a few weeks after you start to work."

Daddy always felt more comfortable with family. We all shared his sense of loyalty. He felt free to speak openly.

Daddy, Mr. Wadley, Hassie, and I traveled by train to Winnemucca. After a day there, Hassie took me aside. "This is no good. We're oilmen. I'm a wildcatter and you're a driller. We have nothing to do here. Let's go to Reno where they have casinos and great restaurants. I'll teach you to gamble."

We had a great time; we were probably the only people that ever visited Reno for six weeks without being there to get a divorce. At first we all stayed at the old Golden Hotel in downtown Reno, then we moved to the new Hotel Riverside. Hassie would stand behind me at the blackjack tables, coaching me while I played. Like Daddy, he was brilliant with cards and numbers.

As always, Daddy located the best places to dine. Cal-Neva Lodge, on the state line, was the "in" place to be. Avocadoes were gaining popularity at that time, and the lodge served avocado cocktails with Russian dressing as appetizers. Helen Morgan would sit on her little white piano singing "Why Was I Born?" and "My Man."

Hassie and I shared a drawing room on the train coming home from Reno. When we were settled and the train had started to move, he sat down next to me, an expression on his face that clearly said that our vacation had come to an end.

"Margaret, Dad has another family besides us."

Fearful that I had misunderstood what he had said, I asked, "What do you mean?"

"There is a woman, Frania Tye. Dad lives with her. Like he lives with Mother and us. As if she's his wife, which she thinks she is. But he told me she's not. They have four kids. A lot of the times when he's away he's with his other family."

He was always kidding me. "Hassie, there are limits to everything!"

"I'm not joking, Margaret."

I felt ill. Staring at Hassie's face, I saw none of the impishness he so often projected. "Dad took me to see them. It's true."

As Hassie spoke, I visualized Daddy at the head of our table three times a day, telling us everything he did—standing at the piano with his arm around Mother, holding her close, singing "Sometimes I'm happy, sometimes I'm blue, my disposition depends on you"—taking us to the oil fields, to the theater in New York—teaching us ...

*Maybe this doesn't really exist. I won't ask Hassie anything else.*

"One kid could be an accident, Margaret. But not four. That family was planned. I could see that by the way Dad treated them and her."

The train was rocking, and I had to hold on for fear it would knock me over. Daddy. With another woman! With children! It was raining outside, and large drops struck the windows and slid down the glass like a thousand tears.

"Hassie?" I finally managed. "Why did you wait all this month to tell me?"

"What was the hurry?"

I was trying to put it all together. I realized that four children didn't happen overnight. "When did it start?"

"He met her in twenty-five when he went to Florida to check on the land boom."

"Why would he take you to see them?"

"I was with him in Shreveport, where they live now. I guess he wanted to see them, so he brought me along. It was convenient."

"Did he explain anything?"

"You know he wouldn't."

"I should think he'd try to keep it a secret."

"Dad's a very unusual person. I don't think he sees anything the matter with having two families. You know that he's always had the idea that he's got super intelligence, super genes that he figures he should pass on."

Daddy always thought he was above a lot of things. He didn't break laws, but he had a high opinion of his worth and he often made his own rules.

I had believed it was because of business that we sometimes didn't see him; even so, we'd always done so much together, spent so much time together. Why was he always sending for me to come to New York, to Washington, making me believe he enjoyed my company? Did he do that with those four other kids?

The train rushed on. Mother! How could he do this to *her?* I remembered the night before Lamar was born, her suitcase packed, her fear of having a child at forty-three, yet understanding Daddy's wish to pass on his genes.

"What about Mother? Does she know?"

"I'm sure she doesn't."

"How are you sure?"

"The way Dad took me there. Like it was a secret between the two of us."

Presumably he'd told Hassie because he was his favorite and he probably wanted Hassie to understand him in a way he would never expect me to understand or to approve.

When Pap died that had been awful. Baby Lyda's death had been difficult too, but I'd been a kid and she had been only a month old. This was the most horrible thing I had ever experienced. I recognized that there was not a thing in the world I could do about it. I couldn't talk to my mother. I couldn't talk to Daddy. I wished I had not known.

I stared out the train window at the houses we were passing—poor people's houses, with naked kids in the yards. A young black woman held a scrawny little kid's hand, staring at the train as we went by in our luxurious drawing room and pointing at us like we were really something.

I wanted to not think about it, to not see Mother's face. Or Daddy's. I wanted to dismiss it from my mind. And to be sure that Mother didn't find out.

Daddy called me at Mary Baldwin. "Why not spend the weekend with me in New York? We can have dinner at the Chambord and now that you speak French you can read the menu for me."

He spoke in the same warm, cheerful voice, as much as saying, "I love you, I enjoy you, I want to see you." It would be the first time we had been together since the Jumbo Gold Mine trip.

After the train ride with Hassie, I'd thought of almost nothing else, trying to figure out what to do about this other family. But I'd come up with no answer. I felt that the kids were threatened. Not I, nor Hassie. We were grownups, and Penrod Drilling was making money. But the kids had nothing. Caroline was twelve, Bunker nine, Herbert six, and Lamar three.

I could rarely get my mind off this woman, curious as to what it meant, what she was like. She was nothing to me. And we were nothing to her. I knew I needed to do something but I couldn't imagine what. Normally, when I had a problem or a question I spoke to Mother. For this I had no one to ask advice.

When I arrived at the Waldorf on Friday evening, Daddy was in the living room listening to Paul Harvey on the news. He turned off the radio. "I have a table reserved for us upstairs." He handed me a list of Broadway shows. "We have tickets to see Beatrice Lilly tonight but you can decide what appeals to you for tomorrow." I looked, unseeing, at the list and wondered how he could be thinking of anything so frivolous as Broadway shows.

As we walked into the Starlight Roof, I heard Xavier Cugat's music. I pretended to feel happy but couldn't possibly.

It was fall and too cold for the roof to be open, but Daddy had a table on the terrace section and we had a spectacular view up Park Avenue. He invited me to dance and we waltzed. Xavier Cugat came to our table and drew caricatures of us both. Mine was remarkably insightful: a glum face trying to look gay. Daddy looked happy as he always did.

He was acting as if nothing had happened, as if everything were as it had always been. And I was pained to realize that it probably was.

At this point, I hoped that he had in mind telling me about his second family and explaining that Mother would never find out—or the kids—or explaining that it wasn't important, that he didn't care about these other people anymore. And then at least I could try to fool myself that it didn't matter.

But he said, "Tomorrow night we have tickets to see *George White's Scandals.* Bert Lahr and Eugene and Willie Howard are in it and they say it is a scream. You are booked tomorrow at ten A.M. for a two-hour lesson at Arthur Murray. Meet me for lunch here at twelve-thirty and then I thought that you might enjoy seeing a matinee of *Boy Meets Girl* while I have a business meeting ..."

During dinner he talked about the oil business and about the Depression, which was all but over. The Waldorf's food and service were wonderful and the music was beautiful and the people enjoying it all looked lovely. Daddy observed, "What a shame that most of the people here are elderly. It is sad that so few people get to experience the nice things while they are young enough to really enjoy them."

On Saturday we had a pre-theater dinner at the Chambord. We'd had appetizers and main courses, and while we were waiting for the crêpes suzette he'd ordered, I summoned up my courage and blurted out, "Daddy, I think you need to set up trust funds for the kids."

He looked at me and listened intently as I spoke. "Hassie and I have a business but the kids don't have anything. Suppose something should happen to you ..."

When I had finished, he nodded his head. "A prudent idea. I will speak to Judge McEntire and he can arrange it."

Of course, I did not say that I knew about the other family. I would never have thought of mentioning it. I had a feeling that he knew I knew. He had to. Why else would I have been asking him to agree to create a protection like that?

By the time I got home for Christmas vacation, the trusts had not been created. I went to see Judge McEntire at his office and told him about my conversation with Daddy. Fortunately, he had been advised but just hadn't gotten around to it.

"Judge, I'll sure appreciate your attention to this right away." I smiled. "As Daddy would say, 'Why don't you cause this to happen ... *at this time?*'"

So in the last days of December 1935, our mother and father set up trusts for the benefit of the six of us and our blood descendants. They intended for the trusts to be protected from creditors and to protect the trustees from suits by us or anyone else.

# *Nine*

MOTHER HAD MADE plans for the three of us to go to Europe in the summer of 1936. Without being actively aware of it I sensed that Daddy would not make the trip.

May 16, 1936

Dear Margaret,

Daddy cannot come to Europe with us. He has well drillings, etc. all summer. Business comes first.

Daddy suggested that we invite Aunt Rose in his place. The only problem with Rose is I am not sure she can keep up with us. There is a great deal of walking and sightseeing ...

*Mother*

From New York, we crossed the Atlantic on the *Leviathan,* a wonderful American ship, landing in Southampton. From there, we took the boat train across the channel and went to Paris. We traveled by rail through Italy, Switzerland, and into Germany. Mother carried a suitcase full of Hershey bars, so whenever Aunt Rose showed signs of weakening Mother would just give her a Hershey bar. Aunt Rose was not a diabetic, though she probably became one by the time we returned home. Surely Mother missed Daddy but she kept herself "up" and gave no indication of it.

We were traveling as part of a college tour group, and when we arrived at our hotel in Nuremberg the receptionist said rather coolly, "You don't have rooms here."

There were thirty-two of us. The conductor asked, "How can we not have rooms? We have reservations." She showed the written confirmations and receipts for money that had been advanced for the whole group.

The receptionist called the manager; seeing our papers, he said, "There has been something unforeseen and unavoidable. I'm sorry. The best we can do is to put you in a Sample Room."

A sample? Of what? It was a ballroom. Big enough for a party of a hundred. They'd put cots in it and made it into a dormitory. The room resembled a barracks with our suitcases at the foot of each bed. There were no dressers or closets. We had two washrooms that normally were the Ladies' and Men's rooms at banquets, and one bath on the floor above—for thirty-two women sleeping in one room.

One of the girls spoke German, and she went out and snooped around. She told us, "The reason we don't have the rooms we reserved is that Adolf Hitler is coming here with his whole entourage. There's a youth sports festival going on and he's arriving late this afternoon. He needed rooms and as we can see, he got ours."

In 1936 we Americans were not impressed by Adolf Hitler. We saw his picture posted all over the place and we heard that he was controversial in Germany and making a lot of changes, but we had no idea what they were and they had not yet had any effect on our world or selves.

I said, "Let's just sit in the lobby, and maybe if we prove obstinate enough they'll come up with private rooms, at least for some of the older ladies like my mother and Aunt Rose."

There weren't enough chairs and sofas, so a few of us sat on the stairs. Every now and then the manager came over to us. "Lovely ladies ... gentleladies, wouldn't you like to go out and see Nuremberg at twilight?"

We said, "Oh, no. Can't move. Tired."

At about 7:30 there was a great deal of excitement in the lobby. Bellboys and managers and concierges began to hurry around; then a fleet of white cars came swooshing into the courtyard. I heard men's voices giving orders and loud footsteps coming through the doors. Up the stairs where we sat came several tall men in white leather uniforms surrounding the small man in black. People in the courtyard were yelling "Heil, Hitler!" and as these men passed us they stabbed their arms into the air and shouted "Heil, Hitler!"

The entourage passed us, and the next thing I knew, we were all standing up and calling out "Heil, Hitler!" It was a perfect example of mob psychology.

That night Mother was deeply concerned. "Somebody is liable to blow up this hotel to get rid of Hitler."

We returned to Tyler in August. Sarah McClendon, the Washington correspondent who today is known as "The Queen of Questions" was at that time working for the *Tyler Courier-Times.* Since anybody from Tyler who had just been to Europe was news, she came to the house and interviewed Mother.

The next day the front page of the paper carried the interview with the headline, MRS. H.L. HUNT PREDICTS WAR! The article stated that we had been in Nuremberg and Hitler had come there and that Mother had seen changes in the country that made it apparent that Hitler was preparing for war. The article quoted Mother as saying that there was a serious situation taking place in Germany of which the American people were unaware.

When I was at home on vacations I occasionally dated a boy named Earle (Bill) Mayfield from Tyler. He wrote letters to me at school and sent them special delivery, which always caused them to be posted on the bulletin board. It was considered a big deal to receive special delivieries in those days.

In November 1936, while I was a senior at Mary Baldwin, Bill invited me to Dallas for the New Year's Eve celebration in the Mural Room at the Baker Hotel with his mother and father and then to attend the first Cotton Bowl game on New Year's Day. I knew that Mother and Daddy had bought tickets for us to go to the first Cotton Bowl game, but the gala at the Baker and seeing the game with Bill appealed to me. I enjoyed being with him though we had a purely platonic relationship. I overlooked the fact that it might irritate Daddy for me to be with the Mayfields because Bill's father, a former U.S. Senator, was big in the Democratic Party. Daddy, rigidly Republican, referred to Bill as "your Democrat friend."

On New Year's Eve, the Mayfields and I attended the dinner and saw the New Year in at the Mural Room. The next day, after a pre-game party at the home of one of his school friends, Bill and I sat with the Mayfields during the game. This did annoy Daddy because our whole family was in attendance as a unit. We always went to football games together. Lamar was only four, but he came to the first Cotton Bowl and never missed one for fifty years.

I was arriving for English Literature class one morning in March 1937 when the assistant dean asked me to come to the office and call home. "The radio said something about a terrible explosion in east Texas near Tyler, and your family's name was mentioned, though my impression is that they are not among the injured."

When I called home Pandora answered the phone. "Your mother and daddy are probably worn out, but they're fine. So are the children. They're here with me. Everyone else has gone to the school in New London or the new hospital in Tyler. Gas exploded in the schoolhouse and killed and hurt a lot of children—teachers, too ..."

Mother called a few hours later. "We are all fine, but a terrible, terrible thing happened at the school in New London, a gas explosion destroyed the school and hundreds of children. Aunt Tot is at Mother Frances Hospital helping the ones who can be helped and I have to get back there ..."

By that evening the radio and the local papers in Virginia had the story of the disaster. In those days gas pipelines ran through the oil field, and if one went past a home and the residents wanted gas they would just tap into it. The New London School had tapped into our gas line. We didn't go to the school board saying, "You're using our gas, we're going to put a meter on and send you a bill." You just didn't do those kind of things. It didn't amount to that much. Since natural gas was viewed merely as a by-product, oil producers were usually pleased to have somebody using their gas. Everybody was looking for a way to dispose of it since there was as yet no market for it. In the 1930s, there was no other option but to flare it.

The school was using the gas to heat the building. There must have been a faulty connection or valve because gas had managed to accumulate in the basement. When it ignited, the explosion had the force of a ton of dynamite.

The other Texas girls at Mary Baldwin and I were waiting when the mail arrived with my March 19, 1937 *Tyler Courier-Times*. The headline was spread across the entire eight-column front page:

425 BODIES TAKEN FROM NEW LONDON BLAST DEBRIS

Workmen Dig in Debris Hunting
for Bodies as Rain Drenches
Scene of Explosion

> Workmen, an average of 250, in a six hour shift, finished wrecking the main wing of the New London School by this morning. The job of digging into the basement has begun, bringing with it the task of unearthing the bodies ...

The paper contained page after page of pictures and human interest stories, among them coverage by Sarah McClendon. As soon as she had the time, Mother wrote to me.

> Dear Margaret,
>
> ... They are saying that an electrical switch in the shop in the basement of the school caused the spark which set off the explosion. At final count there were two hundred and ninety-seven children and teachers killed. More than a hundred were severely injured. Fortunately, there was a County Meet in mathematics so some of the children were not in school.
>
> There is talk of bringing the school superintendent to court but the fact is no particular person can be blamed. It was just a tragic case of escaping gas going unnoticed. Your father says that we will probably be blamed in some way because it is our gas line that the school was tapping. He says that we are blameless as we did not do the tap, the school did it on their own, without asking, and of course we never took a dime from them for the gas they used in the four years the school has been open. However, Daddy says you should be prepared in case somebody serves you with a subpoena because you are an officer of the pipeline company. He agrees that it is appropriate for the authorities to make a thorough investigation of such a tragedy, but he told me to assure you that it will never go to court and therefore do not be concerned should you be subpoenaed.
>
> There is just so much horror in all of this that I hardly know where to begin. The explosion occurred at ten minutes after three in the afternoon. If it had happened twenty minutes later, after

three-thirty, school would have already let out and the building would have been empty of the majority of children.

The proverbial good which they say comes out of everything bad, is that the Legislature is meeting to quickly pass a law which will force odorization of natural gas. If there had been such a law before this happened the leak in the school basement probably would have been discovered before it reached such tragic proportions.

All the doctors from Tyler, Henderson, Kilgore, Gladewater, all of east Texas have come here to help and still there is not enough medical material or personnel. All oil companies turned their men loose and told them "Just work on digging out those children and teachers." The oil field has been left to take care of itself.

The Red Cross, National Guard, everyone, is here helping. As soon as your father saw what had happened he called the bank president—the bank had closed at three—and asked him to open so he could get a considerable amount of cash. We went from house to house of all the Hunt Oil families who were effected to convey our respects and sympathies and help in any way we could and to give them money to pay for the funerals. Most people did not have the means to pay the morticians …

*Mother*

It triggered my memory of Daddy telling me, "The advantage of having money is you can pay for medical help when somebody is sick and needs it." The field had been in for six years, and it had to have been terribly painful for Daddy visiting the stricken families of men he had known over all those years.

COUSIN STUART: *When the New London School blew up I remember Mother* [Aunt Tot] *took over the ward of Mother Frances Hospital in Tyler. The explosion happened the day before the hospital was to open officially. They made appeals for everyone to bring bedclothes and pillows and blankets. People came over all through the night looking for their children. All the children who were still living were brought there in trucks and there weren't nearly enough doctors so all you could do was hold their hands until medical attention was available.*

Typical of Mother, once she had told me the facts she said no more about it. She was neither a gossip nor a moaner. She helped in every way she could, then clearly disciplined herself not to dwell, at least outwardly, on unpleasant things about which she could do nothing more.

The newspapers however, carried the details for weeks. Small bodies were found in pieces and taken out in sacks. A crane lifting a massive concrete slab weighing more than a ton from on top of one child's legs crushed and killed another child who was unseen beneath the other end of the slab.

Walter Cronkite was one of the young reporters covering the explosion. Fifty years later he spoke at a memorial service held by the New London Ex-Student Reunion and Memorial Association and said it was the worst tragedy he had covered other than World War II.

I graduated from college that June. Daddy, Mother, and Kate Bass came for the ceremony. Even though I made average grades at Mary Baldwin, I was awarded a Bachelor of Arts degree. It had been very difficult for me.

Because New York seemed attractive I began to think that it would be pleasant to go to graduate school there and enjoy the museums, theater, and shops, and that unusual freedom that New York afforded—and Texas did not—in which women could do anything they wanted to do.

Coming home on the train, I told Mother and Daddy, "It would be nice if I spent the next year at Columbia in New York City, maybe get a degree ..."

"You will do no such thing," Daddy hastened to reply. "You will come home and go to work. Too much education can be a dangerous thing. It can keep a person from facing life. You have been gone four years and it is time for you to come home and take your place in business."

"Fine, June," Mother agreed. "But first, this summer we are going to Alaska." As usual, Mother had her own educational program.

In August, Mother, Caroline, Herbert, Lamar, and I traveled on the Canadian Pacific Railroad to Vancouver and Victoria. Hassie was at work in the oil fields, and Bunker was in camp at Culver. From Victoria, we took a boat up the inland waterway to Alaska, landing at Juneau before continuing on to Skagway—the boats then did not go to Anchorage.

Herbert and Lamar were eight and five, respectively, and supposed to take naps after lunch. Mother, Caroline, and I went ashore at one of the stops. The stateroom door locks had removable keys; our kidnap scares had left us wary, so we locked the door behind us. The steward assured us he had a key and would be mindful of the boys napping in the stateroom in the event of any problem.

When we returned a few hours later, we unlocked the door but Herbert and Lamar were not there. Not in their beds, not in the bathroom. And the porthole was open.

Mother looked faint.

I said, "Listen, those little kids might squeeze through that porthole but no kidnapper could. Let me look around."

The moment I stepped into the hall I heard familiar giggling. The two boys were hiding around the corner, enjoying the panic they had created. We had connecting staterooms, and Herbert had used the key from our other entrance door.

I glared at them. "Well, I sure hope you're still laughing when we get home and Mother takes a switch to you."

When I got them back inside with Mother I grilled them.

"OK, you little stinkers, what was so funny about scaring us to death, making us worry that you'd been kidnapped?"

Herbert and Lamar were genuinely horrified. Lamar rushed over to Mother. He always called her "Papoose Mooze," a form of "Moo-moo" or "Mooze," which Herbert and Bunker called her. He threw his arms around her and, half-crying with remorse, said, "I'm sorry to have scared you, Papoose Mooze. We would never scare you about kidnappers."

Herbert vigorously confirmed it. "We just wanted to make you think that we'd fallen overboard."

I sent them to their room and called out, "Boy, I feel sorry for your backsides when you get home."

Closing the door, I sat down with Mother. The color had come back into her face. She waved a hand, indicating there would be no punishment of the kids. "They meant no harm."

I laughed in agreement. "Gol-lee! Have you gotten soft! When Hassie and I were growing up, it was spank and paddle. But you let these kids get away with murder."

She sighed and did not deny it. "Your father and I wore ourselves out trying to make you and Hassie perfect, and we are just plain spanked out."

# *Lyda Bunker Hunt Ancestry*

Thomas Macy 1608-1682, Salisbury Wiltshire, England

Mary Macy 1648-1729
married William Bunker 1647-1712

George Bunker 1671-1743

Caleb Bunker 1699-1777

Caleb Bunker II 1736-1810

Capt. Uriah Bunker 1759-1820

Andrew Bunker 1786-1869

Charles Waldo Bunker 1813-1896

Nelson Waldo Bunker 1846-1922

Lyda Bunker 1889-1955
married Haroldson Lafayette Hunt II 1889-1974

| Margaret | Haroldson | Caroline | Lyda | Nelson | William | Lamar |
|---|---|---|---|---|---|---|
| 1915- | Lafayette Jr. | Rose | Bunker | Bunker | Herbert | 1932- |
| | 1917- | 1923- | 2/20/1925- | 1926- | 1929- | |
| | | | 3/20/25 | | | |

Lyda Bunker Hunt, 1912

H.L. Hunt, c. 1916

Lyda Bunker Hunt, 1914

*Left to right:* Mattie Bunker, Lyda Bunker, and friend in Lake Village, 1914

H.L. Hunt, c. 1920

Sara Bunker and Margaret Hunt, 1916

Lyda Bunker Hunt's father,
Nelson Waldo Bunker, c. 1918

Margaret Hunt, 1920

Left to right: Lyda, Caroline, Margaret, and Hassie, c. 1924

The Pines, El Dorado, 1926

Hassie in Montana, c. 1928

Hassie and cousins Sherman and Stuart Hunt, Miles City, Montana, c. 1930

*Clockwise from top right:* Lyda, Bunker, Caroline, Herbert, and Margaret, c. 1930

The H.L. Hunt Family in Tyler, 1932

The Mayfield house in Tyler after restoration was completed by the Hunt family in the fall of 1932

Margaret and Hassie in Tyler, c. 1935

Lamar and Herbert, 1937

Al Hill and Margaret Hunt, spring 1938

Lyda and H.L. Hunt at Petroleum Club Ball, c. 1940

Al Hill, 1955

Lyda Bunker Hunt, c. 1939

Hassie outside Mount Vernon, 1941

Lyda Bunker Hunt, c. 1948

H.L. Hunt in the early 1960s

This photo of Margaret and Al Hill appeared in *Town and Country* magazine. Chevrolet had just introduced the Corvette when this picture was taken in 1953.

# *Ten*

DURING OUR FIRST DINNER HOME in September 1937, Daddy said, "The most advantageous starting point for you is the switchboard. You will place and receive all telephone calls and become familiar with our business associates. Though I expect you to observe normal office discipline, Mom and I emphatically feel that you need never turn down any social engagement or invitation because you are working."

Mother was watching me take a second portion of banana pudding, my favorite dessert—vanilla wafers under a custard sauce that had a few bananas dropped in it, then a layer of sliced bananas on top of that, more custard sauce on top of that, and then a heavy layer of whipped cream.

When dinner was over Mother took me aside. "Margaret, it would be nice if you were to think about dieting and lose a few pounds. Why not make a goal of being able to wear a size twelve?"

Our office was in the People's National Bank Building in Tyler, an eight-story skyscraper. Daddy introduced me to the switchboard operator. "Mrs. Bartholemew, Margaret will be assisting you. Do teach her everything she needs to know."

It was the old-time switchboard with cords and jacks. I sat in front of a board that had dozens of numbered holes. When one of them lit up, I took the nearest of the two cords in front of it and plugged it in. "Hunt Oil, good morning."

"Mr. Hunt, please?"

"May I tell him who's calling?"

"Yes, ma'am, Harold Lovejoy at Tidewater Oil."

"Thank you, one moment, sir." I plugged the second cord into the hole corresponding to my father's line, pushed a lever that rang his phone, told him Mr. Lovejoy was on the line, and then I left the lever open until I heard them speaking.

Other times a hole would light up and it would be someone from our office: "Margaret, will you get me Jack Pew at Sun Oil?" Telephones did not have dials yet. Only the switchboard connected to the central operator, and I would give her the number. After a short while, the outside lines would light up: "Good morning, Margaret, can I speak with your daddy?"

"Good morning, Mr. Pew. Yes, sir, one moment please." By then I knew Jack Pew's voice because I had him on the line frequently, and I knew who Daddy would speak with as opposed to who needed to be told, "I'll see if he's in."

During a normal day the wires crisscrossed like vines in a jungle and I soon knew everybody in the petroleum industry.

I drove my own car to work because I dropped the kids off at their schools on the way. At 11:45 sharp, Daddy and I left and went home for lunch. Almost always we brought friends who seemed to drop by at mealtime. The kids came home, too. I took them back to school after lunch and sometimes picked them up and drove them home.

Driving home from the office one day, I rounded a corner and had a minor accident. Cars did not have shatterproof glass in those days and the window on the driver's side broke. In order to protect my face, I threw my arm up. It was cut so that it needed stiching, so I went to our doctor.

Bunker was twelve then. He saw the bandage as I got out of the car, before I'd had time to change into a blouse that would cover it up.

"What's wrong with your arm, Mahdy?"

I'd had two previous minor accidents, a couple of crinkled fenders. I took a quarter out of my purse and held it up to him. "I'll give you this if you'll keep your trap shut. OK?"

"Sure." He took the quarter.

"Just don't say anything about it."

LAMAR: *When Margaret is sick or has a problem she is the most top-secret person I have ever known.*

That evening we were sitting at the table and Bunker piped up, "I wonder why Mahdy is wearing a long-sleeved shirt to dinner tonight?"

Daddy showed no curiosity. He looked at me blandly and his only comment was, "If I had as many accidents as you I don't think I'd be driving automobiles."

That was about as aggressive as Daddy's criticism ever got.

As we were moving into the living room, I told Bunker, "Give me back the quarter." I snatched it from his hand. "You little stinker."

I did not stop driving but I sure was more careful. Later, after we moved to Dallas, my sister Caroline had a similar experience.

> CAROLINE: *I was given a car when I was sixteen because it was more convenient than having to have someone drive me to and from school, as we lived quite a distance away. On my way one morning I landed in the lake, off a bridge. The car turned over but I got out a window that was open. One of Roosevelt's Civilian Conservation Corps trucks stopped when they saw me all wet and covered with mud. I told them no one else was with me and asked if they'd please take me home. Which they did.*
>
> *I walked in while Daddy was having breakfast and there I was just dripping with mud. He was reading his newspaper. He looked at me but didn't react. "Daddy do you have a couple of dollars I can give these men?" He gave me two dollars. I never asked for another car and Mother and Daddy never gave me another one.*

Mother and Daddy's pointed and rare comments had more impact on us than nagging about what had to have been infinitely clear and self-evident.

Daddy did not force any of us to work, though he did not want me off in New York by myself. He knew that by exposure we would become interested and involved and actively a part of the "business family" he had many times described us as being. When Caroline was home from Hockaday on vacations she worked in the office coloring oil-field maps.

> HERBERT: *Dad was buying some acreage in Florida, and they didn't make county ownership maps at that time. But they had road maps that showed the sections. He'd come home and say, "Here, you want to color on this?" As a ten- or eleven-year-old kid, instead of playing with coloring books I'd read descriptions of leases and learned what the northeast of the southeast of Section two Township three North Range two West would be in such and such a county. They were oil plays. In those days there was not the technology to reproduce things in color, so if you wanted three sets you'd have to color three sets. And*

*I'd color them instead of crayoning in coloring books. He didn't insist that I do this, he just brought it home and said, "If you'd like to work on this, fine."*

Not long after I began work at Hunt Oil, Daddy called me into his office and stated, "You never go out on dates with young men."

"I see Bill Mayfield every now and then."

"Your Democrat friend. It is obvious to me that we need to move to Dallas. You and I ought to go over there next week and find a house and office space."

"But Mother just finished the house here. After pulling up roots from El Dorado she's happy in Tyler, she has a beautiful rose garden that she loves, she's active in the church, she has Mrs. Wilcox—"

"Mom will be even happier in Dallas, Margaret. If you think about it, Mom has to travel constantly to Dallas or New Orleans to enjoy the concerts, antique shops, Neiman's for clothes. I am sure she will be happier permanently installed in a major city. And from my own point of view, the way our business has spread Tyler is not convenient. Dallas has the bank we do business with, trains, and much wider air service."

Cars and streetcars were everywhere in Dallas in the fall of 1937. It had a population of around 250,000 people compared to Tyler's 28,000, which was an oil-boom jump from its 1930 population of 17,113.

Mr. Williford had Daddy and me comfortably installed at the Baker Hotel. There were only a few sizable structures downtown: the Magnolia Building, which had the flying red horse on it, the Cotton Exchange, the Santa Fe Building, and the Adolphus and the Whitmore, the first air-conditioned hotel in Dallas.

A real estate broker drove us around the residential area. Being a family of eight, with three servants, we needed quite a lot of space. We saw several possibilities but nothing that Daddy felt suited our needs. Then the broker took us to a colonial house set on ten acres on White Rock Lake.

It was a replica of George Washington's Mount Vernon. It had a glassed-in cupola set atop the roof just as in Washington's time. I knew immediately that Daddy was going to love it.

He beamed at me, "This is what I have hoped for. A lake. Rather like Lake Village."

"But, Daddy, it's too far from town!"

The broker protested, "Only ten miles from downtown Dallas, Miss Hunt."

"This is the sticks! It took us half an hour to get here. It is just too far from schools for the kids. Talk about me having dates? A man would have to drive ten miles out here to pick me up, then ten miles back to town for dinner or a movie, then ten miles out again to bring me home, then ten miles back to town ..."

Daddy was enamored with Mount Vernon. "What I like about this house is that it faces the lake. I would like to make our permanent home on a lake or on some substantial body of water. Mom would enjoy that, too."

I understood that he was right, that Mother had grown up in Lake Village, which they both had liked, and she would feel at home. Still, I could not quite accept it. "This house looks fine, and the furnace burns oil, but there's no gas. We'll have to buy an electric stove and Gertrude will have to learn how to cook all over again."

Daddy gazed at me quietly, waiting for me to conclude that Gertrude's changeover to an electric stove should not exactly determine where we lived.

The broker said, "The owner of this house, Thomas Y. Pickett, built it in 1930. As you can see, it is an expensive house, yet it has dirt driveways. Mr. Pickett ran out of money toward the end and he's had more severe financial reversals since then. He's asking sixty-nine thousand in cash. However, I know that he would be susceptible to a firm cash offer."

"Mr. Pickett's figure is acceptable to me."

"You could offer him less. Start at fifty—"

Daddy raised his hand, closing the subject. He would never squeeze a man who'd had bad luck and needed to sell his home. He turned to me.

I made one more effort. "Before we decide anything, let's look in Highland Park. Lakeside Drive has beautiful homes. It faces a lake—not as big as this but it *is* water—and it's not so far away from town."

"It's the most prestigious address in Dallas," the broker agreed. "And there *is* one house I can show you on Lakeside, though there is a bit of a complication …"

As we parked in front of it, he explained, "The owner was in the cotton business, lost all of his money, and he's living here alone without telephone, electricity, or water. Those services have been cut off for nonpayment. But, as Texas law does not allow a man's homestead to be taken from him, and as he has no money to move anywhere else, he is making do. However, he can become volatile if provoked by a creditor, all of whom he sees as enemies who have stripped him of everything."

Walking through the overgrown, neglected brush, Daddy slowed down, musing, "This man has had such terrible troubles that upon seeing us he might assume us to be creditors …" He stopped walking, stood still, and looked at me. "If he has a gun he could conceivably start shooting at us. I am not comfortable. We should get out of here."

In the car the broker said, "I regret that I have no further listing that meets your requirements."

Daddy turned to me. "White Rock Lake?"

I nodded. "White Rock Lake."

We went back and looked through Mount Vernon again. We entered the front door of the classic colonial structure into the traditional hallway running through the house. On the right-hand side was the dining room, beyond that the breakfast room. Just past the dining room was a hall and then the kitchen. On the left-hand side of the main hall there was a large living room, and behind it a small sunny sitting room that Mother could turn into a morning room. Behind the living room was a large library. It had fourteen rooms in all.

Accepting the decision, knowing Daddy was right, I could appreciate the beauty of the house, the setting, and even the location. In spite of the distance from the center of Dallas it was anything but "the sticks."

While we were waiting for the papers to be drawn, we rented office space in the Santa Fe Building.

On December 22, 1937, Daddy entered into a contract of sale with Mr. Pickett to purchase Mount Vernon for $69,000 cash. A letter of agreement was made a part of the contract.

> Confirming our agreement and contract, it is understood that I am to deliver you the sprinkler equipment, mowers, etc., two peacocks and all chickens except those belonging to Juliet Jane, one cow and calf, all of which is a part of the contract price to be paid for my house and 10 acres located at 4408 Lawther Drive, on White Rock Lake, and all draperies upstairs, downstairs, sun parlors, including curtains in full, etc. also all lighting fixtures.

Daddy sighed, "I did not expect the poor man's cow."

Mother was amused, "I have lived in the country, but I never had a cow. Not till we decide to move to the big city."

Though I could never have imagined it at the time, that cow would figure in my future.

Mount Vernon was deeded over to H.L. Hunt on January 1, 1938, the day we moved from Tyler to Dallas.

Before we left Tyler, Daddy was determined to sell our house even at a bargain price, which he did, to C.M. Miller, an independent oilman. We should have given our El Dorado house to the city as a public library, but in the rush to east Texas it was overlooked. Later we learned that the beautiful house Mother had built had been vandalized, and Daddy would not allow a repetition of that sad end to an otherwise happy chapter in our lives.

Mother had not looked forward to the change to Dallas because she had made some good friends in Tyler and could not anticipate making friends like that again. Nor did she. Mother appreciated and valued her friends. Once, Mother had memorialized a good friend at a D.A.R. meeting, saying, "Friends are like flowers—they fill our garden and home with beauty and fragrance. Then they wither and fade but the memory of their beauty and the sweetness of their fragrance live on. Indeed as the flower drops into seed to relive another year, so the souls of our friends but return to God who gave them, to bloom again for Him."

Nevertheless, she got right down to the business of moving. "If you have good furniture and good rugs, you can move them almost anywhere. And if you have the man you love and your children, what does it matter where you are?"

It saddened me. But, at least it meant that she was not broken-hearted, that she still did not know or sense that she was sharing the man she loved.

The first thing Mother did was look for the best schools in Dallas. The kids went to Dallas Country Day School and Caroline merely changed status at Hockaday, becoming a day student.

> LAMAR: *The excitement of a new house ... I was six years old. My first recollection of Dallas is the wonderful laundry chute. Herbert and Bunker, who were older and saw the house before I did, had told me about this incredible laundry chute. You threw sheets or soiled clothes into it from the second floor and they went straight down to the laundry room in the basement. The first time there we rushed into the house to the laundry chute. There were the older brothers showing me this neat thing. We didn't care how many rooms it had or how many square feet or how good the kitchen was, the ten acres, the lake. No. The laundry chute.*

Daddy had a room and bath at one end of the upstairs hall. My room was next to his. Mother's, a larger room, was next.

The boys shared the huge master bedroom and bath with a porch. Caroline had a wonderful small room that probably was built as a nanny's room. We planned to build another wing because when Hassie came home from Culver on vacation he had to double up in the boys' area.

What the Picketts were not short of were safes. We had five of them: a walk-in down in the basement, a smaller one under the staircase, two in bedrooms, and another one in the attic. As we never locked up anything Mother took the enormous one in the basement and used it for jam and jelly and San Marino products, which was a super brand of canned goods you could only buy from a lady who came to your house by appointment.

Lamar took over the safe under the stairs and kept his football and baseball in it. I can't remember who used the safe in the attic. I believe Caroline kept her dolls there.

Once Mother had the house and schools in order, she looked into the matter of landscaping and planted many live oak trees, which were still experimental in Dallas. Then she turned to her favorite, a rose garden. When we had moved to our large house in Tyler and had the space,

Mother enthusiastically embraced the Tyler roses and had developed a splendid garden. But she found that the Dallas soil was heavy and not well suited for roses. She solved that very easily. Mother staked out the rose garden she wanted and had all the soil removed. Then she sent to Tyler for truckloads of east Texas sandy loam to replace it.

We continued with our family breakfasts and dinners, but we no longer enjoyed a family lunch as we had in Tyler, except Sundays. The kids ate at school, and the office downtown was too far away for Daddy and me to go back and forth.

We had breakfast at eight and were in the office at nine. Mother filled her days with her garden and church activities.

The switchboard was at the entrance to Hunt Oil, so I was also the receptionist. When people came looking for jobs, I gave them a form to fill out that asked about their qualifications and experience.

One night at dinner I commented, "There are days when it seems there is not a single human being in Dallas who is employed, they are all in our office looking for jobs. Most depressing thing I've ever seen."

Daddy said, "We will hire an appropriate applicant to be the switchboard operator. You move to executive secretary to the president of Hunt Oil."

Obviously Mother and Daddy were concerned about me seeing the more depressing side of life. Though they wanted us to know all of the world as it was, I think that the incident served as a catalyst to move me on to where I could learn more—or perhaps I was not the greatest switchboard operator.

Since I was not capable of being a real secretary—I could neither type nor take shorthand—I became Daddy's assistant with an exalted title. I had an office right next to his. As executive secretary, my job was to decide what papers got to his desk and to handle people he didn't want to waste his time with. Since Daddy believed it was desirable to have the Hunt name on the company checks, I also, as an officer of the company, signed all the royalty and payroll checks.

On my first day as executive secretary to the president of Hunt Oil Company, I was called to the switchboard to greet a Mr. MacDonald who had an appointment. I led him back to Daddy's office and said, "Daddy, this is Mr. MacDonald," and then I went back to my desk.

When Mr. MacDonald had left, Daddy called me in. "Margaret, I believe it would be more professional if when you introduce strangers to me you address me as 'Mr. Hunt.'"

"Yes, Mr. Hunt," I said, and from that day forward I always called him Mr. Hunt when we were in the office or away on a business matter.

Working so close to "Mr. Hunt," watching him facing and surmounting daily problems, I developed a respect for a major portion of his personality that "Daddy" never revealed to his family. At home he made everything easy and comfortable and was always available to us. At the office I watched him close out all abstractions and people around him and concentrate on problems. His ability was to identify what the problem actually *was* and then find a solution.

Occasionally I accompanied him to the oil fields, making notes for him. We drove to Louisiana to be on site at a well that was about to be tested. Daddy pulled over alongside a green field he had spotted. "We need to find a four-leaf clover before we get there."

I did not feel qualified to tell H.L. Hunt how to discover oil, even if he thought it required the help of four-leaf clovers, so we got out of the car and down on all fours, parting the grassy cover.

Searching the ground, he said, "You especially need signs of good luck when you are going to a well that is being tested."

That did it. "Daddy! If we are going to get superstitious about things then I would think that traveling all the way from Dallas to Louisiana to be present at a well testing would be the kiss of death! Did you ever think of that?"

He stopped spreading the greenery and peered at me, poker-faced, his blue eyes giving away nothing. "Why do you think we are here on our hands and knees?"

When we reached the well site, the test was delayed because one of the roughnecks accidentally dropped a slip in the hole. The "slip" is a piece of hardened steel that fits around the drill pipe to hold it in place, allowing the crew to unscrew or make up joints of pipe when coming out or going in the hole. When the pipe is out you must be careful not to let anything fall into the hole. Dropping a slip in the hole necessitates a time-consuming fishing job.

The driller said, "I guess I should fire him."

"Oh, no. He will never do that again." Daddy never fired anybody for a mistake they made because he believed they would have learned and would never make the same error twice.

My father had an appointment with a Mr. Watson from Toledo Pipe and Tube. From my next-door office I listened to the conversation, to learn, as I had been instructed to do.

"We're so desirous to do business with you, Mr. Hunt, that we're prepared to offer you unlimited quantity of six-inch pipe at a nickel a foot for the rest of this year. As you know, that represents a cash loss to Toledo Pipe and Tube, but we consider it an investment. And we guarantee that for Hunt Oil we will always keep our price twenty percent lower than the market."

"Appetizing and flattering, Mr. Watson, but I purchase everything I need from Continental Supply Company."

"Yes, sir, I've been told that. But Continental gets a quarter a foot for the pipe we're willing to provide at a nickel."

Daddy said, "When I was unable to afford a nickel a foot, or a penny, Continental shipped me all the pipe I wanted, on faith. Continental has all of Hunt Oil's business forever."

"But Mr. Hunt—"

"Please have the wisdom, young man, not to waste your valuable time on the impossible."

Daddy frequently had out-of-town callers. One was a senior partner of one of the large trust companies in New York. The elegantly dressed banker said, "Due to your success in the pioneering stage of a great industry, sir, we see fit to offer you the full range of our commercial banking facilities. The Hunt Oil Company can count on us to remove any financial impediments to whatever expansion you deem appropriate."

"This is flattering conversation. However, a few years ago when *nobody* was interested in the Hunt Oil Company, Mr. Nathan Adams at First National took a chance on us."

"I'm sure Mr. Adams is a fine man, but we're talking about a local banker versus one of the great—"

Daddy was shaking his head.

"Mr. Hunt! We are offering you national facilities. First National Bank of Dallas is a local, limited ..."

When the bedazed gentleman had left, Daddy called me in. I expected to hear something about banking. But banking was history, Daddy was on to looking after his "family."

"Margaret, I want to put out a memo to the employees to take flu vaccine. Also tell them—take this down—I have found that if you rub your chest with Vicks VapoRub, then put on a flannel cloth and pat Absorbine Jr. on that, it will have a tremendous effect on loosening congestion ..."

Daddy's response to the man from New York would be repeated in various forms over the years. In 1961, when the Hunt companies were occupying fifty thousand square feet of office space, Nathan Adams asked Daddy to sign a long-term lease to move all of Hunt Oil's companies into the newly planned First National Bank Building on Elm Street in Dallas.

By then Bunker, Herbert, and Lamar were in their thirties and really operating Hunt Oil. The four of us explained to Daddy that it was not a good business move. We had financial projections showing that a Hunt-owned company should construct our own building, rent office space to all the other Hunt companies, and rent out what remained to the public at a profit on our investment. Going to someone else's building was bad economics.

"Our economics are not hurting," Daddy replied. "Nathan Adams has been our friend and he wants to build the First National Bank Building, but he cannot get his financing unless he has responsible tenants lined up. He needs to rent out six more floors of ten thousand square feet each. That is what Hunt Oil and our other companies are going to do."

Placid Oil was then headquartered in Shreveport so it meant moving personnel, but that was what he did.

One of the first things Daddy did when we moved to Dallas was plant pecan trees and buy six deer, which he loved to feed.

LAMAR: *The deer were fenced into an acre-and-a-half area with a twelve-foot fence, but they could virtually jump over anything if they got scared, for example when there was a thunderstorm. We'd have to go out in the car and try to find them and lure them back.*

*We also at one time had a herd of sheep in lieu of lawnmowers. It did not work.*

*We would use fishing poles to knock the pecans off of the trees. We grafted different varieties to make a better pecan with more meat. Dad always had pecans in his hands, cracking them and eating them.*

*Sunday afternoons we'd drive to Winona to see the pecan grove ... or another of the farms Dad had. We'd go look at the cows and steers in the field and Dad thought it was the most marvelous thing in the world. To me it was the most boring.*

*The whole perspective of life was so different in thosed days. You didn't have all the scores coming in and dozens of channels of television shows and "60 Minutes" to watch ... it was a totally different life. All we had was radio. On Sunday nights there was Jack Benny, Fred Allen, Fibber McGee and Molly, and Edgar Bergen and Charlie McCarthy. We listened to them as a family.*

*I used to chart the top ten every Saturday on the Hit Parade. I still chart everything that interests me, stocks, ball games.*

*We often had outdoor parties in the garden with wonderful barbecued chicken. That's where my weight problems started. The food was always wonderful. Lewis had left us to go into the business of selling burial insurance. His replacement was a wonderful man, Armstead B. Smith. Armstead drove and was the most fabulous cook. He made hot, sweet rolls, which were just enormous and wonderful. We called them "stomach-breakers." Bunker, Herbert, and I would eat until we couldn't manage another bite, and then we'd lie down on the floor gasping.*

Hassie was busy buying leases in Mississippi. He had called me recently at the office.

"Why are you not in New Hampshire at school?"

"I stayed long enough to learn how to ski."

Who could blame him? Hassie was an oilman.

One night after dinner, when he was home for a visit, he and Daddy were engaged in their nightly memory contest. They sat at a coffee table in the living room. Daddy put a deck of cards on the table, let Hassie cut them, then turned them over one by one, memorizing their order in the deck. Then Daddy turned the deck upside down and, starting from the top, called the cards as he turned them over. He called every card correctly.

Daddy pushed the deck to Hassie. The competition between them was tremendous. Hassie was always trying to outdo Daddy and Daddy urged him on, rooting for him to win, hoping he would but not giving away an inch.

Hassie shuffled the deck thoroughly, offered the cards to Daddy who cut them and pushed them back.

Turning them over one by one, Hassie was memorizing their order in the deck. I had been standing nearby to see better, but I sat down. When Hassie had seen the last card, he turned them over and began at the top.

"Five of hearts." He turned it over and it was the five of hearts.

"Two of clubs." It was the two of clubs.

Card by card, he called them correctly. He did not make a mistake and he was at the last one.

"Seven of spades."

I waited for him to turn it over. But he paused, looking at my father.

Daddy nodded, "Of course. The only one left."

Hassie smiled. "Of course," and turned over the card. It was the seven of spades.

At breakfast one morning, Daddy began looking at the newspaper and gasped, "Oh, my goodness! Mr. Hubbard's house down on Lakewood—they were held up and robbed, and Hubbard's mother, who is in her eighties, lives with them and they tied her up, tied all of them up, and they were not found until about twelve hours after the robbery."

He looked shaken. "We have safes here. Do we have anything in them?"

Mother shook her head, "We use them for cupboards."

"Let me see."

We all went with him and Mother to the basement. She pulled open the door to the big walk-in safe, which was not locked, and there were her preserves. Then we went upstairs and looked at Lamar's football and baseball in the safe below the stairs, which opened as easily as a cabinet.

After he and Mother had gone up to the attic and come down, Daddy said, "I want every one of these safes fixed so they can't be locked."

Bunker asked, "Why would you do that?"

"I would hate for anyone to get hurt or killed over cash or jewels we do not have. These safes could accidentally become locked, and we would be unable to open them. Some nut could come out here and think we have something of value in them. He could pull out our fingernails, torturing us to open them. Or shoot us if we say we do not know how. Those things can get you in trouble."

He sent for a safeman and stayed at home until the man arrived and locked every safe open.

Daddy stopped carrying money, and he made a point of people becoming aware of that. If he was outside and wanted to make a phone call, he would borrow a nickel from someone.

He invited Hassie to go to an event at the Cotton Bowl with him. As there was limited public parking, the practice was to park in some local person's driveway and pay them. Daddy said, "Hassie, I have no change."

"I've got it, Dad."

Then they went to pick up the tickets, and again, as Daddy did not carry money, Hassie bought the tickets.

On the way home Hassie asked, "By the way, Dad, who invited who?"

When Daddy and I drove somewhere to look at a well, without any of his superintendents in the car as bodyguards, he drove an old Plymouth so he'd look like someone who had no money. "The best security measure is not to be noticed."

> BUNKER: *My mother said, "You often wonder if it is worth working hard and trying to save up money and get ahead, because when you have something it can become a target and people just like to take it away from you." I have often thought about that when I have had problems through the years.*

Dallasites were nice to me. I was blessed when we moved here. Today everybody thinks that I'm a native. They are always stunned to learn I was born in Lake Village, Arkansas, lived in El Dorado, lived in Tyler, went to school in Virginia, and moved to Dallas in 1938 not knowing one soul.

Daddy called John Jenkins, who was an ear, nose, and throat doctor, and asked if he knew any young people he could introduce me to. Dr. Jenkins acquainted me with a very nice bachelor doctor, Hub Isaacs. Hub and I dated a few times and he became a really good friend, though nothing romantic. Hub was a sailing enthusiast, and he interested me in the sport. I bought a small sailboat to use on the lake.

I told Hub, "I'd like to meet some girls." He introduced me, and they graciously invited me to many of their social activities. The next year there were eighteen debutantes and I knew most of them so I was included in quite a few deb parties. I was fortunate. The city was absolutely marvelous to me.

I had no idea *how* marvelous Dallas was about to be.

# *Eleven*

HASSIE HAD BECOME AN ARDENT SKIER when he was in school in New Hampshire. In February, a month after we moved to Dallas, he said, "Margaret, you and I need to go to this new place, Sun Valley, which is opening in Idaho. I hear the snow is fabulous, and you need to learn to ski."

He and I boarded the train for the two days and two nights it took to reach Sun Valley, Idaho. The lodge was still under construction so we stayed at the inn and had two bedrooms with a bath between.

Hassie proceeded to buy me skis and boots and booked ski lessons. The next day the lessons started. If the slope was a thousand yards long, I guarantee you that all of my limbs, every part of my body, had an intimate familiarity with every inch along the way. I don't know where I had gotten the idea that snow was soft.

The next morning when I awakened I couldn't move. When I tried to raise myself from the bed I felt like I was on fire. I shouted, "Hassie!"

He came rushing into my room. "What's wrong?"

"I'm paralyzed."

"You're just stiff from the falls. Today we'll practice skiing, not bouncing." He jerked me out of bed. "Get up, get your skis, and work out the kinks."

"At the swimming pool."

I never put on a pair of skis again. I am not, and never was, athletic.

It was a gorgeous day. The snow was piled up alongside the pool, but the sun was warming and the only risk of falling was asleep. In those days everyone let themselves tan golden brown, and with my olive skin I got a beautiful deep suntan.

When we returned to Dallas, Hub was my escort for the Petroleum Club Ball, which was a major event. This one had a Hawaiian theme, so they had Don the Beachcomber come from Hawaii and decorated the Baker Hotel meeting rooms like Hawaiian villages.

There I was, in a pale blue tulle evening dress, with my golden tan, when I saw a tall, handsome, athletic-looking man coming in right behind us. When we were in the ballroom, I saw him eyeing me from across the room. He was at least six-foot-two. He had dark brown hair. I hoped somebody would think to introduce us.

Hub invited me to dance. As we were two-stepping around the dance floor, I saw that sensational man speak to Ruth Jenkins, Dr. John Jenkins' wife. Then they both looked toward where I was, and I hoped I read his lips to be saying, "... suntan, blue dress ..."

When the dance ended, Hub took me to our table and excused himself. I glanced back toward where the man had been and saw him walking toward me with Mrs. Jenkins. When our eyes met he smiled. *A gorgeous smile.*

"Margaret," Mrs. Jenkins said, "I would like for you to know Al Hill. Al, this is Margaret Hunt." She stayed with us a moment and then went back to Dr. Jenkins.

Al smiled admiringly. "Where'd you get that great tan?" Finding someone in Dallas with a suntan during the winter in those days was unusual, because there were no such things as weekend flights to Palm Springs or Acapulco.

"Skiing. Sun Valley."

"I've read about that. Just opened, didn't it?"

"Yes. The lodge isn't finished yet."

"Are you an ardent skier?"

"No. Not at all, really."

The orchestra started playing "The Lady In Red."

"Would you care to dance?"

Al took me in his arms. He was such a wonderful dancer that I just floated around after him like I was Ginger Rogers.

"I've never skied," he said. "I play tennis. Do you play?"

"I am planning to take lessons." I hoped my nose wouldn't grow a foot long. I said, "Tennis makes much more sense than skiing. You have to go to where the snow is in order to ski. And that's not so easy when you work."

"Where do you work?"

"At the Hunt Oil Company. In the Santa Fe Building."

"I'm in the Santa Fe Building, too. I've worked for Barrow, Wade and Guthrie for eleven years."

"That's an amazing coincidence."

"It's a *wonderful* coincidence. What would you think about having lunch with me on Monday? I usually go out at noon. Just to the coffee shop across the street."

Daddy lunched at the Petroleum Club every day at noon. On Monday I looked into his office and said, "See you later." He glanced at his watch. "It's only eleven-thirty."

"I have a lunch date at twelve."

"A lunch date?"

"Well, you moved us to Dallas so I could get social."

"I did not mean at eleven-thirty A.M."

"Sorry, Mr. Hunt, but I've got to run. I need to fix myself up."

"Why are you so dressed up? Who are you having lunch with?"

"Al Hill."

"I never heard of him."

"That may change."

I looked at my watch as the elevator door opened onto the lobby. It was 11:58. As I stepped out and looked up, Al was standing there, waiting for me. He was wearing a navy blue suit with a white shirt and a white-and-blue checked tie.

"You're on time," he said.

"So are you," I smiled. I had an instinct that this man was always on time. I had grown up with that—Mother and Daddy, even my brothers and sister were always reliable—and it gave me a warm, comfortable feeling.

There was an empty booth at the sandwich shop. "We're lucky," he grinned. "They don't exactly take reservations here."

As we seated ourselves he said, "I usually have a tuna salad sandwich with a cup of fresh fruit and a glass of milk."

"Sounds great. I'll have the same except for the milk."

He ordered our lunches. He had the loveliest hazel green eyes.

"Al, where would you suggest I go for tennis lessons?"

"That would probably depend on where you live."

The last thing I wanted him to know was where I lived, that he would almost need to take an airplane to pick me up for a date. Nor did I want to distance myself economically by waltzing over to the Dallas Country Club, where Daddy was a member.

"What I was thinking," I said, "is that I should take a series of lessons, but if I wait for the weekends it's going to take too long. I can get an hour or two off from the office now and then, so if there's someplace near here … or maybe where you play …"

"I play in Oak Cliff." He smiled. "It's a men's club. Mostly businessmen. But there's a new tennis club that just opened right on Cedar Springs …"

When we'd finished our sandwiches, Al asked, "Do you like dessert? They make excellent coconut cream pie here."

We both ordered the pie and he asked for another glass of milk. I noticed that he loved coconut cream pie as much as I did.

I can't recall what I talked about, only that I was making every effort to be scintillating, and he seemed to be listening—fascinated, I hoped. He commented, "You have a real nice accent."

"Thank you. Arkansas. Lake Village and El Dorado. Well, the fact is I probably also have eight years of east Texas rolled into the way I speak."

"I'm an amalgam, too." He explained, "I was born in Murfreesboro, Tennessee. My father was a telephone company manager, and we went to Colorado when I was a little boy. He organized phone company offices so we lived in a whole lot of towns—Lamar, Colorado Springs—wherever the company needed to open a new office. When I was in high school and college, every summer I worked, of course. I threw concrete, which means shoveled, for street construction.

"One summer, unbeknownst to my father, I applied to the railroad company for a job. I was real surprised when they asked if I was afraid of heights and did I have strong legs? I told them I didn't have any trouble with heights and I thought my legs were fairly strong. Anyway, I got the job immediately, which amazed me because there was a lot of competition for work with the railroad company. The first day on the job I found out why they hired me. They needed somebody who could hang from a bridge and paint."

We both laughed. And I was thinking that Al was a very, very handsome man.

"When I was going to Colorado College my mother moved there to be close to me. I left school and went to work at the Exchange National Bank in Colorado Springs. I needed to earn money for Mother and myself." Al looked straight at me. "I mean to say that I come from a divorced family." He kept looking at me, pointedly. "I just want you to know that."

"Why?"

"Because I hope to see more of you and I don't want there to be any surprises."

It was pleasing that he wanted to see more of me. I was also thinking that I would be the last one to find fault with another person's parental fidelity. I was just happy that mine had stayed together. "What your parents did is their doing, not yours."

"Anyway, my brother Horace and I took over. Mom lives with me here in Dallas. My sister Alyce, too. Horace works in San Antonio."

"Didn't you like banking?"

"I liked it a lot. I was there for a few years."

"Why did you leave?"

"I came to realize that the president of the bank was only ten years older than I was. I knew that I couldn't wait until he retired to have his job."

I laughed out loud and he joined me. "How did you wind up in Dallas?"

He said, "I have a cousin who was living here and he said it was an up-and-coming city. He worked for an accounting firm and helped me get my job with Barrow, Wade and Guthrie."

Al glanced past me at a line of people waiting to have lunch. "Let's let someone else use this table."

An early spring sun warmed the air as we walked outside toward the traffic light on the corner. A man walking in front of us crumpled an empty cigarette package and flipped it onto the sidewalk. Without interrupting our conversation, Al leaned down, scooped it up, and dropped it into a litter basket. We crossed the street toward our office building. Al guided me by the arm protectively through the heavy Dallas traffic.

"It's only a quarter to one," he said. "Would you like to take a walk? Or do you need to get back?"

"Since I work for my father, I can get away with murder. I don't, but I could." I didn't want him to get any surprises, either. "My father is H.L. Hunt. He's in the oil business." Why had I taken a breath and all but blurted that out?

Al's voice was warm. "I know who H.L. Hunt is. And I knew that you were his daughter. Mrs. Jenkins told me after I asked her to introduce me to you."

On Tuesday when I told the president of Hunt Oil that I was leaving early, he looked at his watch. "Again? You're having lunch with him again?"

"No, Daddy. I'm going to skip lunch. I need to get on my diet and I'm taking tennis lessons at Cedar Springs Tennis Club."

"Tennis lesson? Diet? Cedar Springs? What about the Dallas Country Club?" Daddy was overreacting. It wasn't like him. Yet it was. He had antennae, and they were telling him that something unusual was going on with his daughter.

The telephone rang. I picked it up. "Mr. Hunt's office ... Oh, good morning, Mr. Adams ..." Daddy signaled that he would call him back. I pretended not to notice, "Yes, sir, he's right here." Daddy wanted to continue what he had started to say, but he took the phone—giving me the opportunity to slip away.

The Cedar Springs Tennis Club pro shop sparkled with new racquets and white tennis dresses trimmed in pink and soft yellow. I chose a few nice outfits and tried them on in the ladies' locker room. They were flattering, with little pleated skirts. The tennis professional, Charlotte McQuiston, suggested which racquet I should buy, a Dunlop, and for the next half-hour I showed her that no matter how hard she tried she could not successfully aim the tennis ball to hit my racquet.

She came to the net. "Have you ever played any sports, Miss Hunt?"

"Am I hopeless?"

"No, no, no, no! I've had much worse beginners."

She was lying. I was grateful.

"Tomorrow?" I asked.

She examined my right hand. A world-class blister was building up on the heel of my palm and one on my thumb. "Wait a few days for those to dry. Then wear a glove."

When I got back to the office I went to Daddy's desk, took his Absorbine Jr. and poured it onto my hand. It stung like mad.

Daddy said, "Let me blow on it." He blew very hard. "OK, now you blow hard."

I blew very hard on my hand. "Thanks, Dr. Hunt."

He was neither smiling nor unsmiling, just looking at me with those blue eyes that I had known for so many years and that indicated he wanted to say something to me, something that was not yet within him to articulate.

On Wednesday, when I brought some papers into his office, he looked at his watch. "Eleven-twenty. You are going to be late. You would not want to keep your instructor waiting."

I showed him my hand. "I need to wait a few days. I'm having lunch with Al Hill today."

Daddy sat back in his chair and put his hands in his lap, one thumb rubbing the cuticle of the other.

I said, "See you later." I was halfway through the door when I heard his voice.

"He is too old for you."

I turned around.

"Albert Galatyn Hill is twelve years older than you are."

I couldn't believe my ears. "How would you know that? It doesn't matter. I've always been mature for my age. And how would you know his full name when even I don't?"

"Mr. Williford informed me."

"And how would Mr. Williford ..." Slowly things began to fall in place. "You sent him to check up on Al Hill."

"I suggested that Mr. Williford familiarize himself with the facts concerning a man who is attracting your attention. Those facts are: he is thirty-five years old to your twenty-two. He has never been married ..."

"Well, I'm sure relieved about that!" I glanced at my watch. "I'd better not be late. Poor old Albert Galatyn might just shrivel up and die of old age before I get there to have lunch with him."

We sat at the same table in the sandwich shop. Al was not smiling, nor had he touched his sandwich or the glass of milk he had enjoyed so much the last time we'd lunched. "I'm glad you told me. They said in the office that somebody had been asking about me. I didn't realize that it was your father. Does he do this all the time?"

I wanted to say, "No, but I've never been serious about anyone before." I said, "No, I'm sorry."

He smiled. "That's nice to hear."

"Are you offended by being spied on?"

"No, but I don't consider it very nice. I have a good job with a distinguished firm. If they were to think that someone's inquiring about me because I'm looking for another job then I would not blame them if they decided to make me available to go ahead and *take* another job."

"That's terrible! I'm sorry."

"It's OK. There's been no damage. They know me well enough to have asked me if I'm looking elsewhere, and to believe me when I told them I am not."

"I feel just horrible about this."

"Don't. I can't blame a father for wanting to protect his daughter. There are a lot of shabby people in the world."

I wasn't as forgiving. It didn't say much for Daddy's opinion of my judgment about people. I changed the subject, "Galatyn is a very pretty name."

"Maybe a little fancy. I just call myself Al G. Hill. The original name is Gallatin—double *l* with an *i.* My mother changed it. There's a town called Gallatin, Tennessee. Albert Gallatin was the fourth Secretary of the Treasury of the United States. He served two terms, under

Jefferson and Madison. There's a statue of him on the Pennsylvania Avenue side of the Treasury Building in Washington, D.C. I don't know for sure if my great-great-grandfather was named after Albert Gallatin or even if I descend from that family, because all my family records were destroyed in the Battle of Stones River in the Civil War..."

I interrupted him. "Al, why don't you eat your sandwich and drink some milk?"

"Well, your father might want to know these things." He stopped. "I'm sorry." He made the effort to smile. "I think I've got some cattle rustlers somewhere along the line on the Harding side of my family." He took a bite of his sandwich and quaffed half the glass of milk.

"You enjoy milk," I commented.

"I really do."

I was afraid that if we said goodbye after lunch we might not see each other again, he might just find a doting father too threatening to be worth the trouble. While I was thinking what I could do he said, "I'm going out to Cedar Springs this afternoon. I've got a match at five."

"Oh, that's great. Could I ride out with you? My car's in the shop." This wasn't exactly the truth, but it was the best excuse I could think of.

When we arrived, Al went to the gentlemen's locker room. I did not have an appointment, and the pro was on a court giving a lesson. I hung around the pro shop looking at some cute tennis outfits and saw Al come out of the locker room with another man. They went onto a court and began warming up. He seemed to be making no effort, yet he hit the ball so hard that it sounded like it should have split open. It crossed the net in a straight line to his opponent, and a second later it was on its way back. Whenever I had managed to connect and hit one, it arced in a high semicircle and took five or six hours to land.

When the pro came in, she looked at my hand. "Isn't it too soon?"

It did not matter if my hand fell off. The point was to stay out there and occupied while Al was playing, so I could ride back with him.

This ploy worked successfully six times over two weeks until he observed, "You seem to have car trouble quite a lot." He smiled, understanding perfectly, and not exactly minding it. "Would you like to have dinner and go dancing on Friday?"

"I would love to. Do you know where White Rock Lake is ?..."

Mother said, "Invite him to come for dinner. There is no need for him to spend money feeding you. Then you can go dancing later."

I was torn between wanting to save Al's money and fear of exposing him to Daddy—and the kids. In the end, I figured he might as well see the whole crowd and know what he was getting into sooner rather than later.

We were in the living room waiting for Armstead—who had replaced homesick Gertrude as well as Lewis—to call us for dinner. Daddy was courteous but hardly his ebullient self. I was wishing that Hassie were home. He'd have liked Al and he would have helped me. But Hassie was in Mississippi.

Fortunately, Mother took over. "Mr. Hill—if you don't mind I'm just going to go ahead and call you Al ..." and she proceeded to be charming, warm, and welcoming.

We were called to dinner. Al's six-foot-two frame towered over mother's five feet, but they walked into the dining room like they'd been going to dinner together every night for a year. Mother seated Al at her right. He helped her with her chair, then waited for Caroline and me to sit down.

There was always a glass of milk at everybody's place except mine. Al was effusive. "This is the most delicious milk I have ever tasted."

Mother explained, "When we moved to the city the Jersey cow came with the house."

"Your own fresh milk in Dallas!" Al marveled. "That's fabulous."

Daddy had had enough chitchat. "Mr. Hill, how do you feel about this popular new Social Security program that President Roosevelt has introduced?"

Even the kids knew how much Daddy disliked Social Security. He was testing Al's political leanings, which I already knew were similar to Daddy's and what we had all grown up with. Everybody fell quiet.

Daddy was looking at him benignly.

"Well, sir, there are idealists who think that Social Security is a wonderful thing, that everybody will have this financial security. Having grown up in the Depression, I well know the insecurity of many people's lives. But with all due respect, sir, my opinion is that by guaranteeing people's futures you're taking away their motivation for developing their own abilities, relying on their own energies, saving their money, and shaping their own destinies, which is what made this country great. Besides which, Mr. Roosevelt and his government are not putting that money aside to take care of these people. I believe that time will show that these people's grandchildren will pay to take care of them."

Mother said, "Well, June, I would say that Al has explained it as well as anyone I have ever heard on the subject."

Lamar, who was nearly six years old, said it for all of us. After dinner, when we sat down in the living room, he curled up in Al's lap.

We drove to town in Al's Chevrolet and went dancing at the Mural Room at the Baker Hotel. We danced for hours, and though we didn't say much, we communicated everything that each of us needed and wanted to know.

It was midnight when he brought me back to White Rock. I got into bed going over every minute of the evening. Knowing that Al had gone to work as a kid and carved out a living for himself and his mother with his intelligence and industriousness, and having seen him withstand my father's cynical parental eye, I felt certain that Al Hill stood unafraid in the world, capable of bending life into the shape he wanted it to be, and I was certain that he was a man you could depend upon to do what he said he would do, and to be what he said he was, with no postures, no secrets, no surprises.

I stopped seeing other young men, and Al and I had lunch every day and began dating seriously. The Mural Room was the place we enjoyed the most. It was about the first nice dinner spot there was in Dallas, like a nightclub with a lot of mirrors, and music every night.

Al Hill was a great dancer. The only trouble was that there was a three-dollar cover charge if you didn't have dinner. Six dollars a night, a few nights a week, was a lot of money for a man earning an auditor's salary of, I guessed, around three hundred a month, on which he supported himself and his mother.

When I learned that all the debutantes in Dallas had passes to go to the Mural Room free of charge, I mentioned this to Mr. Williford, who despite being Daddy's spy was a wonderful guy—Mr. Fixit Williford. In twenty-four hours I had a pass to the Mural Room.

As summer was approaching, Daddy decided that the entire house needed to be air-conditioned. I told Mother, "We should also have a swimming pool."

She agreed immediately. "You're in charge of getting it designed and built."

We decided that we also needed a pool house, or guest house, with two bedrooms and dressing rooms.

> HERBERT: *I think ours was the second private swimming pool in Dallas. There was an outfit called Paddock Pools that came from California to build it. Two fellows literally camped on the job until it was finished. It was exciting watching the hole being dug. There were no bulldozers in those days, they used a scoop and a team of mules. The mules would pull a bucket and scoop up the earth.*

The day the concrete was poured, covering the sloping bottom of the pool, the Paddock foreman went off to see a neighbor who was inquiring about building a pool. Bunker, Herbert, and Lamar discovered the freshly poured cement and used it as a sliding pond. When the foreman reported the disaster to Mother she said, "I'm sorry. I'll pay what it costs. Just fix it quickly, please." She never told on the kids to Daddy. My parents never did tell on us.

> LAMAR: *My dad wanted me to learn how to swim. I loved all stick and ball sports but did not care for water. Dad's idea was safety- and confidence-motivated. He would come home from work in time to teach me. I would hide in my bathroom or the attic but he always found me. He got into a pair of bathing trunks and got in the water with me.*

Al and I continued to use my sailboat with Hub as our captain. One Saturday afternoon when Al came out, there was a lovely soft wind and our captain was out of town. I said, "I'll take you for a sail."

As we untied the boat, Al asked, "Do you know how to operate this?"

"Well, not really, but it doesn't seem very complicated. There's no motor or anything. If you'll just pull up the sail like you always do for Hub, I'll steer."

We pushed off and glided away from shore. It was lovely being alone with Al rather than sitting on the porch watching the kids and Daddy play in the yard. Floating in my little sailboat, Al and I chatted and laughed and agreed about things and people. And we rested together in silent harmony.

Texas does not have domesticated weather. There is a saying that if you don't like the weather in Texas, stay around for an hour, it will change. Without warning, a powerful wind came up and spun the boat around. I looked at Al. For the first time since I'd known him, he did not appear entirely in control. I panicked. "This was a bad idea. Let's get back to the dock."

Quickly he lowered the sail and took the rudder from me. "What we want is not to be affected by the wind. Don't move around. Stay seated where you are, and I'll balance you over here."

I sat rigidly still as Al began navigating the forty or fifty yards between us and the shore.

The wind swooped back on us and created such a great downward slope in the water that it tossed me out of the boat. When I surfaced, I tried to catch hold of something. I heard a splash and in a second I saw Al alongside me. "You OK?"

I was treading water. "Fine." The boat was too far away to reach.

Al said, "Swim for the shore. Calmly."

We swam steadily, side by side, until we reached the dock. Al put one hand on my arm while his other clung to one of the steel barrels that kept the dock floating. "Grab hold of something."

Obviously we were safe. I put my arms around his shoulders.

"I meant the dock," he said, though not unhappily.

For a while we made no effort to climb the wooden ladder onto the planking, both happy to be there in the water, holding each other.

Al retrieved and tied down the boat. When he returned he said, "I have two suggestions. One, you give up sailing. Two, you marry me before you kill yourself and maybe me, too."

"That's perfect."

Quickly, I sold the boat.

I've often said it's not important where and when Al proposed to me, because from very early on, our getting married was a foregone conclusion.

At lunch on Monday Al stopped talking and looked at me as if he were about to broach something serious. "You need to be sure you can handle a dramatic change in your lifestyle. My salary is two hundred and seventy-five a month. I'll do better in time, a lot better. But for now that limits us to a small apartment and a fairly simple life."

"My salary is a hundred and seventy-five."

"That sure will help."

I didn't want to be a burden. I welcomed being able to contribute my salary and appreciated that he didn't refuse to allow me to work. In 1938, most men felt it infringed on their manhood if they didn't totally support their wives. I thought that Al's attitude was immensely masculine.

"I'm sure happy that my father having some money doesn't bother you."

"On the contrary. Frankly, loving you as I do I would not marry you if I did not know that in the event of an important medical problem your father would be able to provide the care you might need. I can take care of you up to a certain point"—he grinned—"up to colds, measles, chicken pox, that kind of thing. And babies."

He fell serious again. "I've saved money and invested it, and I have a little more than two thousand dollars if ever it's necessary. My salary can feed and house and clothe us, and take us on a honeymoon and to the Baker, and handle minor emergencies. But the unknown quantity of a major illness is not something I would undertake."

"You mean, if Daddy wasn't here you wouldn't marry me?"

"Would you want me to? Should I promise to take care of you without knowing that I can? Should I put you in jeopardy because I love you? That's not my idea of love."

I appreciated what he was saying. And I found it interesting that his main concern about money was similar to my father's. That it was handy in case of illness.

At lunch on Wednesday he said, "I've been thinking that we could be married in the fall. I have not been taking vacations, so I'll have a full month coming to me as of October fifteenth. I spoke to my mother and she's going to live with Horace in San Antonio."

"Won't your mother miss you? And Dallas?"

"Yes. But she understands that I've got to live my own life, so she's willing to move, and with Horace being single that's the appropriate thing to do."

I knew that Al's mother was very attached to and dependent upon him. If he had said that he could not bring himself to abandon her, that he wanted her to live with us, I probably would not have opposed it. Having met Mrs. Hill and spent time with her, I realized what a sacrifice this was on her part. I was touched by the quality of her love for him that caused her to act so unselfishly.

On Friday afternoon, he came out for dinner and to take me dancing. Bunker, Herbert, and Lamar all liked Al, and they hung around us until, for privacy, we went for a walk around the swimming pool.

Al said, "It would be appropriate for me to speak to your father formally."

Mother and I waited in the living room while Al and Daddy went into the library.

The kids straggled in and Bunker asked, "Al's popping the question, right?"

I glared at him. "He's just giving Daddy the courtesy of asking his permission. It's me he 'popped the question' to."

Mother said, "I've been thinking that part of our wedding present to you and to Al will be your silver, and that we can buy it this summer at Georg Jenson when we're in Denmark." Mother always had a positive approach.

Within minutes Daddy and Al emerged from the library. Neither of them indicated anything, so I quickly said goodnight and we left.

In Al's car I asked, "What did he say?"

"He said, 'We'll see.'"

"'We'll see.' That is what he always says." I was outraged. "Well, I'll tell you what we'll see: we'll see that on October fifteenth you and I will be married."

"What if your father won't give the bride away?"

"That's OK. Mother will be there. And the kids'll be there."

We tried to have a wonderful time at the Mural Room. Though Al didn't say anything further about it, I'm sure he wished he'd heard, "Welcome, son." And I didn't say it, but I wished Daddy had come out and kidded me, saying, "Well, you finally did something right."

We danced and we talked about our wedding party. I wanted my best friend, Coleen Baughn, who had married Jesse Johnson, and Julia Bozeman, my friend and neighbor from El Dorado, as my matron and maid of honor. Al planned to ask Chester Donnally to be his best man. They'd played tennis together and had been friends for a good many years. Chester and his wife, Roxy, lived in California where he worked for Western Geophysical Company.

Between dances, Al gave me a blue velvet-covered box. "This is not an engagement ring," he said. It was a small gold charm in the shape of a tennis racquet with a tiny diamond chip. I was delighted with it.

"Someday I will give you the engagement ring you deserve." I hadn't the slightest doubt of that.

On Sunday, Aunt Tot and Uncle Sherman came over from Tyler for dinner. Everyone was enjoying the dessert of Lady Baltimore cake when Uncle Sherman said, "Al, we'd sure like for you to come down to Tyler next weekend and spend a few days with us."

It was the most outlandish thing I'd ever heard. I'm sure I gasped. Mother stared at Uncle Sherman, astonished. Daddy was expressionless, like it was the most normal thing in the world.

Al said, "That's very kind of you, Mr. Hunt, I'll be delighted." But he was not very convincing.

On our way to town Al said, "I think your Aunt Tot is fabulous and I like your Uncle Sherman, but I really don't want to waste a weekend away from you with your aunt and uncle so they can have a look at me and give their vote."

"Well, I sure don't want to spend next weekend without you, either. Don't go. It's ridiculous."

"I have to go, because if I don't it could appear that I'm afraid I can't withstand their test, whatever it is. But frankly, I'm beginning to feel annoyed."

COUSIN STUART: *Uncle June sent Al down to spend a weekend with us in Tyler to get an OK on him. Margaret was the apple of his eye, and Uncle June wanted to make sure everything was all right.*

*Al was probably the best-looking man you've ever seen. Well dressed, always well groomed. A perfect gentleman at all times.*

*Dad and Mother had to give a report to Uncle June, what they thought of him, what all of us thought of him, and he passed with flying colors.*

But Daddy continued to ignore my impending marriage as if hoping it would go away.

"I would appreciate one concrete objection, please."

"The difference in your ages is too great."

I said, "Al is a young person for his age. And I'm mature for mine. We're ideally suited, perfectly compatible. We are in love with each other. He's a hard worker. He is kind and gentle, a gentle man and a gentleman. He's handsome. Clean cut. Well dressed—"

"He's *too* well dressed."

"I need that explained."

"Why does an auditor wear a new necktie every time I see him? I'm wondering about his values. How come an auditor is so interested in clothes and neckties?"

"Maybe because he plans not to always be an auditor. And if a few neckties is the greatest fault you can find with him, then I guess that really isn't so bad."

Silence.

Appealing to logic, I said, "Daddy, this man supports his mother, and he has not been married before because of his sense of responsibility. He is dependable. He has held a job with a fine firm for eleven years."

"Ten."

"Yes, you would know, wouldn't you! OK, only ten short years. Not eleven. To continue: his politics may be even more conservative than yours. He lives in Dallas and is well known."

"He is not from Dallas. Nor from Texas."

"Well, for Pete's sake! Neither are *you.* Neither am *I* ..."

I wanted to say, *Daddy, sit back and relax, you are going to really appreciate this man. He embodies everything you value, politically, every way.* But I said nothing. Logic had nothing to do with Daddy's objection. I said, "I don't care to discuss this any further."

"I appreciate that."

"But I am going to marry Al Hill."

Silence.

"He's fabulous," Aunt Tot said. "I'm crazy about Al."

"Why?" Daddy asked.

"He's smart as a whip. Knows more about politics and has better business judgment than all of us put together. He's handsome as can be, also fun to be with ... and anybody who's as good to his mother as he is has to be a fine person."

And my brothers loved him. I might not have been able to handle Daddy's forceful disapproval without that support. Daddy was always very suspicious of people. And here was this very attractive person who hadn't been around too long.

I kept after Daddy. "It's not like you to be so cantankerous and plain obstinate without some good reason."

"Well ... I have not wanted to say this and hurt your feelings, but he is just marrying you for your money!"

"That's flattering."

"I am not trying to flatter you. My object is to protect you."

"Whatever big deal money I've got is yours. You can just cut me off and I'm poor."

"Your trust fund owns a part of Placid Oil."

"What's that worth?"

"I have no idea, but not much as yet."

"And if my trust owns it, then the trustee is in charge."

"Uncle Sherman."

"Well, he sure won't give me anything you tell him not to. So where's the money Al's marrying me for?"

"You own fifty percent of Penrod Drilling. It is in your name. You and Hassie built it, it is your company. No trustee."

"OK. What's Penrod worth?"

"I would have to look at the books for an evaluation. But you own four rigs, you have valuable contracts ... Penrod is obviously worth a substantial amount of money."

"Gol-lee!"

"But I would not recommend that you sell it."

"Don't worry. I haven't the slightest intention of selling Penrod."

Al was not cheerful when we met for lunch that afternoon. "Now your father has hired a detective agency to check up on me. There is nothing negative to find, but he's turning us into an object of gossip. People who don't even know me are telling other people, 'Al Hill is marrying Margaret Hunt for her money.' This whole marrying-an-heiress thing is awful. It's completely out of hand."

I felt tears of compassion and frustration in my eyes. "Al ... I'm sorry ... I've talked, I've reasoned ... I just don't know what to do to stop him."

"Sweetheart, this atmosphere of 'Al Hill the fortune hunter' is ugly and offensive, and it won't permit us to be happy. I asked a wonderful, beautiful girl named Margaret Hunt to marry me, but the whole of Dallas is convinced that I'm marrying H.L. Hunt's daughter for her money, and that atmosphere will haunt us."

"Don't give it another thought. I've got it all solved."

I held onto his hand. It felt so strong, so solid. I wanted to never let it go and for Al to never let go of me.

Judge McEntire's secretary said, "I'll let him know you're here, Miss Margaret—"

"Thanks, I know the way." I knocked on his door and without waiting I walked in. "Sorry to bust in on you, Judge."

The Judge helped me into a chair in front of his desk. "My office doesn't have a door on it for you, Margaret. What can I do for you?"

I took a slip of paper from my purse and read him a letter I had written. "'I, Margaret Hunt, hereby make a gift of all my interest in Penrod Drilling to the trusts of my brothers Bunker, Herbert, and Lamar Hunt. I am not including my brother Hassie, who already owns fifty percent of the company, nor my sister Caroline because she owns Panola Pipeline. Signed, Margaret Hunt.'

"Judge, will you please put this in proper legal form so that I can sign it as soon as possible."

"Ohhhh, Margaret ... does Mr. H.L. know about this?"

"Not yet, Judge."

"Well, this may take some time ..."

I read him clearly. "Judge, I don't mean to be disrespectful, but it won't take very long to call Daddy. You can call him as soon as I leave. But then, please have this done," I smiled, "at this time; so to speak."

Daddy was waiting for me at the office. "Judge McEntire called."

"I told him to."

"What do you think you are doing?"

"Daddy, I have said it before: it is an inconvenience having money. In fact it is almost wrecking my life. So I'm getting rid of that inconvenience. Al doesn't want it and I don't want it. But he wants to marry me and I swear to you I do want to marry him."

It was one of the rare times I ever saw my father flustered. He spoke to me but as though to himself. "You really will not be influenced by my advice. You would give Penrod ..." He pulled himself together and made another stab at it. "It is impossible to make a gift like that. Have you considered the gift tax?"

"That solves my only other problem. I've got almost fifty thousand dollars in the bank. I'll pay the gift tax."

It wiped me out. All I had was my salary. Perfect.

By June, when Mother and I began shopping for my trousseau, I'd dieted myself down to 136 pounds and wore a size twelve for the first time since I'd gone to Mary Baldwin. While Mother and I planned the trousseau, wedding dinner, and everything else, Daddy continued to pretend that nothing was happening.

The days with Al flashed by faster than normally because there was going to be a six-week period in the summer when I wouldn't see him, when I'd be traveling with Mother through Scandinavia. The trip had been planned before I'd met Al. It was to include the whole family, except for Hassie.

I had been enthusiastic about traveling with Mother and Daddy, but now I certainly didn't want to leave Al and go to Europe. I was considering remaining home but then, as I might have anticipated, Daddy suddenly announced that he had business that would keep him in Dallas. And then Herbert couldn't make it either. Like Hassie and Bunker, he had dyslexia and needed to go to a private summer camp in Michigan to learn how to read in a normal way.

With both Daddy and Herbert canceled out of the trip, there was no way I could back out on Mother.

We took the train to New York and sailed on the maiden voyage of the *Osloford,* a beautiful Norwegian ship. It was a good thing that Bunker, Caroline, and Lamar had each other because there were no other children on the boat. I made an effort to have fun with them but Mother knew me too well and understood that I really had no desire to be anywhere but home. She tried to soften the ache I felt over missing Al. After the fourth day at sea Mother asked me playfully, "Did you ever see so much pickled fish?" Normally she would never find fault with an institution's food. She had elected to travel on a Norwegian ship and she would have considered it extremely bad manners to criticize Norwegian customs and food simply because they were not to her liking.

I groaned, "If I look at one more pickled fish I am going to just die." But in fact I loved having my weight down and was glad not to be tempted to overeat.

The kids were surviving on ham sandwiches.

We landed at the port city of Bergen, Norway. As we checked into our hotel the reception manager handed me a cablegram. I tore it open. "It's from Al."

Mother's face brightened. "After we check in you can read it."

I felt my face flush. "Mother, it's just a few lines. I've already read it."

"Now, Margaret, there are some things we like to read a few extra times. Like good poetry, it gets better each time."

"It's a real extravagance for Al to have done this."

"There are times to be extravagant," Mother stated. "And bear in mind that he does not have the expense of taking you out."

Our travel procedures were always the same. I handled the tickets and the money. Mother counted the luggage and took care of the children. Caroline was fifteen and Bunker twelve, and they really managed for themselves. Lamar was just going on six. Mother had these trips worked out so that we were met at every stop by a car and a driver who was a guide. We toured Bergen, then went through the fjords and arrived in Oslo and on to Stockholm. There were letters waiting for me all along the route. I wrote to Al every day.

When we got to Copenhagen, Mother and I went to Georg Jenson, where she bought us a complete set of flatware for twelve, the Acorn pattern.

On our first night in London, Mother and I went to the theater to see the young sensation Laurence Olivier in a play. Caroline stayed at the hotel with Lamar, while Bunker went across town on a bus to see *Snow White and The Seven Dwarfs.*

Laurence Olivier was marvelous, judging by everyone's reaction to him. Then we had supper at Simpson's-in-the-Strand, lovely paper-thin sliced roast beef served off a trolley. But my mind was across the ocean, and I was yearning for the tuna salad sandwich lunch I had not had with Al.

When Mother and I got back, Caroline was waiting for us anxiously. "Bunker hasn't come back yet."

I called the theater and got a manager who said the theater had just closed for the night. He was nice enough to go outside and look for him but returned to say there was no little boy standing around outside. I thought of going over there and looking for some sign of an accident en route. But I was concerned about Mother's high blood pressure and that would have further alarmed her. She was doing her best to keep calm. "With God's help this will most likely turn out to be nothing. Nine out of ten frights are false alarms."

Then she called the hall porter, who in turn called the hospitals and then the police.

At a wee hour in walked Bunker. I leaped off the couch. "Where have you been?" I demanded.

"I saw the picture twice, and when I got out there was no bus. Nobody told me they stopped running after midnight. I couldn't find a taxi and it took me this long to walk back."

This twelve-year-old kid had walked nine miles across London.

The next day Mother and I went shopping for a reversible coat for Al on Bond Street. Hassie joined us for dinner that evening. He had been in Germany with Mr. Williford trying to buy steel pipe, which he needed for drilling.

Mother had arranged for a chauffeur-guide to drive us to Edinburgh, so we enjoyed the English countryside. Returning on the other side of the British Isles to Southampton, we then boarded the *Empress of Britain.* This famous ship had a tennis court on the upper deck and I thought of how much Al would have enjoyed that.

The ship landed in Montreal. We could have stayed on until New York, but Mother understood that I was in a hurry to see Al so we took the train back to Dallas, which was only slightly faster.

My makeup was done and I was ready an hour before the train pulled into the Highland Park Station on Knox Street.

Highland Park Station was a social spot in those days because everyone's coming and going was a big deal, but my mind was only on Al, who would be waiting for me. With my nose glued to the window, I looked for him but was unable to find him standing there. As we stepped off the train I saw his sister, Alyce. After we hugged, she gave me a letter.

> Sweetheart,
>
> I can't tell you how much I have missed you and wanted to be there to meet you when you returned, but the firm sent me to Marshall to audit the Verhalen Nursery. I tried to get it assigned to somebody else but Verhalen is an account I've audited for several years and they insisted that I be the one ...
>
> *Al*

So I drove to Tyler to see Coleen and Jesse Johnson. Of course, Marshall is a short distance from Tyler.

On September 15, 1938, I mailed off around one hundred letters that I had written inviting guests to our wedding at our home on October 15. My long white satin, form-fitting gown was ready. And the bridesmaids' dresses were made and in their hands. They were going to wear purple, the fashionable color that year. It seems to me that my trousseau was almost all purple as well, and it was fitted and hanging in a closet next to my new luggage. Mother had made sure I had fabulous clothes, including a mink coat and a terrific Christian Dior red satin evening dress with a satin jacket and sable collar, which today is in the Texas Fashion Collection at the University of North Texas in Denton. I was still dieting, but I was an easy twelve.

Aunt Tot and Uncle Sherman and cousins Sherman and Stuart had moved to Dallas in June. Between Mother and Aunt Tot, there was not a loose detail.

On October 1st, I found a note on my desk from Daddy when I got to the office.

> Hassie and I are en route to Washington, D.C. We will be detained there on urgent business for three weeks or a month.

He was fighting me to the finish. Hassie was an unwitting accomplice. Though he was traveling separately from Mississippi, he had been told by Daddy to join him in Washington, but surely not why, nor for how long.

I called Mother. "He no doubt figures if he isn't around it can't happen."

"He's wrong."

I told Al. He had run out of patience with Daddy's shenanigans. "Either we get married as planned, or we'll just stop dating."

"That's my feeling exactly. We will not postpone the wedding. Mother is supportive."

I waited until October 7 before I called Daddy, giving him plenty of time to wonder why I hadn't called immediately.

"I surely hope you haven't forgotten that I'm getting married on the fifteenth?"

"That's not a convenient date."

"Well, that's too bad. October fifteenth is the date I'm getting married."

"That's not really convenient."

"OK. But that's when I'm getting married."

"Postpone the wedding."

"Sorry. Can't. Listen, Daddy, Mr. Williford and his detectives have had since early spring to find something wrong with Al Hill, but he just doesn't have anything the matter with him. Al and I are going to be married on October fifteenth. We'll miss you if you're not here."

It suddenly became convenient. Daddy and Hassie returned to Dallas on Friday, October 14.

A few hours before our wedding, Hassie came to see me in my bedroom where I was sitting with my bridesmaids, waiting to start dressing. He took me aside. "I didn't have time to buy you a wedding present so pick out something for yourself ..." He gave me five one-hundred dollar bills.

He was looking at me with unusual tenderness, my closest brother, my oil-field chum, my sometimes adversary, my former Penrod partner, my dearest friend with whom I'd shared childhood and growing up. He said, "I hope you have a whole bunch of kids."

"Hassie! We're not planning on having any kids very soon. Lamar's only six. I've had *plenty* of kids."

The Wedding March was being played on Mother's Steinway piano. Lamar was sitting on the end of the piano bench, swinging his feet. Dr. DuBois from the Presbyterian Church was waiting to perform the wedding ceremony in front of the fireplace. Daddy and I came down the stairs. He was going to give the bride away after all.

We paused at the landing, and looking straight ahead, I whispered, "Daddy? Thank you."

He looked at me curiously.

"For being here to give me away."

He nodded and whispered back, "I hope he's good enough for you."

"He is. You're going to find that out."

# *Twelve*

AL AND I SPENT THE NIGHT IN Fort Worth. The next day we drove to San Antonio, where we stayed at the Gunter Hotel. The next day we visited Al's mother and brother, who also had driven from Dallas on Sunday. I understood what an emotional wrench it must have been for Mrs. Hill to move from her home with Al, whom she referred to as "Son," whereas she called Alyce and Horace by their names. But as we said goodbye, she said to me, "You and Son have a wonderful time." We did.

In those days, it was unusual for anyone to spend four weeks on a honeymoon, but Al had not taken any vacation time for several years so he had the time accumulated. It also was the slow time of the year for auditors, which was fortunate.

We were adventurous and drove to Mexico City, which took three or four days. After we departed San Antonio, our next stop was Monterrey. Having heard of the beauty of Saltillo, we drove there for a short visit. By the time we reached Mexico City, we had both experienced Montezuma's revenge and were delighted that the new Reforma Hotel had the conveniences of a drugstore and bottled water. In a few days Al discovered the Mexico City Racquet Club, where he played tennis with the pro, whose name was Jesus. We spent Halloween in Cuernavaca, and by this time, Al had become acquainted with a colony of Americans who had moved there to enjoy the superb climate, economical living, and tennis. One of my recollections is bobbing for apples on Halloween in Cuernavaca—perhaps because my head went under water and I resembled a drowned rat.

We visited Taxco and its silver factories and stayed at a large new hotel built on the side of the mountain. After a few days of hearing reports of its beauty, we decided to drive to Acapulco. The road was under construction, which in those days meant driving over sharp boulders. It was a disaster. Al decided we could not chance the tires, and we returned to Mexico City.

We returned to Dallas by November 15 and stayed for two weeks in a furnished apartment at Maple Terrace, the first apartment house ever built in Dallas. It was temporary housing for us because Al's next assignment began on December 1st in Fort Worth at the Texas Electric Service Company, which he had been auditing for years. Al and I had dinner with my parents our first night back and almost every night until we left for Fort Worth.

In Fort Worth we lived at the Worth Hotel. Every morning Al would get up and go to work across the street. He loved to read, and for fear that I might be bored he bought several good novels for me. But I had no fear of being bored. Not only did I meet Al for lunch regularly, I had a friend in Fort Worth, Nancy Lee Muse. She had once dated Al, and I had met her through him. So I lunched with Al and then spent every afternoon with Nancy Lee and her darling mother, Mrs. Ewel Muse; then I returned to the Worth Hotel and looked forward to Al's return from work.

During our monthlong honeymoon in Mexico I had gained weight but Al stayed at his normal 185 pounds. He could eat more than I because of his size. He didn't always clean his plate like I do, but he did include a lot of bread in his diet. But he didn't gain an ounce. In fifty years of marriage Al's weight never changed by more than two pounds—superb metabolism, I'd say.

In Fort Worth we naturally ate out every night, and when it came time for dessert Al would say, "I really don't care for desserts."

"Are you kidding?"

But he was smiling with that scintillating brightness in his eyes, and in a second I realized that he was trying to make it easier for me.

Al had brought his racquet and tennis clothes and played a few times a week after work. I had left my racquet and tennis dresses in Dallas. I had no intention of ever needing them again.

When the audit was completed, we moved back to Dallas and rented a half-furnished apartment on Gaston Avenue, not far from White Rock Lake. Mother said, "Take any furniture we have. You can have anything you want." I took a bed and a few things, enough so that we could get along.

At Daddy's insistence, Al and I came to Mount Vernon for dinner almost every night. After dinner, we'd sit in the library and talk. One evening Al took a long drink of milk and put down the glass, staring at it as if it were something he didn't recognize.

Mother nodded. "I sold the cow. We just did not have anyone to take care of her properly."

Daddy turned to Mother and elaborately interrogated her, "Mrs. Hunt, do you mean to say that you and Margaret courted Al on fresh milk, and then as soon as you landed him you sold the cow?"

"That is correct."

Daddy could not possibly have been spending that much time with Al without growing to appreciate him, as well as seeing that his daughter had never been so happy.

Al was gazing at me, shaking his head gravely. "Are you admitting that you got me under false pretenses?"

I nodded vigorously. "Absolutely."

"However, you wouldn't do such a shady thing again?"

"If necessary. Without a moment's hesitation."

"And do not think it has gone unnoticed that since we've been married you have not picked up your tennis racquet."

"It served its purpose."

There are times when you hear a telephone ring and you get a feeling that it's bad news. We were having dinner out at the house on December 23, 1938, when the phone rang and I had that bad feeling. Armstead said, "It's long distance, Mrs. Hunt. From Lake Village, Arkansas." Mother's back problem was in an aggravated condition and she was especially uncomfortable. Daddy helped her to the telephone in the hall.

When Mother returned to the table she looked sad. "My mother has passed away." Mother's mother, Sarah Rebecca Hunnicut Kruse Bunker, had died in her sleep at eighty-three.

Daddy said, "Mom, you should not make the long car ride to Lake Village. You are not in condition. The rest of us will go. Your mother would understand."

We always had Christmas dinner on Christmas Eve because Mother believed the help should be with their families on Christmas

Day. So we had our Christmas Eve dinner at lunch the next day, then Daddy, Hassie, Bunker, Al, and I drove to El Dorado and spent the night at the Garrett Hotel. I had had a florist prepare a floral spray, which Hassie, Bunker and I held across our laps in the back seat. Al always drove when with Daddy, who sat beside him in front. We arrived in Lake Village before lunch, and Al met all the Bunker relatives.

My grandmother's funeral was Christmas afternoon. I had never heard of anybody having a funeral on Christmas afternoon, but it was.

So Al and I spent our first Christmas together with my family. Every Christmas from then on was a Hunt affair. For thirty-seven years I hosted the family on Christmas Eve. We started in 1942 with thirteen at the table. My baby Lyda was tied in her chair. Today the Bunker–Hunt family has reached 103, but we still celebrate it, at a club the Sunday before Christmas.

When we were in Dallas, I was still working as my father's executive assistant in the next office. Our combined salaries don't sound like much today, but Al had been given a $50 raise, which was substantial (and more than I got from the president of Hunt Oil); with $500 a month between us, we were by no means in dire straits. It was easy for us to be thrifty because we had little overhead beside our rent. Mother had an instinct for when I needed something special and would buy it for me. She gave me clothes for my birthday presents, and Christmas as well. We surely were not spending much on meals.

We managed so well within our five hundred dollars a month that Al joined the Brook Hollow Country Club in early 1939 and paid an initiation fee of $350. How the numbers have changed with time! For a young man to join today could cost $60,000.

In September, we moved to a more spacious apartment at University and Preston Road. We hired a cook, a huge woman named Gertrude, by coincidence. She arrived at noon, cleaned, and cooked dinner.

Caroline got married several years after I did, and she cooked and kept house herself and tended to her children. Later on, of course, I looked after my children, but the cooking and housework were not among the things I knew how to do, and had no desire to learn.

Not only did Al let me get away without cooking or cleaning, but other than Mother's presents Al picked out everything I ever wore. He'd call me at my office. "There's a dress in the window at Neiman's that I think you'd better come down and try on." He'd meet me and come up to the fitting room. Or if I saw something, I'd call him and he'd stop by and see what he thought of it. He was definitely responsible for my being on the Dallas Best Dressed list later on for three years and consequently being inducted into its Hall of Fame.

Always on the lookout for a good investment, Al learned that the McKesson-Robbins drug company had been subjected to embezzlement in their Canadian subsidiary. He thoroughly analyzed their annual report and figured out what would be possible to falsify and how it could affect the price of the stock.

At dinner with my father that night, he said, "Mr. Hunt, I would highly recommend that you invest in McKesson-Robbins. Because of the inaccurately low profit being declared the stock has been greatly undervalued. But now that this huge embezzlement has been discovered and will be stopped, the profits will rise and the stock should soar."

Daddy was shaking his head. "Al, playing the stock market you have just about as much chance of winning as you have if you arrive in a town where everyone is a professional gambler, they all have more money than you, and you're playing with their cards."

Later, at home, Al said, "I respect your father, but I know what I'm talking about. This is not 'playing the market.' This is finding a falsely undervalued stock that is going to rise to its natural value. I'm taking everything I've got in the bank and buying preferred stock."

"I've got a thousand dollars."

"If you want to invest it, you should."

I bought common stock. With the huge leak plugged up, in less than a year the company showed appropriately large profits and the stock began moving up. When I sold it, my investment had tripled. Conservative Al bought preferred, which only doubled, but he was satisfied.

Showing Daddy the papers on my purchase and sale, I needled him, "If you had listened to Al and put fifty or a hundred thousand into that stock it would have tripled."

Daddy replied, "If you had put it in an oil well it might be ten times your investment." He looked at Al, "But to have the ability to read between the lines on financial statements is valuable in business."

There was no doubt that Al's image had been enhanced in Daddy's eyes.

As a family we were growing up and growing out. Though we still saw a lot of my parents, Al and I had our own life.

Hassie had a number of producing wells in Arkansas and Louisiana, but he picked up his stride and hit his big production when the Tinsley Field in Yazoo County, Mississippi, was discovered in late August 1939. He earned a great fortune before he was twenty-two. There were no restrictions on production in Mississippi, no proration or fixed allowables. Hassie drilled a large number of wells, and every one of them was a producer. And his timing was great because in 1939 war had broken out in Europe; though the United States was not yet involved, we were fueling England, so there was a market for anyone who knew how to take oil out of the ground.

People sometimes went to Daddy to say that Hassie had made a bad deal, that he had paid two or three times what he should have for a lease. Daddy never said a word to Hassie, and invariably Hassie's "bad deal" came in gushing with oil and Daddy would smile with pride. "That sure was a bad mistake Hassie made. He paid five hundred dollars too much for a million barrels of oil. The trouble is that Hassie is a genius and people become jealous of him."

> BUNKER: *Hassie was a very smart kid. He had a great personality when he was a young fellow. He'd take me to the oil fields with him, and though he was a bit reckless, he was a good driver. He had excellent coordination and could have been a racing car driver.*
>
> *He had a lot of friends. Guys would call him in the middle of the night and say, "They just hit good sand in a well ... Maybe you should come over here, there may be some leases available ..." and Hassie would take off. He was a big success. He was a naturally good oilman.*

Bunker was touching his teens and too old for Dallas Country Day School, so he began going to school in East Dallas. Mother and I decided that he would be better off scholastically at Culver Military Academy for his high school years.

BUNKER: *They gave me a train ticket and told me, "You're going to Culver. It's a good place to go." I never thought about it twice. I just went. Now when I see parents taking children to thirty different schools to look them over, I think it's ridiculous. How would the child know which one to pick? What can he tell by looking at a bunch of buildings?*

*Culver was a strict, tough military school. Though I was in the navy two-and-a-half years and went to Culver for three years, I'm not a military type of person. I liked Culver. There were a lot of nice fellows there.*

*The tactical officers would write home once a month on each boy's progress, and they were always reporting my shortcomings. Finally, after three years there, my mother said, "I've decided you should go to school someplace else." I said, "Oh, no, I like Culver, I want to go back to Culver." She said, "Well, I get these letters and they're always complaining about you, saying you're not shining your shoes right or keeping your clothes properly cleaned or what not, and frankly, I'm tired of getting those letters. After three years, if you're still not up to their criteria you should go somewhere else."*

*Margaret knew two or three guys around town who had gone to The Hill School in Pottstown, Pennsylvania, and they recommended it to her.*

*My mother told me later, "Since I wrote them you were not going back to Culver I've been getting letters from them telling me what a terrible mistake that was, what a fine military career you would have. The way they are talking they as much as said you were cut out to be a general or something."*

Bunker went to The Hill School. At first we heard he was doing real well; he was happy, studying well, he was on the football team, and the school was happy with him. Then word came they were expelling him.

BUNKER: *I went in to Philadelphia to see a college football game. It was at the end of the season. Pennsylvania was playing Cornell. In those days they were powerhouse football teams. Like Notre Dame and Michigan today. A group of fellows was going in to see the game and had permission to do so, and I just went ahead with them knowing*

*I did not have permission. I had some demerits I was supposed to be working off. I went anyway. I was back at school that night. But I hadn't shown up to work off my demerits.*

*The dean who was kicking me out sort of liked me despite the fact that I'd get demerits. He said, "I've got to call home and tell your mother and father that we have to send you back to them." I said, "Well, don't call my mother. I don't want her to feel badly. Call my father." So he got hold of my father in New Orleans and said he was going to have to send me home, I'd broken the rules.*

*Dad said, "Fine. I understand. Just find another school for him up there and let him transfer. No point in him coming home and missing schoolwork."*

*I was there during the phone call. The fellow was shocked that Dad didn't argue with him. "But, Mr. Hunt, Bunker doesn't have any money to get him over to another school." "Well, I'll send him fifty dollars,"—which was plenty of money then—"and he can go find his own school." Hassie was in New Orleans with my father, and Hassie reaches in his pocket and pulls out a crumpled one-dollar bill and says, "Make it fifty-one." That was the way I departed.*

*The day I got kicked out the whole student body refused to sing in chapel, which was considered very startling. Students had to go to chapel but there was no rule that said they had to sing, so they had "a silent chapel for Bunker." The dean and the other teachers felt badly about it. I went to the Hun School at Princeton, New Jersey, for about a month. Then that Christmas vacation when I came home they asked me to come back to The Hill.*

The Hill School did not know it, but there was a much better reason to have expelled Bunker. We have always been an enterprising family. Hassie had run his taxi service at age twelve; Herbert had sold his no-overhead eggs from home and had a filling station while he was at Washington and Lee; Lamar opened a baseball batting range called Zim-A-Bat when he was at SMU; and my daughter Lyda had a paper route when she was at Stanford. And Bunker definitely had a business enterprise when he was at The Hill School: he made book on the football games.

Years later, at Mercedes and Sid Bass's wedding, I met an Iranian oilman who said, "Oh, I'm so glad to meet you. I went to The Hill School with Bunker and he was so nice to me, he taught me so many things."

I asked, "What sort of things did Bunker teach you?"

He made a fist and shook his hand like he had a pair of dice in it and then gestured as if to throw them out. "Crapshooting." So obviously Bunker had another business.

In the spring of 1939, Al bought a darling blue Chevrolet convertible, the first model with an automatic top. I had always wanted a convertible, and we had a wonderful time with it. Everywhere we went people wanted a demonstration.

Al had never been to New York, so when it was time for his summer vacation we left Dallas in our new convertible. Jesse Johnson was drilling in Centralia, Illinois, where there was an oil play, and we stopped there to see him and Coleen. It made me remember my own boomtown days. Jesse was drilling a lot of producers, and they were making money. But he and Coleen were existing rather than living. It was a dirty, coal-burning town, and the August heat was unbelievable. They had a room over a grocery store. Since there was no room for us, we all drove over to Valparaiso, Indiana, where we spent the hottest night of our lives.

Then Al and I drove on to New York City. We lived it up at the Waldorf-Astoria and went to the fabulous 1939 World's Fair on Long Island. The theme was "The World of Tomorrow," and we saw the General Motors exhibit and the Parachute Jump and Steinmetz Hall at the GE exhibit. And best of all, we ate at the Restaurant Français at the French Pavilion, which—when World War II blocked its return to France—Henri Soulé took to New York City as Le Pavillion. After dinner, we went dancing at the Roosevelt because Guy Lombardo was playing there.

It was hot driving in August. We bought dry ice and placed it under the fresh air vents, but it was not much help. This was before the days of air-conditioned cars.

We stopped in Washington, D.C. to see the monuments, among them the statue of Albert Gallatin in front of the U.S. Treasury Building. After visiting the Capitol and everything of interest in Washington, we stopped by my alma mater in Staunton, Virginia, and returned through Nashville and Murfreesboro.

Around this time, my cousin Tom Hunt, Daddy's brother Jim's son, came to work at the Hunt Oil office. Daddy used to say, "Tom Hunt is the smartest person who ever walked the earth. He's a walking encyclopedia." Tom had worked in the oil fields summers and holidays, enough to give him some background, and Daddy started training him to be a land man.

> TOM: *A "land man" works in the field. They drive out, meet a farmer and literally sell themselves and their company. Particularly if it was a hot area you had to impress that farmer and convince him that he wanted to lease with you and not someone else.*
>
> *Uncle June would tell me, "Now Tom, do not press for the last dollar. Act as if this lease is going to produce and you are going to have to be coming back to see these people and their children for fifty years or more."*
>
> *He would take the trouble to teach you what he instinctively knew or had learned. And he did not begrudge a man moving on. "There goes one of my trainees who's become a millionaire." And he took pride in it. He said as he was hiring people, "Now you realize that people who train under me have a habit that when they leave they make a lot of money."*
>
> *Uncle June inspired such affectionate loyalty that nobody who worked for him could ever do enough for him. We had a porter, Payton Williams, who took care of the sweeping at Goodpine. One time when Payton knew Uncle June was coming down—he always stayed at the commissary—Payton meant to sprinkle some talcum powder on the sheets to make everything nice but by mistake he sprinkled tooth powder.*
>
> *Uncle June had his eccentricities. When you phoned him from the fields on oil business you weren't allowed to say hello or goodbye. For economy you were simply to state your business. W.O. Woodard would say, "Mr. Hunt, the Smackover well in El Dorado—" And Uncle June would say, "Now W.O., give me credit for having enough intelligence to know where I'm drilling a well. You just give me the name and the information." He would listen to what Woodard had to tell him and then hang up. Saying goodbye was a waste of time and money. In those days every dime counted.*
>
> *Uncle June's expletives were on the scale of "My goodness." He would never say damn or hell. But if someone really made a terrible, horrible, expensive error, he would shake his head and drop his voice and he would murmur, "Yes ... yes ... analyzing that ... this has to be the record low in poor judgment."*

During the Dallas Fair, while everyone else was out enjoying themselves, Tom was working all alone in the office, day after day. Daddy said to me, "Tom loves baseball. Why don't you get me Jim Norris in New York?"

Norris was famous as "king of the boxing game." Daddy was known as what today we would call "a high roller." So was Mr. Norris, and they were friends.

Daddy spoke to Mr. Norris. Then he called Tom to his office and, in his normal businesslike manner, told him, "If you would really hurry, Tom, why, you could catch the flight to New York, and then if you would take care of my business downtown early, I might know some people who could get a pair of tickets for you to go to the World Series."

Tom caught the 4:30 flight out of Love Field in Dallas, and the next morning went down to Wall Street, took care of Daddy's business, and was met by a man who handed him two box seat tickets to the final game of the New York Yankees vs. the Milwaukee Braves.

> TOM: *Uncle June was demanding: "I want you to do this, and I want you to do that, and if you hurry why you can do this, too …." But he was no pushover, and he was a master psychologist. We had a long-time employee, Martin Pine, who was lazy and sort of a conniver, so he was boiler-housing, putting fictitious production numbers in his record books. Though we didn't like to fire people, I told Uncle June, "I'm going to early-retire Martin." When I explained why, he agreed.*
>
> *The next day Martin called the house. Uncle June answered his own phone and Martin said, "Mr. Hunt, they're trying to retire me over here in east Texas." "Oh, Martin, are you sure?" "Yeah, Tom's doing it to me." Uncle June sort of gasped, "Oh, Martin, if Tom's doing it then there's no one in Dallas who can help you." He sells Martin Pine on the idea that since I was doing it he could not reverse the decision. Martin was mad at me but not at H.L. Hunt.*
>
> *He understood leadership. His men revered him because he caused them to. In the winter of '42 we were drilling in central Louisiana, and it rained and it rained and it rained and it got boggy. The south part of the parish would flood daily. There was a half-hour in which you could get around. Uncle June realized that the men had worked themselves into utter exhaustion, so he told the superintendents, "We're going to shut down for a couple of weeks. We've got the deadline on the leases perpetuated, let the men get back to feeling good." Of course we paid them full salaries. And the men talk still*

*how he shut down so they wouldn't be out in the cold rain while they were working. To this day they talk about that.*

One warm day in March, I began to realize we were getting close to Dallas's hot summer. "Al, it would be great to go to Hawaii this August."

"I've only got two weeks vacation."

"That's OK. We don't want to spend more than that anyway."

So we started saving our money. Every night Al would take all the change out of his pocket and we put it in a box. We cut every corner we could and saved enough to make the trip.

We flew to Los Angeles. In those days the plane would make five or six stops between Dallas and L.A. Everytime it went up or down I would be airsick. I fly without a problem today, but planes were not pressurized then. In Los Angeles we boarded the Matson Line's *Lurline.* It was wonderful traveling on those boats; I wore an evening dress every night, and during the afternoons we shot skeet off the back of the boat. I stood among the spectators as Al fired away and scored twenty-four hits out of twenty-five throws. The man before him had not hit a thing. His wife, a lady I didn't know, standing behind me, explained Al's performance. "That guy has to be a professional."

We had three honeymoon couples aboard: the Henry Fords, the John MacFarlands from Tulsa, and Lily Pons and Andre Kostelanetz. Will Rogers' daughter Mary came to see somebody off, had a few drinks, and ended up a stowaway for the whole trip. Going over, we all became friends. Lily and I hit it off especially well.

We stayed at the Royal Hawaiian. Everyone else had big suites but Al and I were doing it on a tight budget, paying $22 a day, American plan. We lucked into a double room right over the big dining room, where you looked out over the beach with Diamondhead in the background. There were a few buildings—the Moana Hotel next door and the Halekulani—but there was nothing built around Diamondhead. After a few days on Waikiki we had achieved a golden tan. There were no crowds at all, and it was a beautiful way of life.

Sailing back to Los Angeles on the *Lurline,* Lily Pons was always playing the slot machines, and I played alongside her. Once Al came by and noticed a dime on the floor. He picked it up and offered it to everyone, but no one claimed it so he dropped it in a slot machine and pulled the handle. He hit the jackpot and walked away.

"Al," I said, "take the jackpot."

He shook his head. He did not believe in gambling.

Understanding that he was not going to take the money, I said, "At least put another dime in and pull the jackpot off."

"Why?"

"Because nobody'll play a machine that just paid off. You always have to pull a jackpot off."

"You mean so somebody will come along and play this machine not knowing that this has just paid off and probably won't pay off again for a month?"

"Well ... I guess that's the reason."

"Not me."

And he didn't.

"FDR is running for a third term," Daddy said, truly aghast at the idea. Roosevelt had been no favorite of Daddy's since he killed the flexible work week. Nor did he endear himself to Daddy at election time when he came out with his "soak the rich" tax message. However, Daddy could have lived with a liberal president, respecting him for his accomplishments, but he lost all regard for Roosevelt when he broke that longstanding American tradition and ran for a third term in 1940.

FDR's supporters claimed that with a war looming you didn't change horses midstream. But even his vice-president, John Garner of Texas, refused to be a part of this break from a well-founded tradition, and he retired from politics. Roosevelt's hunger for the presidency was so strong that he took an extreme leftist, Henry A. Wallace, as his running mate for his third term.

Al and I didn't want to keep on paying rent forever. The young couples we knew in Dallas were buying houses in Highland Park West, near where the Tollway is today. I told Al, "Let's not do that. You get into one of those small houses and you never get out. Somehow you're inclined to stay there."

At Christmas, Mother and Daddy always gave each of their children whatever the tax-free monetary gift limit was. I think it was $8,000 at that time. Al and I had looked at empty lots with the idea of building our own house. There was one lot we especially liked on Vassar Drive. I took my gift and bought the lot. Al went to the bank and borrowed what we needed to build the house.

Mother suggested, "Why not save some money while you are building your house and move into the guest house at the swimming pool?" It made sense—we were there every night for dinner anyway.

Daddy was revisiting the Louisiana Central lease in La Salle Parish, Louisiana, on which he had previously drilled eight dry holes. His lease was running out, and to perpetuate it he needed to be producing or at least drilling on the expiration date. He still had confidence and didn't want to lose that lease, so he drilled the No. 9 well and it came in producing. It still produces today. Once he had established production on the No. 9 he secured the lease and retained the mineral rights—they did not revert to the land owner. Then the boom started. In 1939, 1940, and 1941, in the entire area of La Salle Parish, there were night and day operations producing thirty thousand barrels of oil a day.

Prior to Pearl Harbor, production from Texas, Louisiana, and Mississippi was being sent to Great Britain and France. There was no Middle East production at that time. The Allies were desperate for fuel. The French fleet had fallen and Europe's salvation rested on its ability to move the British fleet and keep the RAF flying. Winston Churchill had pleaded, "Give us the tools and we'll do the job." The principal tool was fuel. Oil from Texas, Louisiana and Mississippi was making possible the war against totalitarianism.

Meanwhile, the Chinese wanted to begin oil exploration, and Hassie was in Washington working with Chiang Kai-shek's people, trying to bring drilling rigs to China.

In the fall of 1940 Mother and Daddy asked us to go with them to New York for an American Petroleum Institute meeting.

Al was reluctant. "I've had my vacation for this year. I should not ask for more time off."

Mother suggested, "Your firm has numerous oil-related clients. It might make sense to them to have an auditor who is familiar with the inner workings of the API."

Sure enough, the partners welcomed the opportunity for Al to be exposed to the API meetings, so we boarded the train for the two-night trip to New York.

There are moments that wear masks. This one was posing as a simple dinner in the dining car returning to Dallas, between New York and St. Louis. But in fact it was going to change our lives.

We had just pulled out of the station, and the waiter was pouring water in our glasses. Daddy said to Al, "You really should get into the oil and gas business. You know more about the petroleum industry than I did when I took a chance on it, and you know a great deal more about basic business than most people ever know."

I knew how gratifying this was for Al to hear. And I'm sure he shared my sense of pleasure at being vindicated, especially since he had come to really admire and like Daddy. Mother was visibly touched. We all understood that Daddy was saying, "I'm sorry, Al. I was all wrong about you."

"Petroleum exploration is the best business in the world. You are looking for a product that is of great value if you find it. And if you don't find it, then you cap your dry hole and you go somewhere else and try again. There is no expensive carrying charge, no ongoing overhead or inventory that you're stuck with. In fact, I foresee the day when there'll be new tools and we'll be able to go back into dry holes and drill to deeper formations and discover oil where previously it was impossible.

"Why don't you change professions? I will sell you the Bradley well in the Chapel Hill field. It is shut down with no market; you can see if you can find an outlet for the gas. It will be a challenge."

Al said, "Mr. Hunt, I thank you and accept your offer. I will see if I can find a market for that gas."

We both knew a good deal about Chapel Hill through dinner conversations. It was a field with great potential but a major problem. Its high gravity crude was the best, nearly pure gasoline. You would get a good price for that quality of petroleum. The problem was that a large volume of gas was produced with the liquid. There was no market for the gas, and it was illegal to flare it. With admirable foresight, the State of Texas had passed a law prohibiting the waste of a natural resource of such potential value as gas. So presently one could not produce unless there was a market for the gas.

I could feel Al's excitement at the challenge. "How much would I need to invest to own the Bradley well?"

"Your time and resourcefulness. You can pay for it out of the oil produced. As it stands today, the well is capped. It is producing nothing because neither I nor anyone who works for me can figure out how to dispose of the gas. If you can cause it to have value, then you will be doing a service and I will make money on your effort."

Al and I started in Gladewater, the closest potential marketplace. He talked to a meeting of the Gladewater City Council, trying to convince them that they needed the gas and offering it to them for three cents a thousand cubic feet, which was what it would have cost him to put in the pipeline to deliver it. We would be giving the gas away free, but we would make a profit on the crude. Unfortunately, Gladewater had all the local gas they could use for a penny a thousand, or free. We traveled all over east Texas asking every county and city government to buy it. We called on sawmills, toolmakers, everyone who needed cheap fuel for heat or power.

Finally Al made a sale to a sawmill. We had a start, but there was an overabundance of gas already flowing to the larger municipal markets. In later years, Al would sell natural gas for eight dollars a thousand cubic feet, but he started at three cents.

Searching for customers one day, we had stopped for lunch in a sandwich shop in Kilgore. Al was thinking aloud, introspectively, "We're not being creative. We're doing the obvious. There has to be some fresh approach that is being missed …"

As we drove through the east Texas oil fields, we passed well after well that had once produced but were capped for lack of bottom hole pressure, or that were using expensive pumps to bring up the oil.

Al stopped the car near a well and stared at the pump in operation. "Sweetheart, what does it cost to bring up oil that way, with a pump?"

"If you own the pump, then all you need is the gasoline to fuel it and two roustabouts to operate it."

"And if you don't own the pump?"

"Well, figuring on two pumpers, gasoline and rental ... a hundred a month."

Al's face brightened, "I think we're going to come out of this OK."

> TOM: *Al Hill had the idea to unitize the fields surrounding Chapel Hill so that he could afford to build a large and expensive recycling plant. He would unitize the gas by reinjecting it into the wells to create the necessary pressure to lift rather than pump the oil out of a well, and his fee was cheaper.*
>
> *He applied it to wells that had lost their pressure, producing the profitable crude while conforming to the laws of the State of Texas by utilizing the hitherto useless gas.*

Al and I sat in our room in the guest house while he drew a map of the East Texas Oil Field around Gladewater. "Starting here as our base market, we'll bring the crude through a separator which knocks out the distillate which goes into tankage, and then the gas will be transported through a pipeline which I will provide ..."

> TOM: *Reinjecting gas into the ground was sort of unheard of at that time. You needed big compressors to do that, and we didn't have them. Al Hill conceived of the first gas recycling plant in east Texas. He had to do a lot of talking and persuading with a lot of people but he got it done, and by turning Chapel Hill's gas into a "shoe horn" for producing wells that needed pumping he sold his gas service to individual well owners. The price was fifty dollars per well per month.*
>
> *Al would take the gas portion of the Chapel Hill production, which was fifteen miles to the west, and the pressure of that gas was injected into an oil-producing well in the East Texas Oil Field, causing what we term "gas lift."*

Six months after he started, Al had 102 wells leasing gas for $50 a month apiece. If occasionally we lost a customer, we just unscrewed their pipe and set it up elsewhere. Before the year was out, Chapel Hill Gas Systems was servicing two hundred wells. And best of all, we were able to produce 250 barrels of distillate per day at $3 a barrel.

It was one of those rare moments you never forget: Al gazed at me and said, "Sweetheart, our net this month is twenty-six thousand dollars before income tax."

We sat together quietly absorbing the dramatic change in our financial life. "A year ago, as an auditor, if I'd gotten an unimaginable raise to five hundred a month, it would have taken me nearly five years to earn this much money. And I mean *earn.* When you audit a company's books, all those papers and figures, you truly *earn* what you're paid."

"You've worked as hard in the gas business ..."

"It's a pleasure."

Al was always an independent oil and gas operator. Other than Chapel Hill, he would not go into an area where Hunt Oil Company or Placid had an office or any exploration underway. He went to Abilene, West Virginia, and then Michigan, because there weren't any Hunt Oil offices there. West Virginia was a disaster, but Michigan was successful.

He did use the office, telephone, and accounting services at Hunt Oil, which were prorated among the different companies and for which he paid a monthly fee. Hassie did the same. But Al never used the Hunt Oil personnel, land men, or geologists. In the years to come, Al's financial man, Jack Lambert, commenting on the arrangement said, "Al Hill paid for a lot more services than he received." People assumed that since his office was in Hunt Oil he worked for my father. But Al never worked for my father or for Hunt Oil. He never received a paycheck. He operated his own business. Sometimes it was in the red, later it was in the black, but it was always his alone.

Al and Daddy had lunch together every day at the Petroleum Club. Al's office, like my own, was next to Daddy's, but larger than mine; there was a private door between the two officers. We were at the house for dinner many nights. Daddy enjoyed Al because he was conservative and sound. Quickly, Al became a major part of the family. They had become such good friends that Al was always Daddy's first choice as a business trip companion. They made overnight trips to Washington or to oil fields a few times a month. I complained, "My gosh, you didn't marry my father, you married me."

> TOM: *Bunker, Herbert and Lamar were in school, Hassie was away a great deal on oil plays in Mississippi and working in Washington. So the only adult male who was considered family was Al Hill. Uncle June always felt more comfortable with family. He could speak openly. He was even reluctant to speak totally openly with a lawyer. So after a very little while, Al became a valued counselor and something of a son.*
>
> *By 1940 and 1941, as the war loomed, a lease play started in the Panhandle of Florida. All the companies were taking leases for a quarter an acre bonus with a yearly rental of a quarter, which was a normal arrangement for a ten-year term without production. Al Hill found out you could buy this cut-over timberland for a dollar eighty an acre, purchasing both minerals and surface, so instead of taking leases Hunt Oil Company started buying land from the lumber companies for a dollar eighty, which was cheaper than a quarter a year for ten years which would be two dollars and a half. We acquired close to eight hundred thousand acres that way. Later, in 1946 and 1947, we sold most of that land to St. Joe and St. Regis Paper Companies, some of it for as high as thirty-five dollars an acre, but reserved the mineral rights. We were never interested in the timber rights, just the oil and gas.*

Al became the official family turkey carver at Thanksgiving and Christmas. During one Thanksgiving dinner when we were all together, Daddy told the kids, "The rest of you can marry anyone you want, you'll hear no objection from me, because I've never been so wrong about anything or anyone as I was about Al."

> LAMAR: *Al Hill became the trustee for the Lamar Hunt Trust and helped look after my financial interests when I was still very young. He was always a very conservative, sound business man. He was not a risk-taking person.*
>
> *I got a wonderful letter from Al soon after I got out of college. It was a letter pointing out the financial opportunities I had and how unusual they were; telling me I didn't need to try to set the world on fire in business, I simply had to take care of my assets and they would grow at a normal rate.*

*I have taken Al's lead to write similar letters to my children as they have come of age, paraphrasing for my own children the things that he wrote to me.*

In February 1942, I learned I was going to have a baby. Al joked, "If it's a boy maybe we should name him after the Bunkers so he'll be Bunker Hill. Make a great salesman. He'll always get in the door."

I stopped going to the office. Expectant mothers were still not considered presentable, and in addition our house needed a lot of attention as it was nearing completion. So Daddy and Al went to the office, and we all met for dinner at the house on White Rock.

After dinner one night, I noticed that Daddy did not light up his customary cigar. For as long as I could remember he had been smoking a box of La Corona Belvederes a day. "Are you out of cigars?" I asked.

He said, "No. But I went to see a doctor this afternoon and I asked him, 'They say smoking's no good for you, should I quit?,' and the doctor said, 'Oh, Mr. Hunt, you couldn't quit. That would be too much of a shock to your system.'"

Daddy walked out of that office and never smoked again.

Though he continued to be opposed to surgery, his interest in medical advice was unquenchable. One story holds that he once went to Dr. Jenkins and told him, "I'm concerned about my heart."

Alarmed, Dr. Jenkins ordered his nurse to prepare an electrocardiogram. "Do you have pains in the chest, shortness of breath ...?"

"No, none of that. I feel fine."

"Then why are you concerned?"

"Well, several friends who are my age have had heart attacks and died."

Dr. Jenkins waved his nurse away. "You should definitely go over and see Dr. Krasne."

"Is he a heart specialist?"

"No. He's a psychiatrist."

Since Lamar's trust owned stock in Placid Oil, Al looked into that operation and saw that it wasn't doing what it might. He said, "Mr.

Woodard is a land man. Placid needs a head man with technical knowledge and experience in petrochemicals. Your father needs to have educated people in the company, not all people like himself and me."

"Well, why don't you tell that to him? You're about the only one he'd listen to."

Al wasn't so sure Daddy would listen to him on that subject. At an API luncheon once Daddy was given as a joke a book of entirely blank pages. Across the outside the title was *What H.L. Hunt Thinks About Geologists.*

But Al strongly believed in the need for more educated personnel. "I'll give it a try."

Daddy protested, "But our people are experienced."

"We need them educated," Al said. "Then their experience will be worth a lot more."

"Who is it you want to hire? Someone called a 'geologist, engineer, or geophysicist?"

"Yes. A man named W.F. Dalton, but he goes by Dink. He was the head of engineering for Ingersoll Rand when we did the Long Lake recycling plant. We could not have put that gas back in the ground without his technical knowledge to accomplish it."

Daddy agreed, but grudgingly, "Well, bring him aboard ... but just keep him out of the way."

Al brought Dink Dalton in to meet Daddy. They shook hands, but Daddy warned him, "Just one thing, Dink. There are five special men working for us, and you need to know in advance that if anything happens between you and them, if it ever comes to a showdown, it is *you* who would go, not they. I would not say this to them, but I am telling you, they are untouchable. They are five old drillers—young men really, but they've been with me since the beginning when sometimes I couldn't pay them but they kept working."

TOM: *The five untouchables were Jim Woodruff, Bill Dordan, Jim Garrison, and Tom and Dewey Sorell, brothers from Idabel, Oklahoma.*

*Though they never took advantage, each of them would tell people that he was the number one untouchable. Uncle June said, "Well, really, Jim Garrison is number one. There was a day when I had to have a well or I was out of the oil business. Jim Garrison came into El*

*Dorado from this dry hole I'd just ordered him to stop drilling. He had a few grains of sand in an old Bull Durham sack and he said, 'Mr. Hunt, this will make a well.'" Uncle June asked where they were from. "Well, sir, I had a hunch and I thought I'd just keep drilling for another day. Twenty feet later, we hit this sand."*

*He and Jim Garrison had the same birthday. In later years, when Jim was living in Henderson, Texas, he'd call me, "Tom, you go up and tell the major that I want to wish him a happy birthday."*

*"Better still, Jim," I would say, "I can put you on hold and connect you and you can tell him yourself."*

*"Oh, no," he'd reply each time, "he might be busy."*

*So every year I'd have to go up to see Uncle June in his office and tell him Jim Garrison called to wish him a happy birthday. And he'd say, "Well, you call Jim and wish him happy birthday for me."*

# *Thirteen*

I WAS ABOUT TO LEAVE the guest cottage en route to our building site on Vassar Drive when Daddy knocked on the door and came in. "I need you to go somewhere with me." He was very definite.

He didn't tell me where we were going. I didn't question him. I walked with him and got into his car.

Driving toward town, he said, "You know about Frania Tye." It was not a question, though we had never discussed his other "wife" or mentioned her name.

"Yes. I know about Frania."

"She is here in Dallas. She wants to meet you."

I wondered how true that was. In a situation like this, Daddy was capable of making up anything that was convenient.

"She is at the Stoneleigh Hotel. She wants me to marry her, which I have told her I cannot and would not do. To pressure me, she has been threatening to bring our children here and leave them with me. I know she would not leave them. But she has been threatening to call Mom."

"Oh, *no!*" I'd done my best to keep Frania out of my mind—this terrible threat that had hung in the air over Mother for all these years. I had never again discussed her with Hassie or asked if she still existed in Daddy's life. My question was: "Where do they live?"

"I just bought her a lot in Houston, near the River Oaks Country Club, and built her a large house."

That was the dumbest thing I'd ever heard of, "an all-time low in poor judgment," to borrow one of his own phrases. Houston, of all places! The oil business is very small, and Houston and Dallas oil communities are in constant touch.

I understood that he wanted me to speak to Frania, to persuade her not to call Mother, who was still unaware of her existence. Perhaps Daddy hoped that my age, perhaps even my pregnancy, would dramatically demonstrate that there already was an H.L. Hunt family, that it had started long before hers had, and that we were united, not something fragile that could be brushed aside or disrupted.

When we walked into the suite, Daddy said, "This is Margaret."

This woman who had a family with my father was about fifteen years older than I. Though other people might have considered her attractive, I could not have found anything engaging in her person or appearance if she had been a Vogue model gowned in Balenciaga and dripping with all the treasure of Harry Winston's vault, or a Bible teacher and fluent in five languages. She offered her hand, which I took with difficulty. There were no children visible. Incredibly, we small-talked, about nothing, the weather.

"Frania," I said, "we're chatting about trivia when in fact there is something important we want to get out in the open. I understand that you want to call my mother. Please don't do that. You would hurt her severely. Mother is an innocent bystander in this. She does not know about you and Daddy. She has high blood pressure, and the shock of what you would say about yourself and your children with Daddy might be physically damaging to her, to say nothing of what it would do to her emotionally—it would be an indescribable agony for her."

I had to breathe deeply between each sentence. "Most significant for you, I guarantee that no matter how unhappy your news will make my mother, it will not influence her to seek a divorce from my father. She would never, ever break up her family. So you have nothing to gain by calling Mother. Though it would hurt her badly, it would be a gratuitous, uselessly destructive hurt."

"I don't want to hurt your mother, Margaret."

"Then please don't call her."

"But what am I going to do? The children need to be with their father. They love him. You say your mother doesn't know about me. Well, I didn't know about your mother. For eight years, I thought my husband was Major Franklin Hunt and away traveling on business."

I glanced toward Daddy but he averted his eyes.

"Frania," I said, "I can only suggest that you continue your life as you and Daddy have been doing, discreetly." It took maximum restraint for me to be civil. "I'm sure that you have been provided for, as well as the children, and that you can count on that for the rest of your life. But he cannot be married to two people at the same time."

"But he's already married to me."

Daddy spoke for the first time, "Now, Fran, we have discussed that and you know that we did not take out a marriage license, that what we did was simply symbolic of a man and a woman coming together emotionally but not legally, as you understood at the time."

Frania seemed to lose all of her starch and sink into the chair as he told her what she could not deny. Though this woman's existence in our lives outraged me, I did not hold that against her alone. I felt sorry for her. I could think of nothing more to say. I walked over to her and looked into her eyes. "Please don't call my mother." I left the room and waited for Daddy in the car.

Franklin Hunt! I just could not put all that together with the man I'd thought I knew so well. I wondered how old the children were, but I wasn't going to acknowledge it further by asking Daddy anything about them. I sat there trying not to hear Frania's voice nor see her face, fighting them away, willing it all from my mind.

As I saw our house taking shape, I began visualizing it being furnished and living in it. Visiting with Mother one morning, I expressed an interest in some antique furniture.

"Then we need to go to New Orleans."

John Astin Perkins, our architect and decorator, traveled to New Orleans with us. We went directly to Manheim's, where I bought our dining table, fourteen chairs, a chandelier, a breakfront, several marble mantles, and a few living room pieces.

When we got back to Dallas and were in Mother's morning room, she repeated the invitation she had given me after my marriage. "Anything you want in this house, just take. All you want. I would love to buy some new pieces. It would be a pleasure."

Soon I was going over to the construction site daily to supervise the progress. It was on one such morning, as I was getting ready to go, that Daddy stopped by the guest house. "Frania's in town again. She's going to move to Dallas."

"Oh, no! Why? You just built her a house in Houston!"

"Well … someone there was going to introduce her socially but that did not happen. Frania was rejected, I believe because she has been using my name, calling herself Mrs. H.L. Hunt, and someone knew better and was offended. Her plan now is to live here as Mrs. H.L. Hunt." Fran had lived in Dallas from about 1932 until we had moved there in 1938.

For Mother's sake, I was outraged at being asked to support him in this mess he had gotten himself into. But then, he was my father—and we always finally supported each other in everything. And always would. Who else could he turn to?

I reasoned, "But it can only be worse in Dallas. Who's going to accept her here? She must be crazy! No, she's not crazy. She's shrewd. Obviously her point is to make you feel threatened that you'll be pointed at as a bigamist. That's what's going to happen."

"I've offered Fran a million dollars. She screamed at me that she wouldn't sell her children." He looked at me, racked by frustration. "I'm not trying to buy the children. I'm trying to support them. What else can I do?"

"I sure don't know. If a million dollars didn't work, you sure need to think of something powerfully alluring to attract her attention away from you."

The next morning, as I was getting into my car to go to Vassar, I found a note on the windshield.

Please see me before you leave.—*Mother*

I looked for her in her rose garden, where she normally was at that hour. Then I went into the house. She was sitting on a love seat in the morning room, looking out the window, waiting for me. She looked up when I came in. Her eyes seemed to be focused on something far away. This was utterly foreign to the cheerfulness she always displayed. I understood that something was very wrong, and I knew what it might be.

It was almost a minute before she had her attention on me.

"Margaret, I just had a telephone call from a Miss Frania Tye. She said that she and your father were married in 1925 … and have four children." My dear mother's eyes looked as if they had seen hell and been bruised and bloodied by the sight.

"They were never married, Mother."

"You know about this?"

"Yes."

"Why didn't you tell me?"

"Why would I?"

She weighed what I had said, then seemed to accept it. We said nothing for a few minutes.

"How do you know they were never married?"

I told her about my meeting with Frania, about Daddy denying any marriage, and Frania acquiescing.

I stayed with Mother for the rest of the day. For the first time I can remember, she didn't make an effort at cheerfulness. At lunch she said, "Those poor children ..."

*Poor children? Mother! Poor you.* Yet as I was thinking that, I had the parallel thought that my mother was truly a saint. Who else could be so selfless?

"... Daddy always said that his genes were so outstanding that he wanted to leave a lot of them to the world. I am certain that he does not imagine there is anything the matter with this. He is so naive," she said, excusing him to me. "But it is a terrible thing for a child to bear the stigma of being illegitimate. I feel brokenhearted for them. If Frania will allow it I will adopt them so they can have Daddy's name."

I was appalled by the thought. I implored, "Do you need four more children?"

"Heavens, no. But they do need a name. And we can make room for them."

Three days later Frania called again, and Mother spoke to her regarding adoption. She told me that Frania said that it was an impossibility, that she would never give up her children. However, Frania appreciated Mother's goodness, respecting what an extraordinary person she was, and rather than make trouble for her, she returned to her life in Houston.

I had barely contained my horror at the idea of Mother taking on major responsibility again. Her health and her general strength were simply not up to it. She had worked hard enough all her life—too hard. And I surely did not want four more brothers and sisters.

I felt a boiling resentment over what Daddy had done to Mother. How *could* he? All his life, he had controlled everything and everyone around him. How could he have let this get out of hand to attack the person he loved most? Even having known about it for years, now having met Frania, and seeing how Mother took it and what it did to her, I was shocked anew, and disappointed.

But I was all the more impressed and appreciative of Mother's character and spirit, her truly Christian sense of understanding and forgiveness.

I said, "I don't forgive him like you do."

"You must. Do not dwell on something about which you can do nothing. It does not help anything. Or anyone. It makes it worse. Let us have our say now, but then after today never mention this again. When you do not talk about something you have a better chance to keep it out of your thoughts. You rise above things and ignore them. Forget what you do not need in your life. There are a lot of do-needs. Discard tragedy and just get on with what you need to do from day to day. Being happy is a habit."

Mother and I had always spent a lot of time together, but we spent a whole lot more together from that day on. We never again spoke of this situation.

I am certain that Mother never confronted Daddy with Frania Tye. But her pain was apparent. Facing up to the reality of it, Daddy, as usual, found a solution. Handsome John Lee, the accountant who had been diverted from the oil business to handicapping horses for Daddy, courted and married Frania. From then on, the children used the name Lee. Perhaps John Lee adopted them; I do not know. But best of all, Frania and John remained happily married for years.

Daddy also set up the Reliance Trust for Frania's children, with W.O. Woodard as the trustee.

On Sunday, December 7, 1941, Mother and Daddy, Hassie, Aunt Tot and Uncle Sherman, and Al and I were in Denton County testing a well. Hassie had been listening for a weather forecast on the car radio. It was noon when we heard of the attack on Pearl Harbor.

Bunker, the eldest of the kids, was only fifteen, but Hassie was eligible to serve. And eager.

Daddy cautioned him, "You need not join the military. The oil business is listed as a 'vital industry,' vital to the war effort. Producing oil to fuel our country's planes and ships is a greater contribution than being just another soldier. You will automatically have an exemption from service."

"I don't want it. Our country has been attacked."

"Hassie, I need you here. You should begin preparing to take over Hunt Oil—"

"I'll do it later, Dad. Right now I have to help defend my country."

Any father has to dread the idea of his son going to war and wish to prevent it. But in light of the patriotism Daddy had instilled in us from childhood, it was impossible for him to argue.

Unfortunately, Hassie had let his army commission expire. He had graduated from Culver as a second lieutenant in the army. Like all of his classmates who planned civilian futures, however, he hadn't imagined he was going to want or need an army commission and had put his time into the oil business instead of the required periodic refreshers.

Now he felt a fever to get into the war. It was not enough for him that he, independent of Daddy, was contributing ten thousand barrels a day oil production to the war effort. The oil Hassie produced enabled ten battleships to go to war.

We learned that it was possible to reactivate a commission, but there were specific requirements, among them a certain level of physical condition. Hassie's weight had ballooned beyond the parameters of what an army officer was allowed to weigh. He started taking thyroid tablets to burn it off. At that time, there was still little knowledge of calories, carbohydrates, and proteins as they applied to weight loss. In an amazingly short time Hassie lost seventy pounds, took his army physical, and weighed in just under the wire.

Daddy had a flagpole constructed in front of Mount Vernon and he began flying the American flag twenty-four hours a day, lighted at night. Despite the war being removed from the United States by both the Atlantic and Pacific oceans, all Americans felt it, due to family members in the service, the sudden shortages of canned goods, or the ration coupons required for gasoline, shoes, and certain foods like sugar, meat, and butter.

With so many boys being drafted and volunteering for service, there was such a scarcity of men around that Caroline's first job was carrying the mail at Hunt Oil. Until then, girls worked in offices only as secretaries and switchboard operators. Period. Mail delivery and such "lesser" jobs were done by office *boys.* In hotels there were only bell-*boys,* and coffee shops had delivery *boys.* We had not yet arrived at delivery *persons.*

Suddenly Al had to go to Washington every other week to get drilling permits. I complained bitterly to Daddy, but he explained, "It's the government's way of maintaining dominion over all petroleum, ensuring that it be sent where it is most needed. We have so much freedom in America that an unscrupulous oil producer could go ahead and sell to the enemy for a higher price. The drilling permits eliminate that danger."

Hassie was recommissioned and in the spring of 1942 assigned to an infantry company at Camp Beauregard near Alexandria, Louisiana. Hassie was a "hands on" oilman and army officer long before that expression was used. In 1942, the phrase was "gung-ho." That was Hassie. He didn't stand in the shade while his troops drilled. To inspire his men, he joined in and marched along with them, carrying the same heavy equipment as they, working as hard as they. The difference was that Hassie was older and heavier, despite the seventy-pound weight loss, and one August afternoon, in 120-degree heat, he collapsed on the parade ground. The master sergeant under Hassie should have had him treated with ice to reduce his temperature. Instead he just put him in the shade, then brought him to the infirmary where nothing was done for him for more than twenty-four hours while he remained unconscious.

Daddy called. "Hassie's in the hospital in New Orleans. Sunstroke. I just had a call from Sam Sloane, who's in a lease with him in Mississippi. Sam asked me, 'Did you know that Hassie's in the hospital?' Apparently Hassie joked to Sam that he had passed out from the heat in Alexandria and had just regained consciousness in New Orleans. He was calling Sam about their business together." Daddy sounded frantic. "I tried to reach Hassie directly but as he is in a military hospital they would not put me through to him. I have a call in to

Tom Connally"—the U.S. Senator who had fathered the Connally Hot Oil Act in the 1930s—"and I've obtained a travel priority to be on the train to New Orleans this evening. I'll call you from there after I see Hassie."

When Daddy called from New Orleans he sounded deeply concerned. "Hassie does not seem right. Too many jokes, too much hilarity for a boy weakened from sunstroke ..."

As soon as he got back to Dallas, Daddy and Mother came over to our house. We had moved into our new house on Vassar. Al was still at work. Mother was visibly distressed. Daddy's usual slow and methodical manner of speaking was lacking as he blurted, "Hassie is being given a medical discharge from the service."

All of us understood that meant that Hassie was really not well. You do not get discharged from the service for sunstroke. They must have discovered something more seriously wrong.

"They are recommending he be sent to the Menninger Clinic to be evaluated. Is that OK?"

It was more than Mother could handle. She turned to me. I said, "Yes."

The clinical evaluation was that Hassie needed psychiatric treatment for a minimum of two years at the Menninger Clinic—and with little or no contact with his family.

Daddy said, "That's too long. We have to cure my boy sooner than that."

The doctor at Menninger's said, "There is only one way we work. We must call all the shots and there must be no interruptions."

Hassie rejected it. "This is nuts. I feel fine. Great! I'm going back to the oil fields where I belong."

In retrospect, I guess that Mother, Daddy, and I might have been evading reality. In any event, we brought him home. Though he was nervous and erratic, he returned to his business.

Our first child was born at 5:30 P.M. on September 17, 1942, a tiny little thing who weighed six pounds. Daddy exclaimed, "Mom, we never had a baby that looked like *that!* She is so skinny! She looks like a bird. And no hair!"

Al suggested that we name her Lyda after Mother, and today that bald baby has the beautiful black hair of her namesake.

I heard the phone ring in the middle of the night. I heard Al say, "We'll be right over." He put the light on and was out of bed. "Your mother says Herbert has bad stomach pains."

Daddy was in Shreveport. Mother was at the top of the stairs when we arrived. There was no doubt about it. Herbert had appendicitis. He was only thirteen years old, so he was still young enough for Children's Hospital. We piled him into the car and took him there. A Dr. Lee Hudson took out Herbert's appendix. There were no complications.

About a month later, we were having dinner at the house and Daddy asked, "Did you tell Dr. Hudson that it would be acceptable for him to charge fifteen thousand dollars to remove Herbert's appendix?"

Al and I were appalled. The normal-to-high surgeon's fee for an appendix operation in Dallas in 1942 would have been about three hundred dollars. I replied, "The subject of money never came up."

"I thought not," Daddy said. The next day he called Dr. Hudson, and within half an hour Dr. Hudson walked in and smiled broadly at Daddy. "Your boy's appendix operation was an amazing coincidence. At a dinner party someone was talking about what vast holdings you had, and on my way home that night I said to my wife, 'I certainly would like an opportunity to operate in that family,' and would you believe I was called the next day?"

Daddy rolled his eyes over someone both bold and naive enough to say all that. "Now, Dr. Hudson, I am sure that any amount you had mentioned to Mrs. Hunt or Mr. and Mrs. Hill would have been agreed to under stress. But anyone who was anticipating charging such an unusually high fee should certainly have mentioned it in advance."

Dr. Hudson absorbed that. "Well, let's just say I operated on Herbert as a charity patient."

We never knew if he was being sarcastic or if he knew he'd been wrong and wanted to make amends by not charging any fee. In any event, he was sent a check for five hundred dollars, marked PAID IN FULL. He cashed the check.

Daddy said, "People hear about numbers you are supposed to have and they think, 'It would mean nothing to him to give me fifteen thousand instead of two hundred.' But they fail to understand that besides not wanting to be treated like a fool, nobody has enough money to do all the things he wants to do. When I hear about people saying how rich I am, I always hope that Nathan Adams and Fred Mayer believe that, too. I would not find it comfortable for them to abruptly call in what Hunt Oil owes them."

A lot of people think my family is eccentric because we do not particularly enjoy spending money. I like buying things on sale because, first of all, clothes have become unconscionably expensive. Secondly, when clothes first come out they are often too high style for my taste, but by the next season, when they go on sale, my eye has adjusted to them. Also, I don't feel I have to get as much wear out of something I bought on sale.

Caroline is the tightest. She denies it. She says, "Listen, I'm not Hetty Green, we live well, we have a nice house, a maid ..." But the truth is that about twenty-five years ago, Daddy implored me, "Please go buy Caroline some clothes. She is just so tight she will not buy anything." So I went to Neiman's and bought some things for her, among them a good-looking black wool designer dress. Last year there was a party at the Crescent Club at the Crescent Court, a $400 million hotel, office, and retail complex that Caroline developed and owns. She had chaired a benefit for "Dallas Cares," an AIDS benefit, and she turned up at this cocktail party in the black wool dress that I had bought for Daddy to give her all those years ago. I heard several people telling her how terrific, how fabulous this dress was, and she said, "Oh, it's an old dress," and I thought, *Old? It's an antique!*

Though Mother was careful with money she had her own rationale for spending it on what she chose or thought appropriate.

CAROLINE: *There was a parcel of land on which I eventually built the house I lived in for thirty years. But before I bought it, I hesitated because I couldn't imagine spending forty-five thousand dollars on a piece of land. I asked my mother and she said, "If you want it, then go out and get it. Just think of it as being like a dozen Cadillacs. So don't*

*buy any Cadillacs. Buy inexpensive cars and then you've paid for it."*
*I still drive a Plymouth.*

Daddy's secretary rushed into his office excitedly, "The White House is calling. It's the president!"

President Roosevelt said, "Mr. Hunt, I know that you are not a supporter of mine, but I want you to know that I am a supporter of yours. You are a major factor in fueling our armed forces toward our ultimate victory. Your oil production is so indispensable to the United States of America and our Allies that I want you to know that should any bureaucratic or other impediment to your efficiency in supplying your maximum production arise, I am available to you at any time and I am prepared to personally intervene on your behalf to eliminate whatever the problem."

TOM: *Uncle June never came out and said that the east Texas field was fueling World War II, but he took great pride that his various companies produced more oil as Germany had in total from Baku in Azerbaijan, and the Ploesti Field in Romania. Our War Department estimated that Germany had nineteen thousand barrels of crude oil per day, and here he was producing thirty thousand a day in central Louisiana alone.*

*Later, Uncle June enjoyed saying, "My son Hassie and I produced and supplied more hydrocarbons for our military forces toward the winning of World War II than the combined production of all the Axis powers, including Romania's giant Ploesti Field." The Hunt interests were outproducing the combined Axis powers.*

# *Fourteen*

HASSIE WAS LIVING AT WHITE ROCK in the pool house. He felt close to Al, and they did a lot of things together—not in business, but as friends. Hassie, like Al, enjoyed sports and watching sporting events and taking walks in the country. He appreciated the beauty of nature, as Al did. They went duck hunting together in 1943. As meat was rationed, I was at home, looking forward to a nice duck dinner when Al returned empty-handed.

I looked at him dismally. "You didn't get even one duck?"

He was a bit glum. Al was not one to be depressed by not having a duck dinner. So I waited for him to explain.

"Hassie and I were sitting in a duck blind in a marsh. We were with a group of about a dozen hunters. We were dressed for the weather and comfortable. Waiting is part of the fun of it, you talk quietly and you keep alert, but right from the beginning Hassie was impatient. Then one little duck came sauntering in and Hassie shot it before he saw a huge flock of geese coming behind it, which he scared away. He was embarrassed. He said, 'Let's get out of here, Al, let's leave right now before the other hunters scalp me.'"

Lamar was eleven and going to junior high school in Dallas at this time. He was mad about sports, especially football.

> LAMAR: *Bunker was an enthusiastic older brother. He'd throw passes to me and got me a blocking dummy for Christmas, a thrilling present. He also coached me at basketball, helping me practice to be ambidextrous to fool the defense.*
>
> *Bunker was on the battleship Washington, shelling Iwo Jima. I got a letter that said "shooting is coming," and I was very impressed and got all excited and showed it to my mother. Then we read it again and we saw that on the first side of the page it said "Let me know how the left-handed—" and then on the other side "shooting is coming."*

BUNKER: *I wanted to go into the Marine Corps. The marines sounded like more action to me than the other armed services, and I was dumb enough to want action. But navy people were needed at that time. So I was in Task Force Combat for about six months, on a battleship. We bombarded Iwo Jima and Okinawa.*

*I remember that every time we fired a sixteen-inch gun it cost as much to fire that one shell as to buy a Cadillac. In those days a Cadillac cost around three thousand dollars. That impressed me. We'd wail away with those guns. Some days we'd do it in practice. We'd fire thirty rounds and there went thirty Cadillacs.*

In February 1945, I gave birth to our second child, a boy whom we named Al, Jr. Al was eager to start a trust fund for our son, as we had for our daughter. He was drilling a lot of wells by then, and he said, "I'm going to drill one for Al, Jr."

Well, if you are going to put money into a trust fund and then use it to drill a hole in the ground you sure want all the protection you can get. You aren't going to have your baby drilling a well that isn't an offset, meaning adjacent to or between two producing wells.

Al studied his holdings and narrowed his choices down to three producing wells that he had in west Texas, three wells that formed a triangle. He purchased the center for Al, Jr. He showed the map to Daddy, who agreed that there could be no better place to drill.

It was a dry hole, which is proof that nothing is certain.

Al had always loved Colorado. Being in the oil business, we had extra gasoline ration coupons, so in the spring of 1945 we drove to Colorado Springs for a short vacation.

He had often told me about the splendor of a place called Seven Falls, a natural scenic marvel consisting of seven levels of a single waterfall cascading one into another from the top of a granite cliff. He had first seen it when he was a student at Colorado College and he continued to think it was one of the most beautiful places in America.

This was my first chance to see the falls, and it was breathtaking. He brought me there again during a full moon, and it was even more spectacular.

Al was rapturous. "If I owned it, I would light it for nighttime tourism so that more people could have the pleasure of seeing it." He moved his arms, gesturing to a mountain peak, a canyon, the waterfalls. "Can you imagine owning something like this?"

I had the feeling that he intended to.

"Would there be enough income to make it worthwhile?" I asked.

"You bet. When I was working at the bank I used to be impressed with the cash deposits from Seven Falls. Imagine a business where all the customers pay up front and you have no accounts receivable!"

Al told Daddy at dinner, "I'm thinking about buying a waterfall in Colorado Springs."

"For hydroelectric power?" Daddy asked.

"No, as a tourist attraction."

"I know nothing about the tourist business. What are you thinking of paying for this waterfall?"

"Around a million dollars."

Daddy said, "Sounds pretty crazy to me." Quickly he added, "But don't let me discourage you if you think it's a good idea."

On June 1, 1946, after a year of negotiating, Al made a down payment of $150,000 and signed notes payable over a number of years.

A newspaper in nearby Lamar, Colorado, ran an article saying, "These Texans are coming here and buying up Colorado. If we are not careful they will try to move Pikes Peak to the Gulf."

Al wrote a letter to the editor:

> I am complimented to be called a Texan, however you might wish to know that I was born in Tennessee and before moving to Dallas I lived a good number of years in various parts of Colorado, including your city Lamar, which can be confirmed by checking the school truant records, and I attended Colorado College.

The next day the headline was: LAMAR MAN BUYING SEVEN FALLS.

Apparently Hassie needed more than just peaceful surroundings. He and Daddy returned to Dallas. "He flies off the handle without provocation," Daddy observed. "Even I have no influence with him anymore. He is not himself."

Leaving Hunt Oil in the hands of the executives, Daddy dedicated his life to searching for someone who could cure Hassie. He used all of his resources to research the world. He talked of specialists in Germany and Switzerland, but even with the war over, travel was difficult and Europe was just too far away.

We decided on a clinic in New England. After a month there, they suggested building a cottage on their grounds for Hassie and staffing it with a cook, butler, and maids so that he would feel comfortable and at home during his period of treatment. Daddy told Mother and me, "That is equivalent to a lifetime commitment. We have to get Hassie cured and back home."

He went to another clinic and was told, "We will cure your son in one month." They charged $2,000 a week, which would be equal to $16,000 a week today. But the cost was immaterial. Though Daddy was not an easy man to extract money from, I am certain that had someone credible said, "Mr. Hunt, I have the right doctors and equipment. Give me a million dollars and I will cure your son in one week," he would have gotten the money.

Unfortunately the third clinic did not fulfill their early optimism. After three months, they diagnosed Hassie's illness as extreme schizophrenia and discharged him.

Daddy was growing desperate. He was in his mid-fifties now, an age when he wanted someone to take over the company he had founded, someone with the Hunt name. The army had said Hassie needed clinical evaluation, so he was stigmatized and had to be cured. But above all, Hassie was his favorite, most-adored child. Daddy could not, would not fail him.

He took Hassie from clinic to clinic.

"Of course we can cure your son, Mr. Hunt, we'll start electrical shock therapy—"

"—and insulin shock therapy—"

The talk was not cheap. Some refused to quote a price. "I can help your boy. Pay me what you think it's worth." As each clinic failed, they passed Hassie on to a colleague, like a golden volleyball. And we could do nothing but follow their advice, scouring the country for the one doctor who would solve Hassie's problem.

But the result was always the same. Each of them discharged him as untreatable, with the recommendation that he be institutionalized. None of us would hear of that and we continued trying, but the road was narrowing to an end.

> BUNKER: *I had just gotten out of the navy. I went with my dad to visit Hassie in a hospital in Hartford. We met a doctor there whose son had had a prefrontal lobotomy. That was, at the time, the treatment for schizophrenia. There were no medications for mental illness as there are today. This doctor said his boy had been in bad shape, but that after the lobotomy he was much better and was able to hold a job. Matter of fact, my dad gave that kid a job for a while. He was sort of a screwball kid with a lot of leftist and socialist ideas, but he seemed to be all right as far as his temperament went.*

The prefontal lobotomy had been developed in Portugal by psychiatrists and neurosurgeons from all over Europe, many of them Viennese Jews who had fled the Nazis to neutral Portugal.

Daddy came by the house and talked to me. He had reluctantly come to believe there was no other option; now he was asking my permission. "It's the only thing there is left," he said tearfully.

It was killing Daddy, making him old. This was Hassie—his favorite, who had shown all the genius that Daddy could have hoped for in an eldest son, who had been a natural oilman.

The doctor who had endorsed this operation was the dean of psychiatry at a major Ivy League college. After all the failures, how could we not follow his advice?

The operation was performed in Philadelphia. It transformed Hassie from a very outgoing man who was always busy—constantly talking on the phone, speeding around in his car—into someone who did not want to talk on the phone, who made no effort to drive, and did not care to be busy. He lost all interest in the oil business. After the operation he enjoyed reading extensively, catching up on all the education for which he'd had no time or interest earlier. Hassie became pensive and introspective.

> BUNKER: *I don't know that it effected Hassie all that much. I think it helped him in some ways. My father felt that it wasn't a success. Thought it was a bad mistake, later on. He told me that. He said it was a shame that the lobotomy had been done, because when the drugs*

> *became available they were much more effective and would have made all the difference. Nobody had any indication that they were even on the horizon in 1946. I've thought about it a lot as to whether our parents made a mistake with him, but I don't think so.*

Daddy was certain that he had made a terrible, tragic mistake. Yet there is no knowing what damage Hassie might have inflicted upon himself before tranquilizing drugs became available.

Hassie was perfectly happy with his new personality, his new ways. I, for one, missed my fun-loving kid brother. It had been an expensive operation. I did not have the heart to say what so often occurred to me: *Maybe, if we hadn't been blessed with the money to pay for it, it might never have been suggested.*

Daddy shared my misgivings. The road had been long and winding, an excruciating wait for each doctor to fulfill a promise—and if not that one, then the next one, and the next, and the next. When the last hope was gone, Daddy said, "If a serviceman is killed in war, his parents receive the news as horrible, ghastly, but they can finally accept it. If he is missing in action they can, over a period of time, come to terms with it and finally say, 'He's been killed.' But then someone unscrupulous shows up at the door, 'I escaped from the Japanese, I saw your son . . .' and they are caught up again in the net of hope. In our case it was, 'I can help your boy.'

"But I have to wonder, what would have been their recommendations if Hassie had been an indigent? Or just a poor farm boy? I think the doctors have been more interested in operating on my pocketbook than they have been devoted to helping Hassie."

Daddy bought Hassie the Rupe House, which was next door to Mount Vernon, and had it redecorated in a traditional style that Hassie was accustomed to. And every year, as in the past, Hassie and I celebrate our birthdays together—still with one cake.

# *Fifteen*

DADDY BELIEVED AMERICA was going dangerously to the left. He thought that Roosevelt and Churchill had conceded too much to Stalin at the Yalta Conference in February 1945 and that Soviet Russia and communism were a growing danger to the future of America. He said, “Roosevelt’s age and poor health at Yalta left him no strength to oppose Stalin as he might have otherwise.” It underscored Daddy’s belief in the need for a constitutional amendment limiting the number of terms a president could serve.

My father had no political ambitions, but he did have dreams that he hoped to achieve, and paramount among them was a two-term presidency. He and Al went to Washington to seek the help of Senator W. Lee O’Daniel, a former Governor of Texas. As the three men walked through the Senate Dining Room, nobody spoke to Senator O’Daniel. They passed numerous colleagues who obviously knew him, but nobody gave him the time of day.

Al asked, “W. Lee? Do you get lonely here in Washington?”

Senator O’Daniel understood the joke. “Al, I publicly stated that I believe in no more than two terms of office, that a Senator should serve his two terms then go back home and try to live under the laws he helped pass. When I proposed that resolution be made into a bill, nobody would second it.”

Daddy said, “They were afraid of voting themselves out of their jobs.”

W. Lee O’Daniel said, “Yet we’re all businesspeople; we should serve two terms knowing that we must then go home and try to make a living under the laws we have passed.”

“As should the president, which is why we are in Washington to see you,” Daddy explained. “America needs an amendment to limit the presidency to two terms. Chances are you could get the Senators to vote on that. A president being elected four times is something that should never happen again."

With Daddy behind him, W. Lee O'Daniel introduced the legislation to the Senate. The Eightieth Congress convened on January 3, 1947, and took up the issue of a Twenty-Second Amendment. By March, it had passed the Senate and the House.

The rest of us were all at Mount Vernon when Daddy called from Washington with the news, and we cheered and shouted and felt like celebrating.

Mother quoted General MacArthur: "There is no substitute for victory."

When he and Al returned home, Daddy was delighted but realistic. "The big push is still ahead. It has to go to every state capitol and be ratified by three fourths—thirty-six states to become an amendment. That is a lot of politicians to get to agree on something."

Maine was the first state to ratify on March 31. That same night, Michigan ratified. During the first three days of April, six more states ratified—Iowa, Kansas, New Hampshire, Delaware, Illinois, and Oregon. Daddy and Al were hopeful.

Before the end of April, seven additional state legislatures ratified: Colorado on April 12; California, New Jersey, and Vermont on April 15; Ohio and Wisconsin on April 16; and Pennsylvania on April 29. On May 21, Connecticut ratified, and then in the next two days, Missouri and Nebraska.

Bunker attended the University of Texas for one semester before he went into the navy.

> BUNKER: *I got completely turned off within a week or two. I was down at the University of Texas with a good friend of mine, Ray O'Brien, whose father was a big-time oilman in Shreveport. It was a freshman geology class and we were in an auditorium. The professor was known to be a rather brilliant speaker. But in the first class he said, "Frankly, some people might not agree with these views, or might object to them, but I believe that all natural resources should be owned by the federal government."*

*I punched my friend O'Brien and said, "What are we doing here? Learning from a guy who thinks like this?" We never went back to the class again.*

Since childhood, Bunker had always said what he thought even if it got him in trouble, and he backed his convictions even when it was costly. He bought a Kentucky farm that, among other things, produced a sizable crop of tobacco that could have paid the taxes on his land, but he never believed in smoking and would not keep the money from the tobacco. He turned it over to the University of Kentucky for cancer research.

BUNKER: *I didn't feel right making money off of growing tobacco. I could have burned the crop, but that would have been gratuitous. Sixty percent of the tobacco sold in America is imported from all over the world—South Africa, Zimbabwe, South America, what not. Obviously there would be the same amount of tobacco consumed whether I produced it or not. So rather than destroy the crop I let it do some good for the U. of K.*

Only three more states had ratified the Twenty-second Amendment: Virginia, Mississippi, and New York. After that the bill seemed to hang dead; no other state seemed to be moving toward ratification.

I sensed Daddy's frustration over being powerless to complete what he had started, being incapable of moving politicians to accomplish what he believed so strongly was in the best interests of our country. I felt that Daddy was suffering through a period of self-doubt. He kept it to himself, never expressing his feelings with a single word. I thought how presidents, kings and queens, and giants like Daddy can be afraid, uncertain, like everyone else, but somehow some great inner strength keeps them from showing it.

With all of the producing wells that Daddy had he was generating a lot of income that he needed to invest. Still a farmer at heart, he began acquiring farms and ranch land, around a million acres in a dozen states.

TOM: *Uncle June bought the Hoodoo Ranch at Cody, Wyoming, in 1947—two hundred fifty thousand acres. We had this old crusty ranch foreman, Dale Pettit, a hard-bitten Montana rancher.*

*One time Lamar was up there, and Pettit called Uncle June. He was quite alarmed. "Mr. Hunt, Lamar's up here and he wants to spend money building a dam on one of the creeks so it'll help the trout fishing."*

*"Well, Dale, how much?"*

*"Oh, Mr. Hunt, I calculate it has to take the best part of fifteen hundred dollars."*

*Uncle June told Dale he needed to think it over a while. He waited long enough to give the impression that he had really mulled it over, then he called Pettit back and said, "OK, Dale, Lamar's a good boy and if he wants to do that I guess we can afford it."*

If Dale Pettit had not understood Daddy's reply then, he would have no doubt about it a few weeks later, when *Life* magazine came out with a full page snapshot of Daddy on a street corner, with a caption asking, *Is this the richest man in the U.S.?*

The article stated that Daddy's income exceeded a million dollars a week. They must have gotten the figure from their sister magazine *Fortune*, which said that Daddy was "the biggest of the Big Rich, and thus probably the richest single individual in the United States." They estimated that with daily oil production of 65,000 barrels, at an average worth of $2.25 per barrel, Daddy had an annual income of $53,381,250.

Thus began the game of guessing the Hunt family's wealth. One magazine said Daddy's holdings were worth $237 million while another put it at $600 million.

HERBERT: *He was unknown till that story was published. He said he did recall some guy having a camera out on the street but that he expected the guy to hand him a ticket telling him how to order the picture. That was a common occurrence in that day and time. Fortunately, Life misspelled his name. They spelled it Harralson. When all this mail started pouring into the office, hundreds of letters every day, the envelopes that had the misspelled name were put aside to take care of later, so we could get to the business mail first. We had to put on two additional secretaries to open all the mail and acknowledge the letters.*

*There was everything in there from proposals of marriage to "Here's five dollars, invest this for me and send me the winnings." We'd have to send back the money. Even years later, the office still got letters addressed to the misspelled name.*

Shortly after the *Life* article appeared, a man turned up at the office.

"My name is Charles Hunt. I'm a relative. Take me to the treasurer." He showed his driver's license and birth certificate naming him as Charles Hunt.

The receptionist could think of nothing else to do but deliver him to the treasurer who listened to a half-hour hard-luck story, followed by a demand for some immediate cash against his fair share of the Hunt fortune.

It was so ridiculous as to be difficult to deal with. Even if he was a relative, what claim would he have on Daddy's personal earnings? But such logic was getting nowhere with him. Rather than call the police to remove him, more people got into the meeting trying to reason with him.

Finally, Herbert said, "Take off your shoes."

The man who called himself Charles Hunt looked at him, confused.

"You heard me, take off your shoes."

"Why?" he asked suspiciously.

"I'll show you why when you take off your shoes," Herbert promised. "And your socks."

When the man was barefoot, Herbert looked at his toes and said, "You're no Hunt. If you were a Hunt, your little toe would curl in like this." He took off his own shoes and showed him the curled-in little toes. Herbert had cousin Tom Hunt take off his shoes and show him the curled toes. All the Hunts have little toes that turn in rather than go straight, even the grandchildren.

Herbert said, "You're a fraud. Get out of here." And the man slunk away and never came back.

It is amazing—or at least amusing—how fables grow up around people like my father. Like the legend about how the wealthy H.L. Hunt brought his lunch to work in a brown paper sack to save money. And how he parked his car three blocks from the office because it was cheaper. The press has always made us out as quaint and eccentric, as they expected us to be.

Though my father did not waste money, he certainly would not waste his time and energy walking three blocks if he didn't need to. The story about the paper bag lunch was true, up to a point. Daddy liked to eat healthful foods such as apricots and pecans, which he could not obtain at the Petroleum Club or order from a coffee shop. He had put a bread mill in the basement of Mount Vernon and ground the grains for his own bread.

The drastic change in eating habits began around 1951, after a friend gave me Adelle Davis's first book on nutrition, *Let's Cook It Right.* It was a revelation to me. I told Al, "We're lucky we're alive." Appalled at how poorly we had been treating our bodies, we embarked on a serious program of dietary reform. When I brought the subject up to Mother and Daddy, they too agreed to change their "wicked" but delicious ways.

Using Adelle Davis as a guide, I worked out diets for them, including Daddy's lunch in the office instead of at the Petroleum Club. For Christmas of that year, I gave him a package of one hundred little brown sacks printed across the front—*H.L. Hunt Gourmet Lunch*—and he began bringing one to the office each day containing the foods he wanted to eat.

There was one story about a man with a flat tire. He said he saw another man walking by with a brown paper bag, and said to him, "Hey, buddy, I'll give you a buck to do this for me." The story goes that it was H.L. Hunt, and he said, "Sure," changed the tire, took the dollar and continued on his way. Absurd! At that point in his life I don't think Daddy knew how to change a tire anymore, if he ever did.

All the policemen in Dallas knew him. When they saw his car coming, they would stop traffic to let him turn into the garage. They loved Daddy, because as an active writer of "Letters to the Editor" in the Dallas papers he had complained frequently that the policemen were underpaid and urged that their salaries be raised. The policemen, who were stationed on every corner downtown—Chuck Golden, Walter Finnigan, Mark DeWeese, a patrolman called Jonesy—would never have let anyone approach Daddy or have stood by and allowed him to change a tire. They saw him as their champion and treated him as such.

In 1947, the Big Inch Pipeline, built during the war by the government to expedite the transport of crude oil to the eastern refineries, was going to be sold. A number of oil companies wanted to bid as a consortium. Because of his new visibility, Daddy was approached. He was invited by Edgar and Jack Pew, Gene Holman, and J. Paul Getty to a dinner meeting at Larue, a restaurant in New York, and he took Tom Hunt with him. They wanted H.L. Hunt, because he was an independent, to be the front, for which he would receive ownership of a substantial percentage without cost.

Daddy appreciated their offer but declined. When dinner was over, there was a jovial sort of arguing for the check but Daddy argued the best. He looked at the amount. It was $967. He showed it to J. Howard Pew and said, "I understand that wealthy people come here to eat. But if they come very often they won't be wealthy." Then he turned to Tom, "There's a joke that if you have dinner with a preacher you'll get a prayer; if you have dinner with a lawyer you'll get an argument; if you have dinner with a rich man you'll get the bill. So, Tom, you pay this."

When they were alone on their way back to Dallas, Tom asked, "Uncle June, how could you turn down a sweet deal like that? Your piece would be worth millions."

"I know, Tom, but I really don't want people saying 'H.L. Hunt is a promoter.'"

Daddy was impressed, however, with the effect of the *Life* magazine story, and he granted a few local interviews. When a reporter asked how rich he really was he answered, "If you know how rich you are, you aren't very rich." It was not intended as a catch phrase, but eventually it was quoted over and over again. It was simply a financial fact. Oil wealth is unpredictable because of two variables: market price and the life of a well, which might be five, ten, or thirty years.

To Frank X. Tolbert in the *Dallas Morning News* he marveled, "I'm the same man I was before all this publicity, but all of a sudden people treat me even better than they did when I was just rich. Now, being famous, suddenly they seem to think I know answers to everything."

The April 1948 issue of *Fortune* magazine had referred to Daddy as a man "whose quiet habits and abhorrence of cameras make him an unknown even to his fellow Texans." He had always avoided publicity, consistently refusing interviews with *Time, Life,* and other publications. The only time his name had appeared in print with his approval was when he wrote letters to the editor.

Now he said, "Maybe being famous can be put to good use." Hoping that his new celebrity status could give him political potency, he turned immediately to the Twenty-second Amendment. Two years had passed, and only twenty-one of the required thirty-two states had ratified. Daddy put his full time and effort into telephoning, sending telegrams, and traveling to speak to state senators personally, in the hope of influencing their votes toward ratification.

Politicians always need campaign funds, and they rarely distance themselves from potential contributors. His suddenly famous name opened a lot of doors through which he strode shamelessly, and purposefully. "I hope they do see me as a potential campaign contributor. I don't care what they hope I may give them if it will get us a two-term limit to the presidency."

Still, it was hard and lonely work. In 1949, only one State Legislature ratified—South Dakota on January 21—then no more for the rest of the year. The total now stood at twenty-two.

In 1950, North Dakota and Louisiana brought the total to twenty-four states. Daddy kept plodding on, traveling to the uncommitted state capitols, and talking, talking, talking.

He also went to the rural areas and talked to the farmers and working people, pleading with them to take more interest in their government. He brought with him printed letters stating that the undersigned was in favor of an amendment to the Constitution preventing a presidential third term, and he had envelopes with the appropriate congressmen's names and addresses written on them. "Read this letter. If you believe what it says, sign it and send it to Washington. It's your country. The congressmen work for you. Tell them what you want."

By early 1951 the Twenty-second Amendment still needed the approval of twelve state legislatures. Harold L. Ickes, who had been FDR's Secretary of the Interior, published an article in the *New Republic* stating that the Twenty-second Amendment was "dead," that it had only been a "hate Roosevelt" movement.

Daddy was saddened. "Admittedly I didn't like Roosevelt. But the most important reason I did not like him is that he should have loved his country better than to accept a third, let alone fourth, term."

He began what the press eventually dubbed "H.L. Hunt's one-man campaign" to obtain the necessary twelve additional ratifications. He had tried hard before, but now he worked harder still, and Al and I traveled and worked with him.

Finally, on January 10, 1951, Indiana ratified, followed by Montana on January 25, Idaho on January 30, New Mexico on February 1, and Wyoming on February 8.

Seven more were needed.

Arkansas, where Daddy had been a planter and had begun in the oil business, had rejected the amendment. He went to El Dorado and began looking up old friends who could get him to the state senators in Little Rock. By February 12, Arkansas had capitulated and the state legislature ratified.

There were now just six to go.

Georgia followed on February 16 and Tennessee on February 20.

Texas, our own state, had also rejected the amendment back in 1947. It seemed incredible: our two home states had voted against it. Daddy began working on Texas friends and officials, urging, pleading, and even entertaining them at dinners. Due to his efforts, the Texas Legislature reconsidered, and on February 22 they voted for ratification of the Twenty-second Amendment—on George Washington's birthday— and Bunker's birthday as well.

Three to go.

North Carolina ratified on February 23. Then on February 26, Utah and—one hour later—Nevada ratified, becoming the thirty-fifth and thirty-sixth states.

The Twenty-second Amendment was the law of the land.

# *Sixteen*

DADDY CARED AS MUCH ABOUT his country as any other human being who ever lived. He was extremely uncomfortable with the foreign policy of both the Roosevelt and then the Truman administrations. "When somebody just makes honest mistakes, then it's likely that one mistake will favor the right and another will favor the left. But since the war it seems that everything our State Department has done always benefits the left." He was deeply concerned about the effects of communism at home and around the world.

> BUNKER: *My father had a tremendously negative attitude toward communism. I consider communism to be socialism with a gun. He saw it as a sophisticated slavery. And so many wealthy and sophisticated people were conducting themselves as if they were really pro-communist just to keep their status in society. To be outspokenly anti-communist was to become very unpopular in a hurry.*
>
> *I remember a big Dallas socialite coming to Dad's office asking him to contribute to a hospital. Dad turned him down, explaining, "I'm using my money trying to help save people's freedom. If people lose their freedom it's not going to serve much purpose for them to live longer. They'll just be living in slavery."*
>
> *He said to me further, "Somebody's always going to support hospitals, be it the government or the state or private individuals who like to give money to hospitals. But there's practically no one who wants to spend money to help save freedom. So I want to spend my money to help freedom."*

He worked hard toward getting General MacArthur to run for president. At the office, at home, during dinner, on Sunday—constantly—one thought taunted him: "What can we do to convince him he should run? We need his strength. He's needed so badly."

Daddy foresaw the downfall of this country. He foresaw our loss of international prestige, our world benevolence at the expense of our own backyard and our own economic stability.

My father believed that General MacArthur would not let our former enemies overcome us. He had said, "We must not rebuild them to the point at which they, having more aggressive natures than we, will overpower us." He would not have turned the Japanese and Germans loose after defeating them in a war we did not want, financing their return to life and allowing them to win an economic war against us now. Because finally, economics, not latter-day Napoleons or Hitlers, will decide the fate of the world.

In 1952, Daddy got himself elected as a delegate from the State of Texas to the Republican presidential convention, and we went with him. MacArthur made the keynote speech, then turned his back on the convention and walked out. He was a completely demoralized man, beaten down by Truman recalling him so ignominiously. Truman had treated the war hero like a naughty child, which caused him to make that famous address to Congress that concluded, "Like the old soldier of the ballad, I now close my military career and just fade away." And he was living up to it.

When the State of Texas voted at that convention, H.L. Hunt cast the single vote for General MacArthur. It was a landslide for General Dwight D. Eisenhower. Later, when the presidential race pitted General Eisenhower against Adlai Stevenson, Daddy gave his support to Eisenhower.

Neither Daddy, Al, nor I knew much about politics. But when you believe in something, you find the strength to keep trying. Discarding MacArthur as a remedy for the problems he saw, Daddy said, "I just know that if I can get the facts to the people, they will see the obvious. They will educate themselves."

At 7:00 A.M. the following Sunday morning, he called Welch Wright, his secretary. "I need your help on a project. If you could come out here today I would appreciate it." He had never called on anyone to come out to work on a Sunday, but he had an idea and wanted to get onto it immediately.

Welch had just awakened. "Oh, sure, I can come, Mr. Hunt."

"You do not need to have breakfast. We will have breakfast for you out here." He knew how to impart a sense of urgency.

When she arrived at Mount Vernon, Daddy was in the library working on his project, but Mother was waiting for Welch and they had a lovely breakfast together. Daddy came into the dining room. "Anytime you're ready."

Mother said, "Mrs. Wright has not finished her breakfast yet." She turned to Welch, "Do not let yourself be intimidated."

Daddy smiled and went back to his project, which was the creation of *Facts Forum,* a journal for the dissemination of the conservative point of view. He signed his beliefs *Constructively, H.L. Hunt.* Having been accused in the press of being "too conservative," he described himself as a "constructive" rather than a conservative. "How can you be accused of being too constructive?" he reasoned.

He soon had us giving dinner parties in our homes to get people involved. We had meetings at our house continuously. I often had twenty or fifty people for dinner followed by an excellent speaker who presented people with honest information. He was trying to save the United States from the effects of communism at home and around the world.

Shortly, he sponsored "Facts Forum" as a radio—and later, television—program that reached five million listeners and viewers a week. The guests on "Facts Forum" ranged from Senator Joseph McCarthy to Louis Buden, former editor of the *Daily Worker.* Daddy reasoned that if people hear both sides they will recognize what is obviously best for the country.

My father was an optimist. You have to be an optimist to drill a hole in the ground and hope to find oil and get rich—or to try to educate people and do something good for your country. He was still giving people credit for being a great deal smarter than they are.

LAMAR: *I went to a boys' school in Pottstown, Pennsylvania, The Hill School, where Bunker and Herbert had gone. I went there for five years.*

*Bunker is a shameless booster, a great brother, and he came back all the way to Pennsylvania for a couple of my football games. He sent the school sirloin steaks from Texas so that the football team could have red meat the night before the game, which was a big deal in 1947 and 1948. Otherwise we ate what was in the regular mess hall.*

*Bunker also contributed a hundred dollars a game so that the school could take play-by-play films. They'd never taken game films before, which are a good coaching technique.*

Lamar was about to graduate from The Hill School. He was signed up to go to Washington and Lee, where Herbert had graduated with a B.A. in geology. One summer morning in Colorado Springs, at the Garden of the Gods Club, which Al and I had built and which had become a favorite and important part of our lives, I got a phone call from Lamar. "I really don't want to go to W and L. I've been away at school for five years and I want to come home. Would you talk to Mother and see if I can't come back and go to SMU?"

"Why don't you speak to her yourself?"

"Well, I feel like I need representation, some influence in high places."

Since we had bought Seven Falls, Mother had begun to visit Colorado Springs each summer. I located her sitting under the dryer at the Broadmoor Hotel's beauty shop and reported, "Mother, Lamar has just called. He said he really does not want to go to W and L. He wants to come home and go to SMU, and could I talk you into it?"

Mother sighed. "I dread being back in parents' meetings again." But she had a smile in her eye. "Yet, it will be lively to have those college boys around."

I called Lamar. "OK, you can call W and L and tell them no and come back and go to SMU."

> LAMAR: *My big motivation for going to SMU was that Doak Walker went there. When I was a teenager and played football, not very well, I envisioned that I was a Doak Walker. In high school I wore the same number as he did, 37.*
>
> *A few years ago Doak Walker's number was retired at SMU, and at a dinner honoring him I told the story of Doak Walker being my teenage idol and that I wore his number at school. Doak now tells people, "A lot of people don't know that Lamar's number has been retired at SMU."*

Mother had foreseen what was in store for her with a son in college locally. The help was constantly making chicken spaghetti for Kappa Sigma, his fraternity, and the pool house and swimming pool seemed permanently filled with Lamar's schoolmates and fraternity brothers. They called the house *The Huntry Club.*

At SMU Lamar was the only one on the football team who was not on an athletic scholarship. They called him "Poor Boy." He came out every year for four years and took all that punishment without any glory because he rarely got to play.

Bunker used to train Lamar. He would drive the car at ten miles per hour and Lamar would run alongside. They worked at his football together in the yard every Sunday afternoon.

> LAMAR: *When I was at SMU I was on the team for four years, but I really never lettered except as a freshman when I was a starting player. But on the varsity I was just a bench-warmer. In my last year I got into five games for an average of four minutes each. That's twenty out of six hundred minutes.*
>
> *Knowing I wasn't going to get in the game, Bunker used to bring my mother out to the Cotton Bowl an hour before kickoff because the only way she'd get to see me play was when I was out there with everyone else warming up.*

In the same month that Herbert married Nancy Broadus from El Paso, Bunker married a girl from Ruston, Louisiana, Caroline Lewis, whom he met on a blind date arranged by a friend of both their mothers, Mary Rowland Sowell. Though Mother adored both girls and was generous with others, she was not one to be extravagant on herself. She said, "Two weddings in one month? I am going to buy one new dress and wear it to both of them."

That was in 1951. Bunker and Caroline had a baby girl in 1952. They rented a house near White Rock Lake and then moved into Mount Vernon with Mother and Daddy while they were looking for a house of their own.

> BUNKER'S CAROLINE: *One of the first questions Mr. Hunt ever asked me was what the annual rainfall in the state of Louisiana was. I told him, "Too much!" Mrs. Hunt burst out laughing and said she could tell I was a native. But Mr. Hunt felt that I should have known because, as he said, "Water is the world's most important commodity. Oil is valuable and it can fly you places and keep you warm. But water is life and death."*
>
> *Bunker has always been a great teaser. He'd tell his mother, "I've invited the Sultan of Swat to come out for the weekend. Big oil fields. He's only got fifteen wives. Do you think we can accommodate them?" Mrs. Hunt would sit there for a minute, "Well, I'll try ... Let's see, if I..." When she caught on to him he'd take her around the waist*

*and dance her around the room a time or two. He really enjoyed teasing his mother.*

After the navy and a year of college, Bunker was delighted to be living back at home and have everything he liked to eat. And there were no expenses. Naturally, Mother wouldn't let them pay laundry or cleaning or anything. But Caroline hired a girl to come in and help with Ellen, the baby. It was fun for my parents to have a toddler in the house again.

Al and I were overwhelmingly occupied developing the Garden of the Gods Club in Colorado Springs. Al had also become one of the founders of Palm Desert in California. In June 1948, I had given birth to our third child, a beautiful girl who was named Alinda, for her father. Therefore, Caroline was a great addition to our mother's life. I had always been around so much, and all of a sudden I was busy with the children—then ten, seven, and four—school and civic activities, and rushing back and forth from Colorado and California. Caroline says she was a "useful distraction," but in fact she filled a large gap in this family.

CAROLINE: *Mrs. Hunt drove fast and was stopped for speeding one day. The policeman said she looked a great deal younger than her license said. She didn't mind getting* that *ticket. According to her, it was one of the best days she ever had.*

Mother and Caroline went out and looked at every house in Dallas, but Bunker didn't like any of them.

Caroline told Mother, "He is just too comfortable."

"You are so right. We may have to build a fire under Bunker to get him out of this house."

My sister Caroline finally found a house and called Bunker and told him she thought he ought to look into it.

BUNKER'S CAROLINE: *He decided that was the house we ought to have. I was not crazy about it, but I was about to have another baby. Then we had to furnish it. I had never furnished a house before, I was lost. Besides, I was in a strange city.*

*Mrs. Hunt told me everything I needed, where to go, and went with me to get it. She educated me. "The day after you buy a new piece of furniture, it is secondhand. The day after you buy an antique, it is still an antique."*

*Bunker would tease her. "Awww Mooze, they just take these pieces out to the back of the shop and hammer them with a few old nails and beat them up and let it rain on them and hit them with chains. Then they put a fresh coat of wax on them and they sell them to you for just any price."*

*Mrs. Hunt would get so outdone with him! "Bunker, you would not know an antique if it sat on you."*

*She had a good eye for antiques, and seldom if ever did anyone fool her.*

*Mr. Hunt was violently opposed to us moving out and into our own house. He said, "I'd really like for you all to stay out here. We're gone a lot. And it's just good for you to be here."*

*I was afraid that I was being rude by wanting to move out. Whenever I had a problem, I talked to Mrs. Hunt. She gave all the help you wanted but never offered any advice unless you begged for it. You just kind of had to lie down on the floor and die to get advice out of her. You had to ask specifically, "Do you like this chair?" But when she answered she was always totally honest.*

*She said, "Men just have no understanding of these things. I know exactly how you feel about this. After Mr. Hunt and I were married, we moved in with my mother and I loved her dearly but I wanted a house of my own. You need your own house. So we will just move you into your own house and do not give it another thought or feel the least bit badly about it."*

After Bunker and Caroline moved out, there was no one at Mount Vernon. Lamar was at SMU most of the time. It was a startling change for there to be nobody at home except Mother and Daddy. All these years there had always been a big crowd. That sudden quiet is a tremendous jolt when you live in a large house with three servants. And Daddy was often away on business.

Rather than sit alone in an empty house, Mother began traveling more than ever. Rarely did Daddy go with her. I knew that Frania was married and out of his life so I accepted that he was involved in his business and political efforts.

Aunt Tot and Mother drove across the country together, leaving without an itinerary. Another time Mother took her friend Kate Bass to the coronation of Queen Elizabeth. And every summer she spent six weeks in Colorado Springs at the Broadmoor Hotel, which in those days had a regular clientele, so she made many good friends there.

We had worked hard at the Garden of the Gods Club and Seven Falls during the summer of 1952, and when we closed it for the winter some friends persuaded us to meet them in Europe. We took the fabulous once-a-week Constellation sleeper flight from New York to Paris. It was a big deal, with red carpets, photographers, champagne, and berths. We went to Nice and Cap d'Antibes with our friends, then on to Paris by ourselves.

At that time there was a best-selling book called *How To See Europe on $5 A Day.* As I was dressing to go to Maxim's for dinner, Al was reading from the book. There was a review of Maxim's to the effect that if you go there (which, it said, you should not really waste your time doing), you will probably sit next to some movie star or person of nobility and your service will be just terrible because they will get all the attention.

We both laughed and continued dressing. Nothing was going to stop us from visiting Maxim's. Besides, the club had turned Al into a student of cuisine, eager to learn new and wonderful ideas and services that a top restaurant could provide.

We were seated at a banquette table. Our service was superb, the people attractive, and Maxim's was blissful. Then there was kind of a flutter among the waiters, and in came Aly Khan with Gene Tierney. They were seated next to us.

Our service evaporated. After telling the waiter to get him a newspaper, Aly Khan said to Gene Tierney, "Let's go to a movie." She looked like that didn't thrill her at all. He looked at the paper. "Ooooh, have you seen *High Noon?* I understand that it's very good and it's showing over at the so-and-so." She made a very disinterested face. But he told the captain to call and find out what time the film started. Meanwhile the sommelier was busy pouring his wine and waiting for him to taste it. He took a sip and swallowed it like it was castor oil. "Awful, awful ..."

Al kept nudging me; we were fascinated. We didn't mind that our waiters forgot we existed because we got a floor show we hadn't counted on.

A few months later, we were in New York at a party at Lily Pons' apartment at 10 Gracie Square, and Aly Khan was among her guests. When we were introduced, Al said, "I want to tell you a story. I've had a wonderful experience with you." And Al told him about *How to See Europe on $5 a Day* and the whole story at Maxim's, and Aly Khan burst out laughing because he remembered the evening.

# *Seventeen*

ON THE FIRST OF MAY, 1955, Mother called me to say that she was having a terrible time with her back and that she was going to have Jeff, the chauffeur, drive her to Fort Worth to see her orthopedist, Dr. Johnson.

My life was filled with the children, the Dallas Women's Club, Junior League, D.A.R., Dallas Garden Club, the Historical Society, founding the Dallas Heritage Society, and all the Seven Falls and the Garden of The Gods Club activities. It never occurred to me that Mother was in distress and that I should have dropped everything and taken her myself.

Two days later, Daddy called, frantic. "Mom has had a little stroke."

She was rushed to Baylor Hospital in Dallas. I moved into her suite and was there twenty-four hours a day while they ran tests. It turned out that Mother had suffered a large, serious stroke.

A Dallas neurosurgeon was brought in. He diagnosed a tumor on the brain or a cerebral hemorrhage and wanted to operate.

Mother didn't care for him. "He's knife-happy. I do not want him operating on me."

Daddy and I made the decision to take her to the Mayo Clinic in Rochester, Minnesota. Though we owned a company plane, we chartered a large one from American Airlines.

> LAMAR: *It was a DC-6, because speed was necessary and you had to have a pressurized cabin. Private planes were not what they are these days. We all went to Rochester, the whole family.*

The doctors misdiagnosed my mother's illness. They said that she had a tumor on her brain. They operated on her, and she didn't. She'd had a cerebral hemorrhage. Then they performed an angiogram to determine the cause. That provoked the stroke from which Mother died on Friday, May 6. She was sixty-six.

> LAMAR: *My sister Caroline and I were in the room when Mom died. There was another bed in the room, and we took turns staying with her.*

> CAROLINE: *It almost destroyed my sister, because she was instrumental in the decision to bring her to Mayo to get the best treatment.*

You blame yourself. I should have gone with her to Fort Worth to see Dr. Johnson. I should have given her more of my time. If I had been seeing more of her, I would have noticed she was not well.

On the plane back, Daddy was pitiful. Al was sitting beside him. Daddy wept, "I don't know how I'll ever get along without her." He had a lined pad and a pencil and he was writing and writing. He said, "She was my strength. She did everything …"

I was sympathetic with Daddy. But I could not forget that up to the end, though Mother would make two reservations for any trip she planned—one for herself and one for Daddy—always hoping he would accompany her as he had in their early years—he rarely did and she would end up taking a lady friend. I was making an active attempt to be as forgiving as Mother had been. I watched him writing away. I knew what he was doing. Daddy was a romantic, writing his memories of her. This was typical of him.

When we arrived at the Dallas airport with Mother's body, a full half of the Hunt Oil Company employees were waiting there to pay their respects. The office had been closed for the day, but nobody had organized the reception at the airport. The employees had called the Sparkman Funeral Home and found out when and where her plane would land and had each come out of their own accord.

It was a surprise to find among Mother's papers a note she had written.

> I know that you children will have everything you could possibly ever want materially, but these are a few of my things that I think are appropriate for you to have …

Bunker got Mother's portrait plus a copy of the leather-bound family history. There were only two; I received the other copy. Caroline received the piano. Hassie's bequest was the albums of early oil-field photos. Mother had practically no jewelry. I have her string of pearls and Caroline has her nice diamond ring. Lamar got the big old-fashioned 1910 Victrola that plays copper perforated records. He had always loved it.

After the funeral, when I was at White Rock one day, it occurred to me that Mother would have had some cash secreted around the house. I remembered her hiding money in books in the '30s. I checked a lot of books but found nothing. Then I found myself staring at her sewing basket filled with yarn. That was strange, I thought. Mother never knitted. Yet there were all those balls of yarn. Sure enough, rolled up inside the center of each ball were hundred-dollar bills—just in case.

That summer we went to Colorado Springs, and my brothers, Caroline, and I divided the task of responding to the sympathy letters. My share alone was seven hundred letters.

I was emotionally and physically exhausted. In late August, Al took me to New York for two weeks. He rented a sumptuous apartment at the Waldorf Towers and went to the Davis Cup matches at the West Side Tennis Club in Forest Hills. We went to the theater every evening and took tennis friends with us. I slept fourteen hours a night for those two weeks.

Not long after Mother died, Daddy went to Kuwait with Mr. Williford. He thought he had the Kuwait exploration contract. The Japanese, however, offered a larger royalty, which Daddy would have met had he known about it.

Bunker didn't have much luck abroad either. Investing a lot of his money and all of his energy and know-how, he discovered one of the biggest oil fields in the world in Libya. He owned billions of barrels of reserves, making him richer than Daddy, until Colonel Moammar Gadhafi overthrew the Libyan monarchy in 1969 and shortly afterward nationalized Bunker's holdings there.

Daddy went downhill from the day Mother died. His rock had been taken out from under him, and he was a sorrowful figure. My anger abated. Al and I spent as much time as we could out at the house. All of us did who were in town. We all tried to animate him, to give him some support.

BUNKER: *I asked him, "You don't care to play cards anymore?" And he said, "No, not really, I can win too easily. And it's not much fun winning when it's really no contest. And the people you beat, they don't like it."*

One afternoon, Al and I took him for a drive through east Texas. He looked out the window enjoying the sight of everything connected with his early, productive, happy days.

Seeing a watermelon stand, he said, "Al, stop over here for a moment, please." It was a couple of cents a pound for a watermelon. He negotiated the price down a bit, and when we got back in the car I was furious.

"Daddy, that poor man's out there in the hot sun trying to make a living. Why did you bargain to buy that watermelon for a dollar fifty when the man wanted a dollar ninety for it?"

Embarrassed, he said, "I just wanted to see if I'd lost my touch."

Daddy still wanted to do all he could for his country. He expanded "Facts Forum," his radio and television shows, into "Life Line." The liberal press ridiculed his unbending conservatism, but he continued steadfastly backing what he believed was right for the United States.

Earlier, he had formed H.L. Hunt Foods, manufacturing and distributing some thirty products, many of them the health foods in which he believed. He had done this because he needed a sponsor for *Life Line.* It would have created the wrong image for Hunt Oil to sponsor it. However, a company that made food, especially health food, was perfect. It ultimately cost him $58 million, which he lost in the food business. Even with the sponsorship being a form of advertising, it would have been cheaper to have simply paid for the air time.

Regrettably, Daddy did not have twenty-twenty foresight. From being perceived as a respected, hardworking, economically successful American trying to serve his country, Daddy became known as a crackpot. He was too conservative, so much so that he became ineffective. It killed Al and me to hear him ridiculed, but Daddy seemed able to handle that. Maybe voices from his past drowned it out, kinder voices he remembered saying, "H.L. Hunt is one hell of an oilman."

BUNKER: *The press can take a heel and make a hero out of him or they can take a guy who ought to be a hero and make him a heel. There's not much you can do about it. I'm very philosophical about it. I saw them do it to my father. He was a classic example, a guy who really never caused anybody any harm.*

*My father had courage. He was also an unusually honest man. He would never contribute to two people in the same race. Now that would sound fundamental, but many people do, so that whoever wins they're OK. If my father was for somebody, he certainly would not be for his opponent.*

*Dad was always smeared unmercifully by the press, which he understood came with his conservative ideas. I asked him, "Why don't you hire a public relations man and get a better image?" He said, "Well, that's a little dishonest, to pay someone money to get someone else to write something good about you. I wouldn't feel comfortable with that."*

Daddy did not concern himself with his public image. He did not consider himself a public person. We were never selling anything to the public. The Rockefellers had gas stations, but we did not. He didn't care if people disagreed with him. He always felt sorry for them for not understanding. And by then, I felt sorry for him for not understanding that the majority never would.

One evening, a nice-looking young woman came to Mount Vernon. As we were only having family out in those days, I assumed she was a secretary. Al was standing nearby. Neither he nor anyone else introduced us, so I offered her my hand and said, "I'm Margaret Hill."

"I'm so happy to meet you. I'm Ruth Ray."

We chatted, and for want of something better to say, I asked, "Are you married?"

"No. I was. My husband died."

I expressed my sympathy and asked, "Do you have children?"

"Yes," she said, "I have four."

At this point Al spirited me away from her, rushing me through a goodnight to Daddy. The next thing I knew, we were in our car heading home.

It happened so fast that I was bewildered. "What's going on? Why did you pull me away?"

"Sweetheart ... Now, I know this is going to make you unhappy..." He fell silent.

"Al! What is going on?" I insisted.

He stopped the car and faced me. "Ruth Ray is your father's—well, she's his wife without being married to him. They have four children together."

I was astounded, disbelieving, horrified, brokenhearted. As I was about to demand, "Al, why didn't you tell me?," I heard Mother asking me the same thing and my reply: *Why would I?*

Indeed, why would Al hasten this despair to reach me any sooner than it would finally land on its own? How much love, how much gratitude, I felt toward him for carrying this nightmare alone over all these years. He had chosen to live with it in silence and delay giving me this heartbreak.

Immediately I stopped going to see Daddy. I did not make a point of saying, "I don't want to see you anymore," I just was unavailable. I tried to remember what Mother had said: *Keep it out of your thoughts ... You rise above things and ignore them ...* But when I learned that Ray, Ruth and Daddy's eldest, had been born in 1943, I understood that he'd gone straight from Frania to Ruth. He had three families! He was raising fourteen children.

Even though I was angry at him, it was incredulous that he had the capacity to spread himself among so many people. I for one never felt any lack of his time or interest or devotion. He was always there for all of his children.

> CAROLINE: *I never grieved about Mother's early death. Emotionally, she was ready to leave. I felt that God was answering her prayers.*
>
> *Just before she had the stroke she was at my house, and she said, "I can always tell when my blood pressure's down because I feel terrible. I don't have any energy." She was always an energetic person. She added, "It's hard to get into this world, and it's hard to get out."*
>
> *I felt that she was ready to die. Which was a tragedy for all those around her because she was the one who had kept the family together.*

Mother must have known—or at least sensed—that something other than business was keeping Daddy from her.

In the spring of 1956, Al said, "The Chapel Hill field is depleting. I've been offered over a million dollars by Lone Star Gas. I think it's time to sell and take a capital gain."

He had many other properties, but Chapel Hill was where it had all started for him. "Won't you feel a little sad about giving it up?"

"Yes," he smiled in a kind of bittersweet way, "but now the right thing is to sell it. And I have a plan. I'll use some of the money to give you your long-overdue engagement ring. I think after eighteen years and three children, you've been patient enough."

Not having a formal engagement ring hadn't bothered me in the slightest. I had forgotten I didn't have one. However, knowing Al could now well afford it, I enjoyed the idea of having a lovely diamond engagement ring. I looked forward to it. But Al wasn't just going to go out and buy a ring; he knew exactly what he wanted. He had a college friend who was associated with Kazanian in California send stones for him to inspect. Harry Winston in New York sent stones too, and Neiman's came up with still more to be considered.

On October 15, 1956, our eighteenth anniversary, we were in New York having lunch at "21" with our Palm Beach friends Janet and Wiley Reynolds. That was when Al took the velvet box out of his pocket and gave it to me. The ring was an American-cut, round stone.

I didn't take it off my finger all the time we were in New York, though I wore it turned under more than up. Being round, it was comfortable to wear under the palm of my hand. A few weeks later, at home, I took it off to wash my hands, and as I was drying them, the phone rang. Al saw the ring on the sink and put it in his pocket. When I'd finished the phone call I went to get my ring. I couldn't believe it was gone. Al took it from his pocket and put it on my finger for the second time. "Don't ever take it off."

It was fortunate advice because when the burglar they called the King of Diamonds broke into our house in the spring of 1964 while we were sleeping, he stole my other jewelry but did not awaken us. As I had my ring on, he did not get it.

It occurred to me that it would be fun to show it to Daddy and say, "Well, how do you like the fortune hunter, the boy who was marrying me for my money?" But that anger was long gone. I had not seen my father for more than a year, since that last night at Mount Vernon, and the only emotion he could evoke in me was sadness.

When the phone rang, the caller did not identify himself—nor did he have to. I had heard that voice every day of my life—including the past year, in which I had had mental conversations with him daily, recriminating him, hoping to understand him, wanting to like him again.

"I am going to stop by."

Daddy let himself in and sat down on the couch, as he always had. If a stranger had been present, we would have given the impression that we had seen each other only the day before. He did not ask how I had been, and I did not ask how he had been. We both knew. Al saw him every day at the office and told me how he was, and I assumed he told Daddy how I was. Al and Daddy remained best friends. Part of me was glad that Daddy had Al.

"I came over to tell you that I am going to marry Ruth."

He waited for me to say something, but I couldn't.

"You cannot imagine how wonderful the children are, Ray, June, Helen, and Swanee ... They are beautifully behaved, they treat me so well, they never say a cross word to each other, they are just wonderful, outstanding, children." He smiled. "Not like you kids used to be."

"Well, you do need to give them a name, but you're going to find out these kids are just like everybody else's, they fight and fuss and everything, too."

"No, no, no, Margaret, you're wrong, these children are special."

"This is a mistake you have to make."

"By the way, I've been going to church recently."

"I can just see you there, down in the front row, trying to clean up your sins."

It was on the front pages of the Dallas newspapers—a picture of the newlyweds standing next to Mother's piano. I was not invited and I don't know of anyone who was.

Al and I never went to Mount Vernon to see them. Ruth liked to entertain and became an active hostess. My sister and most of my brothers did go. Daddy and Ruth often invited us, but I just never even considered going. It was just too painful for me. The rest of my siblings seemed to have handled it much better than I. It surprised me that Bunker's Caroline and Herbert's Nancy were able to accept it. They had both been very close to Mother.

Obviously, Daddy loved his and Ruth's children and was ambitious for them, or he would not have had them going to Hockaday and St. Marks. They did not leave Dallas to go away to college, they all went to SMU. Obviously, Daddy wanted them to start becoming a part of the community.

Ray, the eldest, made a major oil discovery in Yemen and has been active in real estate development. He is respected in Dallas activities and community affairs. June has a Christian radio talk show called "Hope for the Heart." She is an accomplished guitarist and singer and has appeared internationally. Helen is happily married and lives in New York City and is active in philanthropic activities, and Swanee, a resident of Denver, has been appointed Ambassador to Austria by President Clinton.

> LAMAR: *When I was twenty-six years old, I wanted to become involved in the formation of the American Football League. Dad felt it was kind of a crazy idea. He never told me that explicitly, but I could tell by the way he encouraged me to talk to financial advisors and financial people who worked for the Hunt Oil Company.*
>
> *Dad provided wonderful financial opportunities for me and my brothers and sisters. Our trusts made it possible for us to do things in business that most young people would not have the resources to do. That was done for me when I was three years old. I could never have gotten involved in the formation of a football league unless the thirty-five trusts had provided the basic necessity.*
>
> *But he was very gentle about trying to stricture. He didn't say, you can't do this, or you shouldn't do that, but he got me on the phone with a couple of people he knew who had been in the football business. One of them was a man by the name of Jim Breuil. He had been connected with a football league, the All-American Conference, that ended in failure. My dad knew Mr. Breuil through the oil business and got me on the phone with him. Dad said, "Jim, I want you to get on the phone with my son Lamar, he's thinking about forming a football league, and I want you to tell him about your experience and how you feel about it."*

> *I got on the line, and though he'd lost a lot of money in it Mr. Breuil said, "I think it's something you'll really enjoy. There'll be a lot of challenge and you'll meet a lot of interesting people ..." I'm sure it was not the answer my dad had been anticipating.*
>
> *One of the proudest remembrances I have is how much Dad enjoyed my relative success. He came to Kansas City after the Chiefs had won the Super Bowl, to a dinner at which the team and I were being honored. There were about a thousand people there and a lot of famous football people such as the commissioner, Pete Rozelle. The biggest hand anybody got that night was when Dad was introduced.*

In early October of 1960, Daddy called. "I am coming by." He arrived carrying a small suitcase. "I will need to stay a few days, maybe a week."

I was distressed. "There's nothing wrong between you and Ruth, is there?" Though I had wished their marriage had never happened, I certainly wanted it to be successful.

"No. We are just fine. The problem is that I need to be unavailable for a few days."

Our daughter Lyda had just left for California to begin her freshman year at Stanford, so I put him in her room.

The following Friday morning, Al and I left for Fort Worth to fly with Nancy Lee and Perry Bass to their island for the weekend. As we drove up to the airport, Nancy Lee was waiting for us. She rushed to the car, "Call home quick. You're headed for California."

Daddy explained, "Lyda called here and said she has had an appendicitis attack and is going to have to have an operation. I talked to the doctor."

"What did you tell him?" I asked, anticipating the worst.

"I asked, 'How old are you?,' and he said he was thirty-six, and I said 'You are too young to operate on my granddaughter. I will find an experienced person.' Lyda got on the phone and said, 'Oh, Pops, come on, let him do it. He seems real nice.' She said she was in something they call a Health Clinic, which did not sound good to me."

I was frantic. "Daddy! I know how you feel about operations. But don't you dare inflict that old-fashioned quackery on my daughter. Now you call back there ..." I demanded, gritting my teeth, giving him the strongest instructions I had ever dared.

While we were en route home, he called some doctors in New York and in California and arranged for someone he considered qualified to operate on her. By the time Al and I got to Stanford, Lyda was recovering from a successful operation.

When Lyda could talk to us the next morning, she thought it was pretty funny. "This doctor who Pops wouldn't let operate on me came in and stared at me and he asked, 'Who are you, anyway?'"

# *Eighteen*

IN 1960, THE THREE BOYS were all officing at Hunt Oil. Bunker and Herbert were especially eager and active in the oil business. By contrast, Daddy was seventy-one and showing it. His health was not good, and he had lost the old desire to change the world.

TOM: *He enjoyed looking at the old wells and remembering the primitive methods employed to bring them in. But he never cared to look at anything that Hunt Oil had done without him. He could spend all day looking at old equipment or at a well that might be producing ten, fifteen, twenty barrels a day, maybe with luck earning a thousand dollars a month. We had new wells that were producing ten or twenty thousand dollars a month but to him they weren't his.*

*He still had the creative curiosity and the intuition that had made him. When we were at the point of the fall bidding on the north slope State of Alaska acreage in the Prudhoe Bay field, we were in a combine with several other companies, and Uncle June told us, primarily Herbert and me, that though he thought it was fine to bid, he did not want his personal account nor Hunt Oil Company to be included. "That could be like putting your money in a deep freeze."*

*The "deep freeze" referred to environmental constraints in developing the field, plus the building of the pipeline. There was a delay of five years in getting on production, and the original bid of two hundred fifty million dollars would have increased by forty percent from interest alone.*

President Kennedy was scheduled to appear in Dallas in late November 1963. Through Hunt Oil's security people, Daddy learned that demonstrations were being planned against the president. Fearing a repeat of the recent demonstrations against Adlai Stevenson in Dallas, Daddy wrote a letter to the editor that no newspaper published but that he circulated to other conservatives, urging against demonstrations that would create sympathy for the Democrats.

It was a Friday. The presidential motorcade was en route to a luncheon at the Apparel Mart. Daddy and Al stepped over to the office window and watched it pass down Main Street. They were not pleased by the administration that others regarded as "Camelot." They saw no magic in it.

Through "Life Line" Daddy had warned that the Kennedy administration was bypassing the laws of Congress, following policies pleasing to Moscow, suppressing those who spoke out for freedom, and causing American taxpayers to subsidize communism around the world.

Bunker had always been open about his political beliefs and had added his name to a full-page newspaper ad that opposed the administration's policies. Because it paraphrased the doctrines of the John Birch Society, of which he was a member, he contributed two or three hundred dollars toward the cost of its publication. The ad began *Welcome, Mr. President* and then asked some embarrassing questions.

Al was on his way to meet me for lunch in the Zodiac Room at Neiman Marcus. As he walked across the street, police sirens and motorcycles sped by. A woman rushed up to him, "I just heard Kennedy was shot. You think that could happen?"

More police and motorcycles sped down the street, and he thought, *Obviously something has happened.* The killing had occurred about a mile away. By the time he arrived for lunch, it was on the radio, and the news spread instantly. We left and went home.

The Dallas police called Daddy at White Rock Lake and told him he was not safe and to get out of town immediately.

He said, "I do not get along well with being scared. I am safe in my home."

Then the FBI called and warned him that mobs were singling out all conservatives who had been vocally anti-Kennedy as Daddy had been in his radio broadcasts. Convinced, Daddy and Ruth left within hours.

We worried about Bunker, who had done nothing more violent than add his name to a newspaper advertisement that asked questions. We feared for anyone named Hunt. It was traumatic for the family to wonder if somebody was going to seek us out in revenge. In lock step, the media adhered to the story that Daddy had created an atmosphere of hate around Dallas toward Kennedy. It lasted two or three weeks. There were no attempts, though we did receive some hostile phone calls and a lot of hate mail, which naturally caused concern.

As much as any other Americans, we were upset and sad about the assassination. And we grieved for the worldwide vilification of Dallas that resulted from being the site of the killing. It was mindless. JFK was not shot by a city or by its inhabitants. He was murdered by a man who came to Dallas to kill him because that was where he was going to be.

Lyda had graduated from college and was to make her debut in 1964. I debated whether to invite Daddy to her ball.

Al said, "Forget what you're hurt about. Lyda is his first grandchild."

Even though I knew that we all had our own lives and homes and he was entitled to companionship, I still could not accept any substitute for my mother in his life. It was wrong of me. Sadly, that was my emotion, and I could not overcome it.

Finally, we did invite him, and he came alone. It was the first time I had asked him to anything since he'd married Ruth, and he was pleased. That made me happy.

In September 1974, Al and I were coming home to Dallas from Colorado Springs. Whenever we returned home, Al always went immediately to the office.

Daddy's secretary rushed up to Al. "Mr. Hunt has been sitting here all day waiting for you. He's sick. I think he's got fever. We've tried to get him to go home, but he wouldn't leave until you got here. He's been just craving for you to get home, Mr. Hill."

When Al went into Daddy's office, his poor, feverish, tired face lit up with pleasure. But it was clear that he was very sick. Al said, "Mr. Hunt, you need to go home, you're not feeling well."

So Al called Ruth, and she said, "Take him to the doctor's office and I'll meet him there."

Daddy's driver took him to his doctor, and Al came home, wishing not to intrude on Ruth. By seven o'clock we had a call from the doctor that Daddy had been taken straight to Baylor and that he was really quite ill. After a week of extensive tests, the doctors called all the family members together—Ruth and Ray and all of us. We gathered in one room at the hospital for the doctors to give us the results.

Daddy's principal illness was advanced cancer of the liver. The doctor's detailed everything that was the matter with him, and we all came to the same conclusion: there was nothing to be done. He had so many problems that no operation would do any significant good. Further, his body just could not have stood it.

He reached the point where he couldn't talk. He'd be conscious sometimes, and sometimes not. I would go and visit every day and stay thirty or forty minutes, and so did Al. Baylor Hospital had suites for family members, and Ruth stayed there with him to the end.

He died November 29, 1974, the day after Thanksgiving. He was eighty-five.

The end was a relief. Knowing him as the powerful force he had been, we had found it painful to see the gradual deterioration that had become noticeable shortly after our mother's death.

For many years, Daddy's will had stated that everything was to go into the H.L. Hunt Foundation. Then, shortly before his death, when the foundation law was changed, an in-house lawyer advised him to change his will. The last amendment was made two or three months before he died. It provided that all of his stock in Hunt Oil Company, about eighty percent of the total, be left to Ruth. That was about $100 million.

My brothers, Caroline, and I were advised by a lawyer to go to court and break the will. At a family meeting, Al said, "No. That is not for you to do. Nobody here needs it. You all have enough money, and it would just be unpleasant."

CAROLINE: *When our father's estate was being settled, there was a difference of opinion between Ray Hunt and our family as to what went where. For the most part, we got very little of my father's estate because he felt we were well taken care of with Placid Oil.*

*I remember this high-powered lawyer coming in and suggesting ways we could get more than we'd been left and Herbert stopped him cold. "Now, we want you to get this straight. We do not want one penny more than we really are supposed to have. We're not trying to get anything for goodwill or anything like that. All we want is what we're supposed to have and not one penny more."*

*One might say that it's easy to be fair when you have a lot, but history does not prove that to be the common case.*

# *Epilogue*

WE WERE IN MIDLAND, TEXAS, IN 1976. There is a museum there called the Permian Basin Petroleum Museum, so naturally we went to see it. Later, Al said, "The East Texas Oil Field is the greatest oil field there has ever been. It fueled World War II. Without it, the Allies could not have been airborne. It's just terrible that there is no museum to show its history."

He was so right. All there was at that time was a Texas Historical Marker that says, *Discovery Well (Joiner No. 3 Bradford) brought in September 3, 1930.* The date is wrong by a month, and it's just a stone marker. There was nothing to show any of the hunger, fever, and passion of the men who found and developed all that oil.

It was then we decided to build the East Texas Oil Museum.

The question was: where to put it? Al, as always, reasoned the situation from all angles. "To have a museum out on a highway, as the Permian Basin Museum is, and hope to have people stop and go through it, is unlikely. The ideal would be to mount it on a train so that it could make prolonged stops in every city of the country, giving the most people the opportunity to see it. But that wouldn't work. Too limited in space." He paused, deliberating. "If a museum were on the campus of a college, it would be taken care of and be a part of history, which is what it really is. And that college should be in the heart of the oil field."

We drove to Kilgore, which is in the middle of the East Texas Oil Field. Nearly half a century had passed since I had been there in the boom days, when I'd seen the oil derricks lined up side by side, so closely placed that they had built a little tunnel, so people could get into church because the whole churchyard was covered with drilling rigs. We spent a richly nostalgic hour there as I remembered what it had been like back then in the days before Daddy succeeded in getting spacing passed as a law.

We met with Charles Duvall, who owned the Kilgore newspaper. His wife was Mr. Williford's daughter, Lyde. He brought us to Dr. Randolph Watson, president of Kilgore Junior College, who happened to have grown up in Henderson and worked in the oil fields as a youngster. We told him what we had in mind. He went to the Kilgore College board, and they voted in favor of the project.

We have always had a family meeting once a month. We talked to my brothers and sister and said we wanted to build the museum and get it open by October 3, 1980—the fiftieth anniversary of the discovery of the East Texas Oil Field. At that time we were financing the construction of a substantial activities building for the Highland Park Presbyterian Church; at that moment in 1976, however, the price of oil was $40 a barrel, and we could afford this as well. My brothers and sister and I wanted to do it: so Placid Oil funded the museum.

We proceeded to buy a city block adjoining Kilgore Junior College. It had a filling station on it, which was torn down, and Al and I started working on the plans with the president of the College. The centerpiece of the museum was to be a recreation of the town during the boom days of the 1930s.

We sent a gentleman around to east Texas towns, to all the Rotary Clubs, to explain: "We are going to recreate 1930. We do not need funds, but if you have any objects you'd like to contribute we would be pleased to accept them." Everybody had something from that time—old meat grinders, spectacles, wood-burning stoves. People emptied their garages, their basements. Before we knew it we had two warehouses full of artifacts from the 1930s.

On October 3, 1980, we were up early for the opening of the East Texas Oil Museum. It was being held exactly fifty years from the day the Daisy Bradford No. 3 came in. The ceremony would take place at noon. Governor William Clements was the dedication speaker. Every prominent educator and oil person in Texas had been invited and was planning to attend.

Al and I and Lyda, Al, Jr., and Alinda arrived early and waited outside the museum looking at the authentic wooden oil derrick and rig that stood there like a dinosaur. If I had not known it was authentic, I would have thought an artist had created a piece of retrospective sculpture.

It was at least fifteen minutes before the first guests would be arriving. I went inside alone to make a last-minute check.

Entering the East Texas Oil Museum, there are panels of exhibits in the modern lobby: School, Church, Home, Transportation.

I looked at the school exhibit, at the books we used and one of the desks, with a sunken inkwell in the right hand corner. I remembered: *"Your mother will sign that."* I could all but hear Daddy's voice as I had offered him my report card.

At the church exhibit I pressed a button and listened to the hymns we sang in 1930. In my mind, I heard Mother singing in her strong, clear voice.

Home: the pots and pans and the old wood-burning stove. I could all but see Gertrude in perpetual motion, preparing meals for fourteen people, preventing me from coming in to make fudge.

There was a Model-A parked in the transportation exhibit, near railroad station lights and wooden bulletin boards with train schedules chalked in.

I walked through the Memorial Room, with a statue of our father and a wall noting his accomplishments.

Then I pushed open a door, and I was in Boom Town. I was feeling and hearing 1930 again. My every sense told me that I had fallen backwards five decades in time.

It was all there: the rain for three years; the street a muddy swamp; a Model-T bogged down to its fenders; a team of horses pulling a wagon. There was the Overton Theater and the Arp General Store, and I thought of rat cheese and crackers and eating watermelon *"... because you need the water."* And of riding to the oil fields in the back seat of Daddy's car.

I walked around the city block, past the Pistol Hill Gas Station, the Cross Roads Barber Shop. From a recording I heard the barber gossiping about a new gusher while he was shaving a customer, and in my mind's eye I saw the little girl in her short plaid dress sitting there while the manicurist shortened her nails so she couldn't bite them.

I continued past the Post Office, Joinerville Feed and Seed, the Drugstore with a nickelodeon, past the elevator ride to the center of the earth with a recorded guide explaining the formation of the earth and the location of the oil deposits.

Then I looked into Boom Town Cinema, where visitors would sit on the old-fashioned wooden seats and watch authentic 1930 footage of a big producer coming in. As oil gushed through the tower of the rig the seats in the theater would shake to replicate the way the ground trembles around a well whose oil is bursting free after a billion years below the ground.

Returning to the lobby, I stopped at the Memorial Room and stood in front of Daddy's statue, looking up at his face, which was gazing straight ahead. His eyes seemed to be seeking something that few others could see.

I had long ago forgiven him. You can't hold it against a man for possessing and being possessed by all the component and conflicting parts of being a genius. It's just that sometimes it is difficult for mortals to live with.

The statue was eight feet tall. I laughed out loud, "You always were bigger than life, Daddy."

Not wanting to ruin my makeup before meeting the guests, I left, returning outside, where Al and our children were waiting for me.

# Index